CONTENTS

Acknowledgements   vi
Preface   vii

1 The language crisis   1

2 Negritude: new and old perspectives   10

3 History as the 'hero' of the African novel   30

4 The new African novel: a search for modernism   53

5 Southern Africa: protest and commitment   76

6 Modern African poetry: its themes and styles.   107
   A   The pioneers

7 Modern African poetry: its themes and styles.   126
   B   The moderns

8 African drama: its themes and styles   173

ACKNOWLEDGEMENTS

We are grateful to the following for permission to reproduce copyright material:

Librairie Armand Colin for an extract from *Littérature Nègre* by J. Chevrier; Associated Book Publishers Ltd for extracts from p 53 and 84 *Idanre and Other Poems* by Wole Soyinka published by Methuen; the author's agents for a poem from *Night of My Blood* by Kogi Awoonor; the author, J.P. Clark for a poem from *Casualties: Poems* published by Longman Group Ltd and his poem 'Song' in *Three Nigerian Poets* published by Ibadan University Press; Rex Collings Ltd for extracts from *A Shuttle in the Crypt* by Wole Soyinka; Andre Deutsch Ltd for an extract from *The Interpreters* by Wole Soyinka and extracts from *Zulu Poems* by M. Kunene; East African Publishing House Ltd for a poem p 16 *Song of Lawino* by Okot p'Bitek, a poem p 52 'Letter from a Contract Worker' by A. Jacinto and a poem pp 60–1 'I want to be a Drum' by J. Craveirinha from *When Bullets Begin to Flower* edited by M. Dickinson; Heinemann Educational Books for an extract from the poem 'Ancestral Faces' by Kwesi Brew from *Messages: Poems from Ghana* edited by K. Awoonor and G. Adali Mortty and an extract from the poem 'Questions and Answers' from *Dead Roots* by Arthur Nortje; Heinemann Educational Books and Holmes and Meier Publishers Inc for extracts from the poems 'The Passage' 'Initiations' and 'Paths of Thunder' from *Labyrinths* by C. Okigbo; L'Harmattan and the author's agents for extracts from *The Poems of T. U'Tamsi* by T. U'Tamsi translated by Gerald Moore published by Heinemann Educational Books Ltd, reprinted by permission of A.D. Peters & Co Ltd; Index on Censorship for an extract from 'Six Poems' by Don Mattera in *Index on Censorship* Vol 3, No 4, 1974; Knox Printing and Publishing Company (Pty) Ltd for extracts from poems in *The Valley of Thousand Hills* by H.I.E. Dhlomo; Mbari Publications and Farrar Straus and Giroux Inc for an extract from the poem 'Off the Campus' from *A Simple Lust* by Dennis Brutus; Methodist Book Depot Ltd for extracts from *Cocoa Comes to Mampong and Some Occasional Verse* by D.F. Dei Anang; the author's agents for extracts from *West African Verse* by A. Nicol; the author, G. Okara for an extract from the poem 'Piano and Drums' from *West African Verse* edited by D. Nwoga published by Longman Group Ltd; Oxford University Press for an extract from a poem by L.S. Senghor from *Selected Poems* by John Reed and Clive Wake, extracts from the poem 'Cahier d'un retour on pays natal' by Aimé Cesaire from *Senghor: Prose and Poetry* selected and edited by John Reed and Clive Wake (c) OUP 1965, an extract from *Sounds of a Cowhide Drum* by Oswald Mbuyiseni Mtshali (c) Oswald Joseph Mtshali 1971, extracts from *Dear Parent and Ogre* by R. Sarif Easmon (c) OUP 1964, extracts from *Oda Oak Oracle* by Tsegaye Gabre-Medhin (c) OUP 1965, an extract from *Sons and Daughters* by J.C. de Graft (c) OUP 1964 and an extract from *Ozidi* by J.P. Clark (c) J.P. Clark 1966; Presence Africaine for extracts from *Antsa* by Jacques Rabemananjara 1961 and an extract from 'Le Renégat' by David Diop in *Coups de Pilon* 1956; Solofo Rabearivelo for an extract from the poems 'Postlude' 'Filao' 'Zakana' and 'Traduit de la Nuit' from *Translations from the Night* by Jean Joseph Rabearivelo; Editions Seghers for extracts from *Légendes et Poèmes* by B. Dadié (c) Editions Seghers 1966; Stockwell Publishers for an extract from a poem by J.R. Jolobe in *Thutula* and an extract from a poem by Dennis Oradebay in *Africa Sings*; Tanzania Publishing House for extracts from poems by A. Neto in *Sacred Hope*; Witwatersrand University Press for extracts from the poems 'Because' 'The Gold Mines' and 'I Hear a Singing' reproduced from B.W. Vilakazi *Zulu Horizons* translated into English by F.L. Friedman from the literal translations of D. McK. Malcolm and J.M. Sikakana (c) Witwatersrand University Press 1973.

Whilst every effort has been made we are unable to trace the copyright holders of extracts from a poem by M. Serote from *Tsetlo*, a poem by Dei Anang from *Ghana Glory*, 'Our God's Black' 'Negro Heaven' 'The Human Race' and 'A Letter to an African Poet' by Dei Anang in *Between the Forest and the Sea: Collected Poems*, 'Chansons sur mon pays' and 'Le Retour au Bercail' by F. Ranaivo, an extract from *Three Malayasy Martyrs* by A. Stratlon and an extract from 'Poetics and the Mythic Imagination' by S. Macebuh from *Transition IX* and would appreciate any information which would enable us to do so.

TASKS

THEMES A

LEWIS NKOSI

TASKS AND MASKS
THEMES AND STYLES OF AFRICAN LITERATURE

Longman

LONGMAN GROUP LIMITED
Longman House,
Burnt Mill,
Harlow, Essex, U.K.

First published 1981

British Library Cataloguing in Publication Data

Nkosi, Lewis
    Tasks and masks
    1. African literature — History and criticism
    I. Title
    809'.896   PL8010

    ISBN 0-582-64145-4 Csd
    ISBN 0-582-64146-2 Pbk

Printed and bound in Great Britain by
William Clowes (Beccles) Limited,
Beccles and London

PREFACE

Tasks and Masks is a result of many accidents and conjunctures. In 1971, after many years of reading African literature as a part-time activity, I was suddenly appointed visiting Regents Professor for African Literature at the University of California (Irvine); during the short time I spent in California I was able for the first time to read many of the texts and to meditate on many themes, questions and problems posed by African literature. At the end of my stay at the University of California I desired to set down in writing some of the insights which had come to me then; at least, to raise some of the questions, if nothing else.

Some time later when I was researching a book on African cultural survivals in the New World, I was asked if I had any thoughts about writing a book on African literature, then conceived more as an introductory textbook for students than as a work of general criticism. This seemed to me an opportune moment to put to use some of the reading I had been doing in African literature. The result was the writing of *Tasks and Masks* which, as the subtitle suggests, is a study of the themes and styles of African literature.

The book is also, hopefully, more than this; for in some of its chapters, in the many 'asides' and parenthical pauses of breath, it is intended to provide a primary sketch of the *ideology* to which African literature is attached. As such the book tries to go beyond the scholarly proprieties of African literature in which the object of criticism is seen merely as the paraphrasing of novels, plays and poems or as the discreet application of the exegetic method to texts which are supposed to remain obscure without such determined glossing. Hence the slightly polemical note which frequently creeps into these discussions; for I agree wholeheartedly with Louis Althusser (*Reading Capital*, New Left Books, 1970, p. 18) when he says '*there is no such thing as an innocent reading*'. What we see in a text is what our ideology has equipped us to see.

But if a literary work cannot breathe a pure air, untainted by the ideology out of which it has issued, it does not mean that a work of literature is entirely reducible to its ideology as some bad Marxists have tended to imply. In his *Critique to Political Economy* Marx specifically denied this; both Trotsky and Lenin followed him, the latter in his discussion of the works of Tolstoy. Today the semi-autonomy of a work is recognised not only by bourgeois critics but by most literary theorists of Marxist persuasion. What the text reveals to us may often contradict both the theories and the wishes of its author; that is why the debate which followed Wole Soyinka's Stockholm address in 1967 (and my subsequent remarks on commitment), a debate which still reverberates in many discussions of African literature, can now be seen not only to have been totally misconceived but to have been hopelessly shallow in many of its theoretical assumptions. My only regret is that during that debate, in my desire to demystify the role of a writer, I presumed too much on the participants' sense of humour. African writers take themselves a lot more seriously than their works sometimes justify. In any case, in retrospect I think I overstated my case and tended to underplay to an unacceptable degree the writers' role in any ideological struggle. Nevertheless, then as now, my main thesis seems to me to have been unassailable: although a literary work is linked both to history and its author, its ultimate meaning and significance cannot be determined by factors outside the text itself.

In passing I feel I must make a few comments on what is sometimes called 'African aesthetics'. In the interest of some exclusivist notion of African 'culture', we are now being asked, in evaluating some African literary works (most of them written in European languages, some clearly using European models), to apply to them only those criteria based on 'African aesthetics'. In judging modern African works, which are by definition only too aware of the outside world, we are not simply asked to broaden our terms of reference sufficiently in order to take into account certain African cultural facts, but it is being suggested that African critics ought to eschew 'Western' criteria altogether and instead use indigenous critical apparatus.

How this great feat, this *cordon sanitaire* around African art and criticism is to be accomplished, nobody is saying. What we get are mainly assertions: 'African literature. . .exists on terms totally independent of any other tradition but the African one, and cries to be examined on these terms. (B. Ezuma Igwe). My friend, Joseph Okpaku, who has had periodic bouts of this malady, became so ambitious that he wanted us to build 'a body of African critical standards for not only African literature, but all literature'. Clearly, one wing of this school (presumably they would also exclude the Marxist approach to literature) wish to establish an 'African trading company' that trades with no one; and the Okpaku wing wants to put up tariff barriers against foreign goods and still be in a position to send theirs everywhere in the world.

But to return to the issues raised by Ezuma Igwe: confronted as we are by the initial fact of language alone, the fact that much of African literature is currently produced in English, French and Portuguese; and given the fact that many African authors, through background and training, are inheritors of a dual tradition, both African and European, how can anyone speak of the works of Achebe, Ngugi, Okigbo, Clark, Senghor and many others, as existing on terms 'totally independent of any other tradition but the African one'? For does not even a writer like Achebe, so heavily steeped in the tradition of his people, betray a partial debt to his European mentors! Even Achebe's dissatisfaction with Joyce Carey's novel, *Mr Johnson* (which, as he told me in 1962, 'was a most superficial picture not only of the country, but even of the Nigerian character'), was it not in some way an acknowledgement of this debt to another tradition, for had this European literature meant nothing to him why should he have cared enough to want to improve on it or even to challenge it? A not very astonishing fact, of course, is that as soon as Mr Igwe had proclaimed the 'independence' of African literature, and presumably the critical norms by which it should be judged, we only had to turn over the page of his manuscript to discover a quotation from a Canadian critic, Northrope Frye; six pages later

Mr Igwe is hard at work, dredging out Freudian symbols from African verse. For instance, we are told that John Pepper Clark, in his poem, *Girl Bathing*, 'has worked into the scene another composite image — that is, the log as a male (and the phallus)'.

The point of the matter is that with the vast spread of communications — forgetting for the moment the dialectical process of mutual transformation that goes on at all times between the culture of the coloniser and the colonised — art is crossing frontiers more rapidly than even before, each idiom modifying the one with which it comes into contact. The spread of new materials and technologies has had a profound bearing on changes in styles and artistic techniques. The role of the critic is not to stand sentry guard at the thinning frontiers between one art and another, trying to arrest the process of intercourse which is radically altering one local idiom after another. His function is to identify the varieties of human experience embodied in each idiom, to note what is vital and useful, and where his critical skills enable him to assist his people in preserving the best from their tradition and absorbing the best from outside. I confess this sounds dull and less radical than the demand for a clean sweep of the slate. So be it!

Bold and incautious and still very young, I once suggested that African writers ought to be judged with the same rigour as their Western counterparts. This was interpreted in certain quarters as advocating the use of Western criteria in African criticism. Many essays were written and published by many people who did not bother to find out what, in fact, I had said. I eventually traced the source of the misinterpretation to an essay by Joseph Okpaku in his journal, *New African Literature and Art*: 'It is as undesirable to plead for leniency in criticising African works as it is absurd for Lewis Nkosi to ask that Western critical standards be used.' Where I had said this Mr Okpaku never told his readers.

On the contrary, no one has been more assiduous than myself, sometimes at the risk of self-contradiction, in attacking an over-reliance on Western techniques where African ones are superior, more vital or more relevant as, indeed, my writings on the theatre will show; equally I have always unhesitatingly accepted those influences from other cultures which are fructifying and relevant to the African situation. And that includes those critical notions which have helped to shape modern African works.

Finally, the reader picking up this book is entitled to ask: 'Why the title 'Tasks and Masks'?' Since the early 1960s I have been obsessed with the idea that African authors were easily divisible into two main groups: first, those who looked at African society in an essentialist way as unchanging in its important elements, rather like a 'mask' one turns perpetually in one's hands, each time revealing nothing more than what it is, the work of some skilful carver who originally imparted to it its outstanding features; the second group consists of those writers who for the most obvious political reasons are to be found mostly in East and Southern Africa; they have conceived of the act of writing as the carrying out of social tasks, almost desperate ones, without which undertaking the development of African societies would be handicapped. In actual fact, this schema is only useful as a broad classificatory category but quickly breaks down when applied too rigorously to all African authors; this is so because even those writers like Camara Laye (in *The African Child*) who are mainly interested in the projection of the folkways and rituals of African societies can be shown to be carrying out an important 'task' in making available a certain image of African society. In some of the writers the two functions, that of simple representation and that of active criticism of African society, overlap.

In ending, this book is presented to those many lovers of African literature on whose patience and goodwill a critic so easily presumes, but also with very special affection and gratitude to Sandra Barkan with whom I worked for a short time at the University of California (Irvine) and to whom I promised that I would write up the remarks I was making with such recklessness before those who came to hear me lecture. Particular thanks are due to Alexa Wilson who throughout the writing of this book worked on the preparation of this manuscript.

London, 1979   L.N.

CHAPTER ONE

THE LANGUAGE CRISIS

African literature as a university discipline, as a subject of numerous textual exegeses, or simply as an object of serious critical comment, has only come into its own during the last twenty years or so. Though some writing by Africans, chiefly memoirs of ex-slaves, dates as far back as the eighteenth century; and though there is some evidence of literary production by African 'exiles' in Renaissance Europe,[1] modern African literature as such can be said to have achieved its present status concomitantly with the maturation of the long struggle for political independence and the achievement of the modern state in Africa.

The point needs emphasising because modern African writing has its origins in the politics of anti-colonial struggle and still bears the marks of that struggle. That observation alone yields another more astounding recollection, that in asserting their right to self-determination Africans had to employ the languages of their colonial masters; that the rhetoric of political demand they adopted was better understood in Europe among both rulers and the common people, than among the African masses for whom, presumably, the demands were being made.

That fact alone has been responsible for a considerable weakness in the political institutions of African societies and finally suggests the limits to the kind of support African leaders can reasonably expect from ordinary people who, after all, were largely excluded from the dialogue between the *evolués* and their masters. In literature, at least, that historical development has planted the seeds of the present crisis.

Let me state at once that to speak of a crisis in this connection is not to be unduly alarmist. It is now an open secret that much of African literature written in the European languages — by far the most influential from the perspective of developing national consciousness — has been, and continues to be, created in a barely concealed state of profound anxiety, even panic. The anxiety stems in large measure from an uncomfortable feeling that this literature, however deeply conscious of its responsibilities, somehow lacks relevance for 80 per cent of the African people who enjoy no literacy. Quite conceivably, the majority of those who can read could easily handle vernacular literature but cannot be expected to deal with the complex forms of modern fiction and contemporary verse, written in the European languages.

Already, one can anticipate an immediate objection to this line of argument. A retort could be made, and quite rightly, that even in European societies people who read serious books form a depressingly small minority; that the majority, for lack of intellectual training or through choice, confine themselves to the world of the newspaper, radio and television. What ordinary people in Europe, however, share with their educated elites is a common tongue, which does mean that a great deal of information, usually a whole set of assumptions which form the common currency of the educated classes, do filter down, in whatever debased form, to the ordinary man in the street. Listen to working people talk in any European city, listen to individuals who have never struggled through the psychoanalytical theories of Freud: you will be amazed to hear how so-and-so is 'fixated' on one or other of the parents, or how this or that person is supposed to have made a 'Freudian slip'. Language then becomes a living organism, forever changing to accommodate concepts and ideas which, in time, become the common heritage of all those who grow up speaking the same language, whatever their class or educational background.

In Africa, quite the contrary is true. The masses are effectively sealed off from the educated elite who, through training and the constant use of an official language in creative and intellectual discourse, constitute an objectification on African soil of another culture and its values. 'The effect of the colonial presence (in Africa)', writes the Kenyan novelist, Ngugi Wa Thiong'o, 'was to create an elite who took on the tongue and adopted the style of the conquerors.'[2] This presents the writer with something of a dilemma. If in trying to rehabilitate their smashed-up cultures African writers are forced to write in foreign languages their task must obviously remain incomplete: for it is one of the bitterest ironies that even when an assault had to be made on those opposing values which the masters used to control their colonial subjects, values which constituted the very underpinning of the colonial system, that war had to be waged by Africans in the same languages that were used to enslave them: in French, English and Portuguese: as such, if not in mental attitude, at least in the tool of its production, the best of African literature reflects a former colonial dependency. Similarly, even at its most complex and formally competent level, this literature presents to us the aspect of a cultural hybrid in which African and European concerns are inextricably mixed through the twine and woof of a common language.

The political and cultural consequences of this historical development are, of course, enormous: the Tunisian Jewish writer, Albert Memmi, on the whole not nearly so pessimistic as other commentators on this question, has nonetheless underlined the irony:

Ces peuples ont été opprimés pendant des dizaines d'années, quelquefois des siècles. Le resultat pour l'écrivain, pour le professeur, pour l'homme de pensée, c'est qu'il a été culturellement aliéné . . . Le resultat, c'est que dans une carrière intellectuelle, il était obligé d'adopter la langue du peuple dominant, d'adopter même, d'une certaine manière, des valeurs institutionnelles et culturelle de ce peuple.[3]

[These people have been oppressed for dozens of years, sometimes for centuries. The result for the writer, for the teacher, for the man of ideas, is that he has been culturally alienated . . . The result is that, in an intellectual career, he is obliged to adopt the language of the dominant people, even to adopt, in a certain manner, some of the institutional and cultural values of that people.]

The relationship between language and national cultures cannot be too strongly emphasised. Like other peoples, black Africans possess a rich and living heritage in philosophy, ethics, religion and artistic creation, the deepest roots of which are embedded in the rich soil of African languages. To re-possess that tradition means not only unlocking the caskets of syntax, disentangling metaphysics from poetry and proverb; it also means extracting social philosophy and habits of moral thought from the rhythm, imagery, repetitiousness, sometimes from the very circumlocution of native African speech. A good writer like Karen Blixen, out of a deep sympathy with people and place, could only express the intimations of this other separate, irreducible experience: 'Until you knew a Native well, it was impossible to get a straight answer from him. To a direct question as to how many cows he had, he had an eluding reply — "As many as I told you yesterday".'[4] But just as ignorant Europeans used to find African music, especially drumming, repetitive and boring, in the hands of an infirm and uncertain talent the attempt to reproduce the exact equivalent of African speech in a novel written in English would probably result in the grinding down of its entire machinery in a distressingly mannered but highly revelatory acknowledgement of its sources.

Talent here is, of course, everything, but I think some critics grossly underestimate the nature of the difficulties.[5] Translating from an African language into a European one has grave risks; even in the sure hands of a sophisticated writer the undertaking can prove quite treacherous. Language is usually the first to betray him: African peasants speaking unlikely periods of Victorian or Elizabethan English.

At the Fourah Bay Conference on 'African Literature and the Universities', Gerald Moore quoted two examples from J.P. Clark's play, *The Masquerade*, in which one of the characters, a fisherman, uses the word 'phenomenon' and phrases like 'being privy to a certain secret'.[6] Moore is unusually indulgent in this case and seems to accept Clark's argument, for example, that the absence of social stratification in traditional African society as reflected in speech, justified that particular piece of dialogue. My own feeling is that it does not; but Clark, an extremely competent playwright, is constantly betrayed by his training in another language and tradition — much more so than his compatriot, Wole Soyinka. Moore was much closer to the truth when he wrote recently that the African writers are being asked to 'define and describe in English, cultures of which that language and its associations form only a superficial part'.[7] Speaking of the African dramatists particularly Moore further noted that 'the English speech given to their characters (which, for the dramatist, means the whole of his text) can be no more than equivalent for words, tones and rhythms in which their originals habitually speak'.[8]

In the face of these difficulties, it would seem that the advantages of writing in the African languages would prove overwhelming: that the most sophisticated and articulate of modern African writers feel unable to do so has created, I suggest, both for the writer and his African audience, a situation of extreme cultural ambiguity. This realisation was borne in upon me some while ago when I was asked to review a new novel, *This Earth, My Brother*, by the Ghanaian poet, Kofi Awoonor; in many ways quite an outstanding novel of its kind.

3

This novel represents a man's physical and spiritual journey from childhood to his death by suicide. It depicts, by use of realistic narrative as well as dream and fantasy, the internal disintegration of its hero, Amamu, a lawyer and intellectual; this disintegration is matched only by the corruption and disintegration of the external society surrounding him. In some later chapters I shall deal more adequately with this extraordinary book; here it is only necessary to pay some attention to certain of its features which point to the kind of profound cultural dislocation that I have been talking about.

One quickly notices, in fact, that though genuine enough and wholly supported by the facts of the situation, the despair of Awoonor's hero is not that of the Ghanaian people who in coup after coup have gone on forever like Tennyson's brook. True enough, the intelligentsia of any country, precisely because it is well equipped by training, reading and reflection, ought to act as seismograph of that society's internal movement: consequently, one is not surprised that Amamu feels so thoroughly depressed by the slow decline of hope in his society, which in turn impinges and disturbs the tenor of his life. But with each reading of the novel, the despair seems to me too excessive, almost synthetic, the result of too much reading of contemporary fiction in other languages, the general movement of which is toward certain recognisable forms of metaphysical despair and lack of belief.

In fact, we have it on the authority of an American English professor that Awoonor's novel is nearly 'a novel of despair'[9] and that the Accra it invokes is closer to Joyce's Dublin and Faulkner's Jefferson than the one we know. John Thompson, the reviewer, further notes: 'There is much guilt in the brilliant English of the best African writing today; see how Chinua Achebe and Awoonor deal with the problem of translating into their English the African tongues of their people.'[10] I agree with Thompson that a novelist like Chinua Achebe is always conscious of the immense debt he owes to his society, if that is what Thompson means by 'guilt'; but with *This Earth, My Brother*, I found there existed at its core unhappy alien demons. The very quality and tone of its language, the surrealistic break-up of its narrative structures and the mixture of realism and fantasy, gives the novel an air of that distressing alienation all too common in modern European fiction.

This must not be taken as a criticism of the novel as 'false' in the general sense of the word: its air of 'falsity', if that is what it is, has a perverse kind of 'truth' since it is an accurate depiction of that feeling of despair among a certain class of the intellectual elite in Africa today, most of whom spend a great deal of their time abroad; the novel's sense of 'alienation', therefore, reflects a painful rupture between the African elite and the people in whose name that elite supposedly speaks: for, let me say at once, I am prepared to argue here as I have done elsewhere, that African society has not yet reached the straits that reading a novel like *This Earth, My Brother*, would lead us to suppose. Throughout the continent, despite an almost uniform betrayal of the people by their leaders, despite an outbreak of war and violence, African society is distinguished by its immense hopefulness, gaiety and cheerfulness.

If you want to examine the springs of this general sense of optimism, you will have to look finally at the traditional African philosophy and religion, with its profound faith in the negotiability of fate through the intervention of magic and the intercession of the ancestral deities, which make it impossible for the people to accept that everything is ever truly lost. If things are going wrong there is always a chance that a greater magician, a more powerful shaman or priest, will come along to snatch the kola nuts out of the fire. For centuries this has been the basis of the people's faith in the face of adversity and the fecundity of the unexpected.

The feelings of dislocation that reading certain African novels induces finally leads one to question the very *appropriateness* of the novel in recapturing the true feel of traditional African society; the anxiety is caused by the knowledge that inherent in the novelistic form itself, as it has come to us from the European tradition, is a view of life that is essentially hostile to African traditional society. Consequently, when we read a novel about African traditional society we are looking, as it were, through a mirror which continually refracts African experience according to its own optical 'illusions' — if not actual delusions. The prisms of that mirror impose their own shape on the reality they try to view; the judgements on African values are therefore already inherent or built-in in the form itself.

For instance, the novel — the traditional novel at any rate — proposes the 'individual' as its centre. To be truly dynamic, to have progression, the novel further proposes as one of its essential mechanisms 'conflict' between 'individuals' or between an individual and a group, between the individual and his environment. Its main characteristic is the exploration of individual character and as such it is an art form that best serves bourgeois society or manifestations of incipient bourgeois society. The novel, it has often seemed to me, must distort the African past and tradition in order to contain it within its framework. At this stage no one needs to be told that certain notions inherent in bourgeois society, in particular the greater regard for individual rights over those of the community as a whole, would have been considered a perversion and an evil in a traditional African society; also that competition between individuals was regarded with a great deal of unease as a basis for considerable disharmony in African traditional society. Naturally, the art forms that any society develops are intimately related to the kind of social structures which it has built up. Thus the kind of art which was prized above all others in the Old Africa was the one which promoted *harmonisation* of the potential areas of conflict within the community by psychological projection or the externalisation of opposing forces of good and evil through ritual and communal forms of art. The novel, much more than drama, represents therefore a radical departure from native art forms.

So far as I know, only one critic of African literature has recognised the anomalous character of the novel in the face of a social system such as I have been elaborating. In *Transition*, Number 18, the Nigerian critic, Obi Wali, wrote:

In a real sense, the chief obstruction to the three characters [discussed in his essay] is the community, with its tyranny and incomprehensibility, the community where the individual does not exist in his own right but is compelled to lose his identity for the sake of social cohesion. In a certain technical sense then, we say that the character in traditional African society

5

does not exist, yet the African novelist in order to make his craft possible is forced to hammer out characters from this social block which is amorphous in many ways.

All this may lead the reader to suspect that the situation of the African writer using English or French is necessarily a hopeless one. The reader may further suppose that given the complexity of his linguistic situation this kind of African writer has insurmountable obstacles placed in the way toward full expression, and that therefore he could only falsify African experience or at best create something that falls short of the genuine article. In a way, any writer always falls short of his true ideal: his struggle with his materials, the attempt to wrestle from language the true meaning of the world he seeks to depict, is always endless and incomplete. Incomplete, because in describing the true lineaments of what the writer sees with his inner eye language can only approximate the shapes and figures of his imagination. In this respect, therefore, the situation of the African writer is not unique. It is the same struggle with language. But clearly what the African writer lacks in this enterprise is the silent *complicity* of his people, the majority of whom still use African languages to express their most intimate thoughts and emotions; in writing in a European language the African writer is alone, operating outside the boundaries of either his own society or that of his adopted language, therefore always on the outside, looking in, increasingly in need of some more specific corroboration of his vision through language that can be consented to, or the authenticity of which can be attested to, by his people. The fact that the people about whom he makes up these stories cannot corroborate the truth of what he is saying is finally what makes his situation intolerable. Certainly, it is an ambiguous one; it may even be said to be critical: at the same time it imposes upon the truly creative writer the kind of discipline which is quite beneficial: his search for form, his straining for the sort of distillation of language which will accurately reflect the movement of African society, will be even more relentless, just because in some hopelessly tragic way it cannot be truly fulfilled: and this search can only be steadily reinforced by good criticism and the writer's own sense of what is fitting.

Technically, some partial answers to the problem of language have already been suggested by several writers, two of whom are quite outstanding in their own ways. The two writers I have in mind are Chinua Achebe and Amos Tutuola, both Nigerians, each of whom starts from the opposite end of the scale: Chinua Achebe, because his sense of responsibility to African material had led him to put his Western training and reading of English fiction at the service of a rigorously selective intelligence which is forever trying to widen the possibilities of what the structure of the English language can support of the African experience; Tutuola, because his lack of self-conscious sophistication and training has permitted him to take the kind of liberties with the English language which no sophisticated African writer could have allowed himself.

Strangely enough, it is just because Tutuola gets so close to the past and the traditional modes of story-telling; and it is just because he has let standard English collide with the syntactical structures of his native Yoruba, that Tutuola seems even more outrageously modernist and experimental than any of the consciously experimentalist writers. My guess is that his technique will appeal increasingly to younger African novelists and poets who may recognise in Tutuola an accidental but happy convergence of the extreme forms of European art such as 'surrealism' and the predominantly anti-naturalistic African models. But as I said, the answers provided by writers like Amos Tutuola and Chinua Achebe are only partial. Until a bridge of communication can be built between the African writer and his native audience, African literature, it seems to me, is likely to continue to exist in a state of perpetual crisis and tension for the foreseeable future.

Dr Abiola Irele is surely right to argue, as he did recently, that the peculiar position of the new literature of Africa written in the European languages, 'involving, at first sight at least, a divorce between the substance of this literature and its linguistic medium, is in itself a reflection of what I would call the state of incoherence which our societies are passing through − of which we have several objective indications'.[11]

Indeed, there are times when to speak of African literature is itself so problemmatical that one can understand the current reluctance to even ask the question: 'What is so *African* about this literature?' A definition such as the one proposed at the 1962 Congress of African artists in Accra seems to me futile if only because it begs so many questions.[12] To begin with one is not sure what 'authentic handling' of an African setting implies. Stories like Camara Laye's *The Radiance of the King* which leans so hard on fable and fantasy, would make it very hard to apply a hard-and-fast rule about 'authenticity'. At the same time a work like Karen Blixen's *Out of Africa* seems to me unquestionably authentic in the way that some books by native Africans are not; but any definition that would include within its compass Chinua Achebe and a Danish baroness seems to me scarcely useful.

There is a further danger that in defining too closely what African literature ought to be or ought to include we may end up being prescriptive in a way that will inhibit true creativity and originality. Just because a work inhibits that area of experience which is considered 'authentically' African does not make it automatically better as a work of art than another which exhibits the results of contact with Western culture. As the late Christopher Okigbo put it: 'Where you have this African feeling summoned for the occasion − put on like Sunday clothing − you have a bastardisation of the idea of negritude.'[13] Black South African literature has for some time now suffered unjustly from this prejudice against its urbanity: critics, mostly Europeans bored with the familiar, have sometimes assumed that anything to do with mud huts, masks and fetish cults is somehow superior to works dealing with modern Africa − an unjustified conclusion that has had at least one deleterious effect of encouraging a proliferation of ersatz novels about magic, religious cults and other lurid tales, all laced with the obligatory proverb on every page. Clearly, the problem of language and form cannot be solved by an adoption of such crude methods. Indeed, the very grounds upon which writers are attempting to discover solutions to this problem are forever shifting as new political choices are made administratively.*

* Tanzania finally opted for Swahili for an official language. Into that language President Julius Nyerere translated Shakespeare's *Julius Caesar*.

It is, of course, entirely natural that African writers, increasingly aware of the impossible situation in which they have been thrust by history, are tempted to favour extreme but impractical measures to meet the situation. The Nigerian playwright, Wole Soyinka, in his characteristically quixotic manner, proposed at a UNESCO conference:

> . . . That a meeting be summoned of African writers and linguists, representations in equal numbers from every state in Africa who shall decide, at a closed session, on an official language for the black continent, including the black peoples of America and set a time-limit for the adoption of this language by all African states.[14]

Were politicians to balk at this suggestion, Mr Soyinka would have this unlikely collection of individuals resolve in advance 'not merely to boycott but to create a boycott of all creative activities in those countries until such politicians of reaction are re-educated'.

One may admire the sound democratic impulses and social concerns which have led Mr Soyinka to present his hasty solution without being convinced by its practicality. What Soyinka's proposal does suggest is that in the final analysis the solution does not lie with the writers themselves but with political leaders capable of taking radical decisions.

For instance, given the number and variety of native African languages and dialects, African leaders could decide to increase the efficacy in the use of European languages by putting more resources in the hands of language teachers; they could shift their priorities dramatically by embarking on massive programmes designed to bring large sections of the African populations to acceptable standards of literacy. Beyond that, we can only agree with the maxim of the Senegalese novelist, Sembene Ousmane, that 'What cannot be cured must be endured . . .'

REFERENCES

1   Janheinz Jahn, *A History of Neo-African Literature*, Faber, 1968, p.30−1.
2   Ngugi wa Thiong'o, *Homecoming*, Heinemann, London, 1972, p.10.
3   Albert Memmi's remarks are contained in the report of the Scandinavian Conference, *The Writer in Modern Africa*, edited by Per Wastberg for the Scandinavian Institute of African Studies, 1968; see p.80.
4   Karen Blixen, *Out of Africa*, Putnam, London, 1937, p.19.
5   See Eldred Jones, 'The Decolonization of African Literature', one of the papers contained in *The Writer in Modern Africa*, p.72: 'The use of the foreign language then need not embarrass the African or the European. As everyone knows, English and French are the two foremost African languages. The African writer need not therefore be dominated by the language of his adoption, though it is perfectly possible that he may be. It is possible that with the adoption of his new language he may become mesmerised by the material in it and quite unconsciously reflect ideas and attitudes not really his own.'
6   Gerald Moore, 'The Language of Poetry', paper presented to the Conference on African Literature and the Universities at the Universities of Dakar and Fourah Bay College, Sierra Leone, 1963; published by the Ibadan University Press, p.108.
7   See Gerald Moore's Introduction to his book, *The Chosen Tongue*, Longman, London, 1969, p.xix.
8   *Ibid.*

9   See Dr John Thompson's review in *New York Review of Books*, 23 September 1971.

10   *Ibid.*

11   Abiola Irele, 'The Criticism of Modern African Literature', paper read at the Conference on African Literature held at the University of Ife, 1968; published by Heinemann, 1971.

12   See T.R.M. Creighton's 'An attempt to Define African Literature', in G. Moore (ed.), *African Literature and the Universities*, Ibadan University Press, 1965, p.84: 'It [the Congress] accepted a definition of African literature as "any work in which an African setting is authentically handled or to which experiences which originate in Africa are integral" '.

13   See Lewis Nkosi's report on the Conference of African Writers of English Expression, held at Makerere University College, 1962, in L. Nkosi, *Home and Exile*, Longman, 1965

14   Quoted from an address by Wole Soyinka to the UNESCO Conference on *The Influence of Colonialism on the Artist, his Milieu and his Public in Developing Countries*, held at Dar es Salaam, Tanzania, July 1971.

CHAPTER TWO

NEGRITUDE: NEW AND OLD PERSPECTIVES

1

No work purporting to introduce the student to African literature can be said to have accomplished its task without some explanatory remarks on the theory of negritude. Admittedly such an undertaking is an onerous one, requiring as it does an amount of patience, fairness and impartiality that is often beyond the capacity of any one critic. Why this should be so can at once be fully grasped by taking into account the mass of confusing, often contradictory statements, the passionate assertions and counter-assertions, that have characterised the negritude controversy these past ten years. A useful starting point in any discussion of negritude is a brief survey of some of the pronouncements that have been made for and against its general philosophy.

In what must surely rank as the understatement of the century, the black American critic and poet, Samuel W. Allen, once observed of negritude that it was not 'amenable to easy definition'.[1] The term, said Allen, appeared to 'serve in somewhat varying roles' those who employed it. While acknowledging this difficulty Allen made a brave attempt to provide various definitions of negritude. 'It represents in one sense', he said, 'the Negro African poet's endeavours to recover for his race a normal self-pride, a lost confidence in himself, a world in which he again has a sense of identity and a significant role.'[2] According to Allen: 'The Negro is denied an acceptable identity in Western culture.'[3] And

> . . . this preoccupation with the situation of the Negro in a culturally alien world common to the vast majority of Negro African poets has given birth in the French language to the central concept of *négritude*.[4]

It is now common knowledge that the man who invented the term negritude is the great Martinican poet, Aimé Césaire, co-founder with Léopold Senghor of *L'Etudiant Noir* in the Paris of the 1930s. In a most illuminating interview describing the precise conditions which gave rise to the negritude concept, Césaire told the Haitian poet, René Depestre, during the Havana Cultural Congress in 1967:

> We lived in an atmosphere of rejection, and we developed an inferiority complex. I have always thought that the black man was searching for his identity. And it has seemed to me that if what we want is to establish this identity, then we must have a concrete consciousness of what we are — that is, of the first fact of our lives: that we are black; that we were black and have a history, a history that contains certain cultural elements of great value;

and that Negroes were not, as you put it, born yesterday, because there have been beautiful and important black civilizations. At the time we began to write people could write a history of world civilization without devoting a single chapter to Africa, as if Africa had made no contributions to the world. Therefore we affirmed that we were Negroes and that we were proud of it, and that we thought that Africa was not some sort of blank page in the history of humanity; in sum, we asserted that our Negro heritage was worthy of respect, and that this heritage was not relegated to the past, that its values were values that could still make an important contribution to the world.[5]

As a movement of political revolt against the tyranny of Western culture over those who were colonised by Europe; as an attempt to restore pride and dignity to those denuded of either hope or racial identity, negritude was fairly easy to understand or defend: and if the objection is made, as it is so often made, that the great mass of white people who made up the white West were themselves victims of economic oppression and exploitation, then the blacks, in the words of Césaire, 'were doubly proletarianised and alienated: in the first place as workers, but also as blacks'.[6]

It was for this reason that in his monumental poem, *Cahier d'un retour au pays natal*, Césaire put all his passionate lyricism at the service:

> of those who never tamed steam or electricity
> those who did not explore sea or sky
> but who know in their innermost depths
> the country of suffering

The poem was a great paean to the humiliated and oppressed blacks; also a noble attempt by a great poet of the French language to reclaim for these 'down-trodden' and 'wretched of the earth' a certain measure of human dignity. Seen from such a perspective, and apart from its profound historical consequences for the black literature of Africa and the New World, negritude was primarily a movement of political reaction: indeed, most of the leading theorists of negritude have at one time or another emphasised the essentially political aspect of the movement's concerns without denying its cultural dimension or its undoubtedly fructifying results for black literature, especially the poetry of the period between the two world wars. Even those figures in the movement now regarded as fundamentally conservative have been no less emphatic on this point. M. Léopold Senghor, the poet-president of Senegal and the movement's most celebrated spokesman and theoretician in Africa, has insisted: 'Africa's misfortune has been that our secret enemies, in defending their values, have made us despise ours.'[7] This conclusion led Senghor to assert, somewhat controversially, the primacy of African values in everything concerning Africans or people of African ancestry:

The spirit of African civilization animates, consciously or unconsciously, the best Negro artists and writers of today, both in Africa and America. Insofar as they are aware of African culture and draw inspiration from it, they rise to

11

international status. Insofar as they turn their backs on Mother Africa, they degenerate and are without interest.[8]

Senghor's exposition of negritude is extremely complex, suggestive, poetic, even subtly conjectural. In contrast to the rest of his pronouncements on negritude his most quoted definition is at once breathtakingly simple and impossibly panoramic: 'Negritude', he has told us, 'is simply the sum total of civilized values of the black world',[9] a proposition which explains everything while explaining nothing. Senghor is not content, however, to leave matters at that: his definition soon narrows down sufficiently to give us some clue of his rather detailed ideas as to what he means by negritude. Senghor's negritude, at any rate, is not simply a matter of political protests; it also involves an African ontology, an essential African way of perceiving reality and the relations between beings or forces inhabiting the universe.

For instance, at his most controversial, Senghor distinguishes between what he calls 'African rationality' and that of the European races. The European, says Senghor, is distinguishable from the African by his worship of the 'objective intelligence'. To understand the world he must analyse, and to analyse he must kill and dissect. 'White men', says Senghor, perhaps enjoying the inversion of a long-standing joke, 'are cannibals.' The African, on the other hand, is 'shut up inside his black skin . . . He does not begin by distinguishing himself from the object, the tree or stone.'[10] The Negro or the African uses 'intuitive reason', he abandons himself to the object: 'Classical European reason is analytical and makes use of the object. African reason is intuitive and participates in the object.'[11] Furthermore, the African, according to Senghor, 'reacts more faithfully to the stimulus of the object. He is wedded to its rhythm. This physical sense of rhythm, rhythm of movements, forms and colours, is one of his specific characteristics, for rhythm is the essense of energy itself.'[12]

These and other similar assertions by Senghor have been the source of a major dispute among African writers and intellectuals. His pronouncements have been variously pronounced as 'racist', 'unscientific' and worse. Nonetheless, Senghor does enjoy formidable support among certain English-speaking African intellectuals who see nothing 'unscientific' in the proposition that Africans possess certain unique characteristics which distinguish them from Europeans or Asians. One of the most articulate of these intellectuals is the Nigerian literary critic, Abiola Irele, a product of English schools and the Sorbonne, a fact which probably explains both his skill in handling abstract categories and his sympathy with some of his French-speaking African colleagues who are the main proponents of the negritude theory. However, Irele's re-interpretation of Senghor's thoughts acquires its peculiar force from a trenchant style, at once aggressively polemical while relying to some extent on what may be termed the 'objective facts' of the situation. His interpretation begins with the hypothesis of a Pan-African 'cultural world view' according to which, despite some obvious internal differences, all African cultures can be said to be united into a single Pan-Negro whole. 'A fundamental basis of negritude', he has asserted, 'is the unity of African culture.'[13] Irele acknowledges there are certain objections to this view, but goes on to argue: 'Surely there is something in common, in the way of perception that distinguishes the Negro-

African from the European and the Asian. The unity of African culture does not exclude internal variations.' Irele then goes on to develop the argument at some length:

> Apart from empirical considerations such as those dictated by racial affinity, there are objective proofs of a fundamental African world system, which embraces Bantu, Akan, Yoruba, Kikuyu and Zulu together in one cultural family. This fundamental conception of the world is expressed in languages, music and art that are related, and that are surely distinguishable from European and Asian, and more profoundly still in the religions of the African peoples.[14]

The writer insists that these differences are objectively ascertainable, and challengingly asserts: 'I find nothing to contradict the thesis of a unified African universe.'[15]

Indeed there is already a considerable body of ethnological data to support the belief held by many contemporary scholars of African societies that there is a certain 'ensemble of African cultural values' which constitutes a so-called 'Pan-Negro cultural universe'. Such a universe is predicated, first of all, upon the essential 'unity of African cultures', until recently a much disputed concept. Not only is the 'unity of African cultures' an often disputed concept but some critics of negritude have gone further: they have rejected any suggestion that there are unique elements in African cultures which are not discoverable in one form or another in other human cultures. On the face of it, there appears to be a lot in this argument but I think most commentators would agree with Senghor when he argues that even those features which African cultures share with other cultures 'are not found elsewhere united in the same equilibrium and with quite the same illumination'.[16]

Even those scholars who for convenience tend to divide sub-Saharan Africa into specific 'culture areas' concede that despite the apparent variety of African cultures there is a certain underlying unity which collectively distinguishes them from West and Eastern civilisations. In his work *Civilizations of Black Africa* Professor Jacques Maquet who, as must be obvious from the title of his book, believes there is not just one but several African civilisations, is equally prepared to concede that 'to the degree to which more similarities are found between the various cultures of Africa than between African and non-African cultures, it is justifiable to place the African cultures in a separate category';[17] and the Ghanaian philosopher, Professor W.E. Abraham, observes that African cultures belong to a 'world view to which can be related all other cultural concepts, including those of religion and theology, morality and social organisation'.[18] It is just upon the validity of this hypothesis of a 'Pan-African world view' that any basis can be found for supporting any idea of a possible cultural link between New World Negroes and Africans; and it is upon this link, in turn, between New World blacks and their ancestral African cultures, determined on a purely objective basis of ethnological findings, that the theory of negritude stands to benefit most.

Ironically enough, it was Jean-Paul Sartre, a French philosopher and a white man, who wrote what has become a seminal essay[19] for any further explorations of the philosophy of negritude. When Sam Allen observed in passing that negritude was 'unsettling to many because it puts into the realm of the explicit that which might more comfortably remain in the area of the implicit', he was merely repeating what Sartre had already stated in more forceful terms in a work to which most commentaries on negritude have since become unusually indebted. In his famous preface to Senghor's *Anthologie de la Nouvelle Poésie Nègre et Malgache de Langue Française* (1948) Sartre stated categorically that the Negro writer 'can scarcely express negritude in prose'.[20] Enlarging on what he described as 'the folly of the enterprise of speech' Sartre saw language essentially as prose, 'and prose, in essence, failure,'[21] so that negritude could only be evoked by words 'always allusive, never direct'. For Sartre, the source of all poetic experience, especially a poetry trying to express the essence of Negro being, was this 'feeling of failure before the language when considered as a means of direct expression'.[22] Thus Allen, too, contrasting poetry with the demands of realism in the novel, speculated that it was probably 'not by chance that this concept, negritude, originated among the poets rather than among those working in prose'. The poet, according to Allen, 'has probably a greater chance to penetrate, at once without apology, and without a setting of the worldly stage, to the deepest levels of his creative concern'.[23] Later on, we shall see in fact that it was precisely for this reason that Freudian psychology and the artistic movements such as surrealism held such fascination for the adherents of negritude. Negritude, after all, was nothing if not an exploration of the collective dreams of black men who had only just awakened from the nightmare of colonialism; and poetry, with its direct visceral routes to the psyche, or because of its spontaneity, became the essential medium for the expression of the 'negroness' of Negro people.

If it is true, as one writer has suggested, that negritude covers 'a variety of frequently conflicting tendencies', it is in Sartre's great analytical essay that all the various strands, political, cultural and aesthetic, are finally gathered together to illuminate that murky area between theory and experience. Sartre's analytical tools are a Marxist outlook deepened by his subjective existentialism, one balancing against the other. For Sartre negritude is both objective and subjective, an act of 'becoming' by black people who, victims of colonialism and the trans-Atlantic slave trade, have been denied an autonomous existence by an exploitative bourgeois West. Negritude is a 'myth', if you will, but a 'myth' that becomes reality through a massive effort of political will: the desire of black people to free themselves from white standards of Western culture by a militant assertion of their independent humanity. The African 'must compel those who for centuries have vainly attempted, because he was a Negro, to reduce him to the status of the beast, to recognise him as a man'.[24]

Sartre accepts the provisional and temporary aspect of negritude; after all, as a Marxist he believes in the ultimate unity which will gather into a single combative mail fist all the oppressed of the world, black and white; but equally Sartre recognises that before the blacks can join the white oppressed in a common struggle there must be what he calls a 'moment of separation or of negativity'.[25] Rhetorically, Sartre asks:

Can black men count on the aid of the white proletariat, distant, distracted by its own struggles, before they have united and organised themselves on their own soil?[26]

There must, therefore, be an interim period in which the Blacks learn to express their claims 'in common', when 'they think of themselves as black men'.[27] This Sartre calls 'anti-racist racism' which he hopes finally will lead to the abolition of the differences of race, of all racism. However, a 'myth' created for political purposes is only one aspect of negritude: Sartre also insists that 'there exists in effect an objective negritude which expresses itself in the customs, the arts, the songs and the dances of the African population'.[28]

It is impossible to suggest in the course of one chapter the full range of Sartre's analysis of negritude, the startling variety of his poetic insights and the resourcefulness of his mind in the face of the mute and unknowable. His essay deserves the reputation it has acquired over twenty-five years since it was first published. It is not just a skilled enterprise of intellectual analysis; it is also a supreme effort by a Western intellectual to enter imaginatively into the world of black men.

2

The first concerted attack on negritude began partly as a result of a general dis-enchantment with the political conservatism of some of the movement's leading ideologues in the post-independence period of African politics and partly as a result of increased exchanges between French-speaking African intellectuals, with their slightly different experiences of colonialism. For several reasons, some of which will be obvious later, English-speaking African writers have generally been hostile to negritude even to some of its literary production.

The debate on the meaning and function of negritude finally reached its most absurd, sometimes hilarious, but all the same potentially dangerous, climax in March and April of 1963 during the sessions of the Dakar and Free-town conference on 'African Literature and the Universities'. I say 'potentially dangerous' because the sometimes justified criticisms of negritude as an 'aesthetic' movement were to assume in Dakar and Freetown a groundswell of reaction, at least among English-speaking critics, in which reasonable men were compelled to adopt extreme positions, even to confuse ideas with personalities, and there seemed to exist no broader understanding of the tendencies of literature to draw inspiration from ideas or ideologies that are later found to be inadequate, if not questionable. Who, for instance, can deny the validity of a work like *Germinal* merely on the grounds that Zola's pseudo-scientific naturalism has been found wholly inadequate as a theory of litera-ture? The extreme reaction to negritude, on the other hand, created an atmo-sphere in which rational men, worrying about the impurity of the water, were inclined to throw the baby out with the bath-water.

At any rate, after the acrimonious proceedings of those two conferences the Negritude movement, if it still had any life in Africa, was generally declared to be 'dead'. As the Congolese poet, Tchicaya U Tam'si was to put it to fellow delegates: 'Let us have done with this question of negritude once and for all!' Sembene Ousmane, the Senegalese novelist and film-maker, summed up what has now become a standard response of the Marxist Left to negritude in Africa. 'There was a time', said Ousmane, 'when negritude meant something positive. It was our breastplate against a culture that wanted at all costs to dominate us. But that is past history.'[29] Ousmane went some way to admit that there were values or qualities that 'characterised the black races' but maintained that no one had yet worked out exactly what they were: no really thorough study of negritude had ever been undertaken. The reason, according to Ousmane, is that 'negritude neither feeds the hungry nor builds roads'.[30] Elsewhere,[31] Newell Flather, who interviewed the author in Dakar, was to repeat Ousmane's strictures of negritude in more specific terms. According to Flather, Ousmane is critical of the negritude movement because 'all too often in Afriːa there is a divorce between words and acts' and 'those who preach negritude most ardently are often most closely allied with those who profit from Africa's backwardness'.

However, to be truly inclusive, any survey of the critical literature on negritude must include, at least, the writings and speeches of Ezekiel Mphahlele, the South African writer and critic who, in English-speaking Africa, at any rate, has been the spearhead of a whole attack on negritude. If nothing else, the value of his contribution to the debate on negritude has been to open up a dialogue between French- and English-speaking Africans.

Mphahlele's difficulties with the more fervent adherents of negritude, and they with him, are as much the result of emotional entanglements as they are the consequences of genuine intellectual disagreements. For instance, as a black man who has lived and suffered great disabilities under the apartheid regime Mphahlele tends to see negritude simply as another version of the racist ideology of the Afrikaners. Reed and Wake, in their preface to the Senghor book,[32] are right to emphasise this aspect of the South African contribution to the debate on negritude; but they are seriously wrong to underestimate the interaction between white South African perceptions of colour differences and the role they assign to indigenous African cultures as a result of it.[33] Mphahlele's objections to negritude are not simply because this ideology reminds him of the superficial aspects of the race ideology of South Africa; time and again Mphahlele has made it clear that his reservations have something to do with his approach to culture as a human activity: for example, he regards South Africa, despite its apartheid programmes, as having gone some way toward providing a model of 'acculturation' in Africa. Such a process is inevitably not without some conflict, and for black South African intellectuals this conflict is expressed in the following dilemma: 'Would it be preferable to call a march back to indigenous culture and thereby help the Government (of South Africa) to reconstruct ethnic groups and help work the repressive machinery, or leave things to drift as they do at the moment, leaving it to individual cultural activity to go the way creative genius guides it?'[34]

Personally, I think this argument has serious flaws, but the weakness is not the one attributed by Reed and Wake to the South African critics of the theory of negritude. The weakness in Mphahlele's argument lies in its negative nature, which seems to suggest that no matter how valid the case for negritude may be, if it can be shown that white racists will benefit from its expression it must therefore be suppressed. Surely, this is conceding too much to white racists: it is virtually to permit them to dictate the shape and the future of the black South Africans, culturally as well as politically; for to be seen as always reacting to what white racists might think of your pronouncements on the black cultural situation scarcely suggests an independence of mind. On the contrary this reminds one of the time when black Americans used to deny that they could dance better than white people on the grounds that such an admission would reinforce the stereotype of the blacks as being 'more rhythmical'. The arguments for negritude are either valid or not valid, and their validity does not depend on what white people make of them.

On the whole, Mphahlele's critique of negritude, has never been an occasion for deep political analysis. In contrast to his thoughtful commentaries on the artistic questions raised by negritude, Mphahlele's contribution to the debate on the relations between black literature and politics is most perfunctory. Indeed, both Mphahlele and some of the left-wing critics of negritude have yet to apply themselves seriously to the kind of analysis of race and class such as Jean Paul Sartre so challengingly offered in *Orphée Noir* or by Aimé Césaire in the Havana interview* and elsewhere. It is upon the aesthetic problems raised by ideological affiliations that Mphahlele's criticisms strike their target most consistently. His objections in this area derive from the sensibility of a creative writer, who is, above all, properly suspicious of any ideological prescriptions that would tend to impose certain restrictions on the artist's creative instinct. A clue to the drift of Mphahlele's thinking on the subject can be discerned in even the most casual remarks that he makes on the relationship between negritude as a principle of black art and the actualities of creative effort as they are experienced by the individual artist. Referring to the negritude controversy at the Makerere conference of African writers, for example, Mphahlele reported: 'We did not dwell on the delegate's defence of négritude because we were not interested in poetry that is written in accordance with a cultural ideology or programme . . . Indeed much of negritude poetry has killed itself.'[35] He has warned us further: 'We should not allow ourselves to be bullied at gunpoint into producing literature that is supposed to contain a negritude theme and style.'[36] Again, more emphatically, 'I say, then that negritude can go on as a socio-political slogan, but that it has no right to set itself up as a standard of literary performance.'[37]

At times Mphahlele seems to be merely raising objections, no doubt rooted in a certain empiricist Anglo-Saxon tradition, against the need to theorise about the obvious or, if not the obvious, the intangible. What most writers have failed to notice, however, is the distinctly anti-intellectual strain running through most of the Anglo-African criticism of negritude — as indeed there is

---

* At that time I criticised the Communists for forgetting our Negro characteristics. They acted like Communists, which was all right, but they acted like abstract Communists. I maintained that the political question could not do away with our condition as Negroes. We are Negroes, with a great number of historical peculiarities.

There are people, even today, who thought and still think that it is all simply a matter of the left taking power in France, that with a change in the economic conditions the black question will disappear. I have never agreed with that at all. I think that the economic question is important, but it is not the only thing.

in English culture generally, an inherent suspicion of metaphysics which can be seen clearly in the tendency to treat with disdain what is obviously a deeply felt need amongst French intellectuals to construct theoretical models about even the most nebulous phenomena. After Dakar Mphahlele wrote with bitter irony mingled, one suspects, with a genuine puzzled curiosity about French-speaking critics of African literature:

> As one listens to the vocabulary of this criticism one experiences various emotional responses: irritation, admiration, humility, because one suspects there is a profound philosophy beneath it all that escapes one, and irritation in turn because of this failure to grasp it. [38]

Mphahlele's own presentation of the issues is beguilingly simple and unpretentious:

> If there is any *négritude* in the black man's art in South Africa, it is because we *are* African. If a writer's tone is healthy, he is bound to express the African in him. Stripped of Senghor's philosophic musings, the African traits he speaks of can be taken for granted. [39]

A sometimes exasperatingly superficial thinker, Mphahlele nowhere examines the implications, among others, of using a foreign language; nor does he pay any attention to a phenomenon common to the colonised: the adoption of models, whether linguistic or narrative structures, which have been bequeathed to them by the colonising masters. The point is hardly original, several writers having already commented upon it, from Sartre to Frantz Fanon:

> Every colonised people – in other words, every people in whose soul an inferiority complex has been created by the death and burial of its local cultural originality – finds itself face to face with the language of the civilizing nation . . . The colonized is elevated above his jungle status in proportion to his adoption of the mother country's cultural standards. [40]

And Sartre puts it even more provocatively when he observes:

> ...it is this language (French), for them half dead, that Damas, Diop, Laleau, Rabearivelo pour the fire of their skies and of their hearts. Only through it can they communicate; like the scholars of the sixteenth century, who understood each other only in Latin, the blacks rediscover themselves only on the terrain full of the traps which white men have set for them. [41]

Mphahlele has a simplistic view of literary production: to hear him tell it, a handful of literary primitives, unaware of antecedent literary examples, cheerfully sit down to write and while doing so automatically exhibit their African qualities. But of course it is not as simple as that: the literature of black people, in Africa as well as the New World, affords numerous examples of writers who in attempting to express the soul of black people were not only betrayed by the language of their colonial masters but sometimes deliberately chose to suppress those spontaneous qualities, which make up the emotional content of their lives, in order to gain acceptance into the metropolitan cultures.*

In Mphahlele, above all, we discern, as I have already suggested, a hostility common among Anglo-African critics of negritude to the type of ratiocination which is characteristically French; if there is any quality to be thought of as negritude, it is said, it must be grasped as part of an artistic feeling within the work itself and not as an object of intellectual inquiry. Hence Wole Soyinka's now famous maxim: 'A tiger does not proclaim his tigritude!'

3

What I now propose as a new perspective in the discussion of negritude is to regard it not as some aberration by a group of racially inspired black men but as part of an old, legitimate, even respectable intellectual tradition which goes back to Kant and the *Critique of Pure Reason*. Anyone who is conversant with the history of the Negritude Movement and its origins; anyone, that is, who is even vaguely aware of the acute dissatisfaction felt by the founding members of negritude with the serene classical detachment of formal French culture, with its cool stately control and rigorous suppression of boisterous emotion – or what one black writer characterised as 'the abominable system of constraints and restrictions . . . generally known by the name of Western civilization'; indeed, anyone who can at all understand the restless quest for the wells of authentic Negro expression which these writers felt were being dried up in the fruitless attempt by the colonised blacks to adhere to the bourgeois norms of a discredited system; such an individual will surely read with a surprised recognition Henry D. Aiken's exposition of a similar, though not identical, sense of frustration among certain 19th-century philosophers, with the rationalistic norms of Western culture, chiefly those concerned with the modes of intellectual inquiry. In his introduction to *The Age of Ideology* Aiken writes:

> In fact, when one looks beneath the forms of words, one finds that what they were attempting, in effect, was a basic critique not only of reason, but of the entire system of norms and principles of Western culture. This task did not and could not be accomplished simply by using the 'rational' methods which had been traditionally employed in philosophical speculation, for those methods themselves formed a principal part of the culture whose norms were being called in question.[42]

* In his autobiography, *A Long Way from Home*, Claude McKay provides an excellent example of the black writer's effort to stifle his own originality: 'In Mr Braithwaite's writings there was not the slightest indication of what sort of American he might be. And I was surprised one day to read in the Negro magazine, *The Crisis*, that he was a Coloured man. Mr Braithwaite was kind enough to write me a very interesting letter. He said that my poems were good, but that, barring two, any reader could tell that the author was a Negro. And because of the almost insurmountable prejudice against all things Negro, he said, he would advise me to write and send to the magazines only such poems as did not betray my racial identity.' (*A Long Way From Home*, an autobiography by Claude McKay, Harcourt Brace and World, New York, 1970, p. 27).

This dissatisfaction with the rationalistic boundaries of philosophic inquiry and the equally tranquillising effects of neo-classicism in literature, led to a general rebellion, of which Romanticism was merely a part, that culminated in the extreme forms of 20th-century 'irrationalism' as exemplified in art by the worship of 'super-reality' of the surrealist writers and painters and the playful, nihilistic gestures of the Dadaists. In philosophy as well as in art, with varying degrees of intensity, these movements were to provide a continuous challenge to the long reign of Reason as the sole arbiter of what constituted 'reality'; sometimes, as with the surrealists, an effort was made to dethrone Reason altogether in favour of other 'non-rational' means of gaining access to 'reality'. Consequently, it should surprise no one that Jazz, traditional African art, the pre-logical or non-logical structures of verbal communication, became so much the vogue; traditional African art primarily because of its anti-naturalistic bias: and it is in this respect, of course, that the psychoanalytical ideas of Freud and Jung became so crucial; their elevation of the 'unconscious' to an important place as an alternative route to the sources of Being was to furnish the modern artist with the means for uncovering the authentic personality behind the careful surfaces of civilised life. We are not, I think, called upon to minimise certain grave dangers inherent in these 'irrationalist' tendencies in order to appreciate their importance in the development of twentieth-century art and philosophy.

At any rate, it ought not to be too difficult to see a connection between the riotous excesses of these movements at the beginning of the century and the equally turbulent birth of negritude as a gesture of rebellion against the stranglehold of Western culture. After a period of apprenticeship in which they had tried to imitate literary forms that had more to do with European pre-occupations than with those of the people among whom they lived, black writers, too, were in a rebellious mood. Perhaps 'imitate' is too strong a word since some of these writers, through education and outlook, genuinely thought of themselves as 'French' and did produce some works of exceptional quality; all the same, as the great Haitian scholar, Dr Jean Price-Mars, so felicitously put it in his essay on Haitian culture, art and literature: 'Haitian literature was like a distant echo of a great organ whose sonorous waves spread out in splendid harmonies over the lands of France.'[43]

In the French Antilles, at any rate, after a century or more of flirtation with neo-classicism or the so-called Parnassianism, these writers discovered they had only succeeded in submerging their individuality beneath metrical verse forms that had nothing essentially to do with the noisy, crowded chaos of black life or its fierce, orgiastic rhythms. To write this type of perennially polished verse the black poet had, metaphorically, to still the memory of the tom-tom in his blood: for Parnassian serenity and its formal objectivity could only pacify the abrasive anger and diminish the affective power of black verse in the interest of calculation and restraint. It was to this dilemma that Léon Laleau, the Haitian poet, referred in *Trahison*, when he wrote:

> This haunted heart which does not fit
> The language I speak and the clothes I wear
> This heart upon which squeeze like a cramp-iron

> Sentiments and costumes borrowed
> From Europe: can you sense the suffering
> And that despair to which there is no equal —
> To tame with words from France
> A heart that came to me from Senegal.

Exile and alienation: they were the starting point in the poetry of negritude from which spun out the themes of self-recovery, self-vindication and a return to Africa, to the source of all Negro inspiration. The Haitian poet, Jacques Roumain, expresses this feeling of exile and return in his poem, *Guinée*:

> It's the long road to Guinea
> No bright welcome will be made for you
> In the dark land of dark men:
> Under a smoky sky pierced by the cry of birds
> Around the eye of the river
>   the eyelashes of the trees open on decaying light
> There, there awaits you beside the water a quiet village,
> And the hut of your fathers, and the hard ancestral stone
>   where your head will rest at last.

If we move to North America we find there, too, in the work of a poet of the Negro Renaissance such as Countee Cullen, that the theme of exile was sufficiently strong to require a similar poetic enactment of a symbolical return to a mythical Africa, a sort of 'literary Garveyism more romantic than convincing', as the editors of the *Negro Caravan* once defined this poetry. However, the sense of loss was very real. As Cullen explained his predicament in *Heritage*:

> My conversion came high-price
> I belong to Jesus Christ,
> Preacher of humility;
> Heathen gods are naught to me.

However, beneath this apparent Christian decorum lay the authentic feelings, the poet's actual negritude, if you wish, which were so volatile that you can palpably feel the poet drawing back from their expression:

> All day long and all night through,
> One thing only must I do:
> Quench my pride and cool my blood,
> Lest I perish in the flood.
> Lest a hidden ember set
> Timber that I thought was wet
> Burning like the dryest flax,
> Melting like the merest wax,
> Lest the grave restore its dead.
> Not yet has my heart or head

In the least way realised
They and I are civilised.

Yet if we examine the poem closely we begin to see a conundrum at its centre. If you compare the poem with lines from Césaire, for example, *Heritage* suffers from a certain stiffness of metre and regularity of movement which are clearly in conflict with the turmoil that the poem is constantly hinting at. Even the rhyme draws our attention away from the turbulence of emotion that lies just beneath the surface of the verse. It was this dichotomy between form and content which, among other things, began to attract the attention of negritude poets of the French language.

The immediate problem then for the black poet was how to recover his authenticity, how to express that 'beleaguered heart' which came to him from Senegal, in an alien language that was for his purposes frustratingly cold, objective and analytical: or to put it in another way, the question for the black poet, especially the kind of poet who considered himself the victim of the French language, was how to shatter the carefully polished Apollonian surface of French verse in order to descend once more fully into his unconscious past, a Black Orpheus in search of his Eurydice:

Do you know my other name, that comes to me from that vast continent,
the name that bleeding and imprisoned, crossed the ocean in chains . . .
Ah, you cannot remember it!
You have dissolved it with immemorial ink.[44]

The instruments that lay close on hand were no different for the black writer than those which the Western artist, in his accumulating frustrations with the proprieties of Western bourgeois society, had already fashioned out from a conglomeration of ideas and techniques, from Marxist economic theories to Freudian interpretation of dreams, from 'free association' to verbal *non-sequiturs* or surrealist techniques. I am indebted to Frederick J. Hoffman, the literary historian, for a vivid picture he gives of the spread of Freudian ideas in the 1920s and the 1930s, to which we must link such artistic movements as Surrealism, Futurism, and Negritude itself, and the consequences these ideas had for the literary mind. The works of Freud, Hoffman reminds us,

...called the attention of writers to the need for a new language − a language based upon the devices of condensation, displacement, multiple determination, and secondary elaboration. In so doing, it suggested to experimentalists the idea of employing 'absurdities' in their writing − that is, a repudiation of what is logical and syntactic, for what is illogical and ungrammatic.[45]

Such a programme suited the militant black writers in the 'thirties and the 'forties even better. After all, their search for 'a new language' to express the nightmare of Negro life had more desperate roots; equally, the search for new forms had a more revolutionary purpose. That in their efforts to liberate themselves from the 'civilised decorum' of Western culture these black writers were obliged to make use of the weapons which that culture had itself furnished points, of course, to the irony which we are at liberty to enjoy while appreciating the always underlying drama in the dialectic between coloniser and the colonised.

4

In June 1932 there appeared in Paris a 'thin brochure' produced by a group of young West Indian students from the French island of Martinique: the journal which was called *Légitime défense*, intemperate in language and radical in tone, delivered a broadside against the 'suffocating' institutions of the 'christian, bourgeois, capitalist world' and the young contributors decided they would no longer 'make peace with this surrounding ignominy'.[46] Taking as their masters Marx, Freud, Rimbaud and Breton, they attacked European rationalism, the foul bourgeois conventions and hypocrisy of the capitalist world; instead they wished to recover for the black man his original personality, and their programe would include the deliberate rejection of existing European models in art and a revolt against the colonial capitalism in politics. But their most violent attack was reserved for the black middle class they had left behind at home, whose principal crime, apparently, was slavishly to imitate everything French, in social manners as well as in art. The literature written by and for this class was 'an indigestion of French spirit and the French classics', and they mocked cruelly 'these chatterboxes and the sedative water of their poetry'. The manifesto was signed by Etienne and Thelus Lero, Jules Monnerot, René Menil, Maurice-Sabat Quitman, Michel Pilotin, Simone Yoyotte, all Martiniquais and aged between twenty and twenty-three. Etienne Lero wrote of his elders' outpouring in literature:

> The outsider would look in vain in that literature for a profound or original accent, for the sensual imagination darkened by Negro life, for the echo of the hates or the aspirations of an oppressed people.[47]

This literature, said Menil, would please neither the whites nor the blacks, the whites because it is a pale imitation of French literature, and the blacks for the same reason.[48] And if there is any doubt as to the impact of the new revolutionary techniques, that were very much the rage in France, upon these young blacks one can only draw the reader's attention to sections of the manifesto:

> We accept without reserve the surrealism to which—in 1932—we tie our future. And we would refer our readers to the manifestoes of André Breton, to the whole work of Aragon, of Breton, of René Crevel, Salvador Dali, of Paul Eluard, of Benjamin Peret, of Tristan Tzara, of which we must say it is not the least shame of this time that they are not known wherever French is read.[49]

Three of the principal founders of negritude, Aimé Césaire from Martinique, Léon Damas from French Guyana and Léopold Senghor from Senegal, were all directly influenced by the ideas of the new review. Surrealism was to become, technically, the principal weapon of self-discovery because of its tendency to go directly to the unconscious in order to tap the authentic reservoir of Negro feeling long buried beneath the tamed classicism of French verse and its tired metaphors: in the words of Breton 'the clear cut intention (was) to deal the fatal blow to the so-called "common sense" that has impudently usurped the title of "reason" '.[50] Césaire, who was to write the first serious poem to embody the negritude theme and the French surrealist manner, has explained in the already mentioned Havana interview:

> My thinking followed these lines: Well, then, if I apply the surrealist approach to my particular situation, I can summon up these unconscious forces. This, for me, was a call to Africa. I said to myself: it's true that superficially we are French, we bear the marks of French customs; we have been branded by Cartesian philosophy, by French rhetoric; but if we break with all that, if we plumb the depths, then what we will find is fundamentally black.[51]

Cahier d'un retour au pays natal, Césaire's long poem which was first published in Paris in 1939, not only affirmed the racial identity of its author, at that time considered a sufficient indiscretion to require a rebuke, but the poem was a-clear celebration of all those qualities which negritude poetry was to enthrone as the most important in the hierarchy of human values: an organic connection between the Negro and the world of nature; unashamed, even aggressive, eroticism; a concern with virility and fertility; the community of all living beings and a recognition of the stultifying effects of the mechanistic, technological civilisation of the Western world.

> Négritude is neither a tower nor a cathedral
> it thrusts into the red flesh of the soil
> it thrusts into the warm flesh of the sky
> it digs under the opaque dejection of its rightful patience
>
> Eia for the royal Kailcedrat!
> Eia for those who invented nothing
> for those who have never discovered
> for those who have never conquered!

Not surprisingly, most negritude verse shares certain striking affinities with a strain in English verse which runs from Blake to D.H. Lawrence. The aggressive sexual imagery or the 'emotional surge of the rhythms' in D.H. Lawrence or the hot passionate intensity in Blake, with its mystical undertones, find their echoes in much of the poetry which characterise as belonging to the negritude mode! The distinction, if there is any distinction to be made, between negritude poetry on the one hand and romantic, or Lawrence's 'organic poetry' on the other, subsists almost entirely in the curiously violent but understandable reversal of colour values to which negritude poets felt themselves committed by virtue of their racial identity. For the first time we find the colour of blackness elevated to a principle not only of immense vitality and fecundity but also of great beauty and majesty; and in the exuberant emotion of self-discovery even the God of the white Christians is somehow transformed into a black God:

> Black of eternal blackness
> With large voluptuous lips
> Matted hair and brown liquid eyes . . .[52]

The blackness becomes, finally, a colour of absorbing sensual richness and aggressive virility, often contrasted favourably with the pallid weakness of the devitalised white hue. This glorification of blackness as the colour in which 'life' inheres led Jacques Roumain, a mulatto poet, to cry out in bitter anguish:

> Listen to those voices singing the sadness of love
> And in the mountain, hear that tom-tom
>   panting like the breast of a young black girl
> Your soul is this image in the whispering water where
>   Your fathers bent their dark faces
> Its hidden movements blend you with the waves
> And the white that made you a mulatto is this bit
>   of foam cast up, like spit, upon the shore.

The contrast is further insisted upon in Léon Damas' poem, *Limbe*:

> Give me back my black dolls
> To disperse
> The image of pallid wenches, vendors of love
> going and coming
> on the boulevard of my boredom.

Or in Senghor's famous poem, *Manhattan*, in which the city is divided into Black and White, into Night and Day, White Manhattan staring at herself in the mirror of a Black Harlem, and the poet sums up the white city:

> All the birds of the air
> Fall suddenly dead below the high ashes of the terraces
> No child's laughter blossoms, his hand in my fresh hand
> No mother's breast. Legs in nylon. Legs and breasts with no
> sweat and no smell.

But Harlem, ah, Harlem hums 'with sounds and solemn colour and flamboyant smells' and the pavements are 'ploughed by the bare feet of dancers'. Harlem belongs to Night rather than Day, belongs, that is, to the 'Festival of Darkness'.

> I proclaim there is more truth in the Night than in the day.

In Brazil curiously enough, negritude was linked not only to the Modernist

Movement, with its sudden lurch into neo-realism after the suffocating influence of European (Iberian) classical and romantic forms; but the country's strenuous attempts to free herself from European tutelage drove writers like Mario de Andrade and Jorge de Luna to emphasise non-European elements in the formation of the Brazilian character.[53] Necessarily, this struggle for cultural autonomy had the further significance of releasing Afro-Brazilian writers from their colonial dependence and was to propel them toward investigating in their prose and poetry the lives of black Brazilians who had hitherto appeared only as exotic 'relief' in Brazilian literature. It also explains why this literature embraces themes of anti-colonial protest in which the expulsion or suppression of African traits in the national literature are seen as a 'supine, colonial mentality, for they passively allow a European model to serve as a national image'.[54] There is an easy transition from the odes of José Craveirinha, an African from Mozambique, protesting against the colonial mentality of his people, against the

> intolerant love of their Gospels,
> the mystique of glass beads and gunpowders,
> the logic of machine gun chatter,
> and songs from lands we do not know.[55]

to the angry cry of an Afro-Brazilian, exhorting his black brothers:

> cast aside your tame glances, your timidity, and your
> eternally happy smile . . .
> be hard, black man
> hard
> like the post on which they lashed you a thousand times
> Be black, black black
> marvellously black.

And, quite evidently, we have come full circle to the great anti-colonial poetry of Césaire himself. Not only did Césaire introduce a new word to the French language, but his poem had immense influence on other young poets, in the Caribbean, Africa and Latin America. Its rhythms, the explosion of imagery and the frank avowal of racial pride and identity, was to set an example that other poets felt obliged to follow.

In the triumvirate that included Césaire and Damas, Léopold Senghor had the distinction of actually having lived the life that Western blacks could only recreate from books. Again it is Césaire who acknowledges the debt: 'At the time I knew absolutely nothing about Africa. Soon afterwards I met Senghor, and he told me a great deal about Africa. He made an enormous impression on me: I am indebted to him for the revelation of Africa and African singularity.'[56]

There is some dispute among critics as to how successful Césaire and others were in employing the surrealist techniques of free-association and semi-automatic writing as a means of mining the Negro psyche for racial memories of the African Past. Roger Bastide has argued convincingly, it seems to me, that even if there was such a thing as a 'collective memory' the sense in which Jung employed the term implied memories of the 'human' rather than a particular race. According to Bastide, 'Africa' in Césaire's poetry is a 'willed construction of his creative imagination, by way of reading' and 'not a dictate of his subconscious'.[57] Césaire, says Bastide, is a 'White poet', albeit a very great one.[58] It is also said, I think rather questionably, that there is something too deliberate about Césaire's technique for it to be an unconscious rendering of negritude: but, surely, surrealism, except among the madmen and poseurs, was never intended to imply a complete abandonment of technical control. What Césaire and other poets of the negritude school achieved was to restore vitality to the French language: they did so by infusing French with the robust rhythms of the West Indies, by exploiting imagery and metaphors whose nightmarish quality had justification in the actual objective conditions of Negro life. If one sometimes found echoes of 'Africa' in their works it was because some of these writers had made the conscious effort to saturate themselves in the living folklore of West Indian peasants, the descendants of former African slaves who are by all accounts the single most important source of African inspiration in the New World.

5

What I have been at pains to show here is that both the philosophical assumptions underlying negritude and the strategies which negritude writers were compelled to adopt in the actual production of their work, came out of a specific intellectual tradition; they were part of a particular climate and a particular mood. It may be embarrassing to those worshippers at the shrine of negritude, who see it as the embodiment of a racial distinctness, to be reminded that negritude is really a bastard child whose family tree includes, apart from the living African heritage, Freudianism, Marxism, Surrealism and Romanticism.

Has negritude, as has sometimes been argued by its critics, outlived its role? Frankly, I think not. Whatever intellectual problems are raised by negritude, its importance for black literature in places as different as Africa, Latin America and the Caribbean, has been enormous; with the present growth of the 'black consciousness' movement in South Africa, a wholly new political and cultural phenomenon, a reassessment of the *négritude* movement and its origins, may once again be in order. In the United States, a resurgence of a black cultural nationalism, with its insistence on a re-evaluation of the role of the African heritage in the experience of black Americans, has resulted in radical changes in the structuring of academic courses and the selection of their contents that is bound to influence new scholarship as well as stimulate a fresh creativity on the part of the young blacks.

Whatever the case may be, negritude as part of a history of ideas, as much as for its past and present influence on black writing, must continue to provide an area of legitimate interest for any student of African Literature.

REFERENCES

1   S. W. Allen, 'Tendencies in African Poetry', published in *Africa as seen by American Negroes*, Présence Africaine, Paris, p.182.
2   *Ibid.*, p.182.
3   S. W. Allen, *The American Negro Writer and His Roots*, American Society of African Culture, New York, 1970. p.9.
4   *Ibid*, p.182.
5   Aimé Césaire, 'Discourse on Colonialism', translated by Joan Pinkham, *Monthly Review Press*, New York, 1972, p.76.
6   *Ibid.*
7   John Reed and Clive Wake, (eds.), *Senghor: Prose and Poetry*, Oxford University Press, 1965, p.97.
8   *Ibid.*
9   Opening address by President Senghor at Dakar Conference on African Literature and the Universities, April, 1963, published in *African Literature and the Universities*, Ibadan University Press, 1965.
10 Reed and Wake, Senghor, p.29–34.
11 *Ibid.*
12 *Ibid.*
13 Abiola Irele, 'A Defence of Negritude', *Transition*, March – April, 1964.
14 *Ibid.*
15 *Ibid.*
16 Reed and Wake, Senghor, p.76.
17 Jacques Maquet, *Civilizations of Black Africa*, Oxford University Press, London and New York, 1972.
18 W. E. Abraham, *The Mind of Africa*, Weidenfeld and Nicolson, London, 1962, p.45.
19 Jean Paul Sartre, *Orphée Noire*, Gallimard, p.24.
20 *Ibid.*
21 *Ibid.*, p.25.
22 *Ibid.*, p.24.
23 Allen, *The American Negro Writer*, p.12.
24 Sartre, *Orphée Noire*, p.15.
25 *Ibid.*, p.15.
26 *Ibid.*
27 *Ibid.*, p.16.
28 *Ibid.*, p.31.
29 Sembene Ousmane, talking at a Conference on African Literature; published in *Papers of the Dakar and Freetown Conference of African Literature*, Ibadan University Press, 1965.
30 *Ibid.*
31 Newell Flather: interviewing Ousmane at Dakar, in *Africa Report*.
32 Reed and Wake, *Senghor*, p.12
33 *Ibid.*
34 Ezekiel Mphahlele, *The African Image*, Faber, London, 1962, p.36.
35 Mphahlele, remarks on the Markerere Conference.
36 Mphahlele, reply to W. Jeanpierre, 'Negritude and its Enemies', *Papers of the Dakar and Freetown Conference on African Literature*.
37 Mphahlele, *The African Image*.
38 Mphahlele, 'Postscript on Dakar', *Papers of the Dakar and Freetown Conference*.
39 Mphahlele, *The African Image*, p.53.
40 Frantz Fanon, *Black Skin, White Masks*, Grove Press, 1967, p.18.
41 Sartre, *Orphée Noire*, p.22.
42 Henry D. Aiken, *The Age of Ideology*, New American Library, 1956, p.21.
43 Dr Jean Price-Mars, *De Saint-Domingue à Haiti*, Présence Africaine, 1959, p.17.
44 'The Name' by Nicolas Guillen, *Black Orpheus*, No.7, (June 1960).
45 Frederick J. Hoffman, *Freudianism and the Literary Mind*, Louisiana State University Press, 1945, p.114.

46   As quoted in Lilyan Kesteloot's definitive study, *Les Écrivains, noire de langue française: naissance d'une littérature*, Université Libre de Bruxelles, 1963, p.25.

47   Lero as quoted by Kesteloot, p.30.

48   Menil as quoted by Kesteloot, p.30.

49   Kesteloot, p.44

50   André Breton's Preface to Césaire's *Cahier d'un retour au pays natal*, Présence Africaine, Paris, 1956, p.24.

51   Césaire, 'Discourse on Colonialism', p.68.

52   See Ras Khan, 'The Poetry of Dr. R. E. G. Armattoe', *Présence Africaine*, Feb – March 1957.

53   See Richard A. Preto-Rodas's essay, 'The Development of Negritude in the Poetry of the Portuguese', included in *Artists and Writers in the Evolution of Latin America*, University of Alabama Press, 1969.

54   *Ibid.*, p.58.

55   *Ibid.*, p.62.

56   Césaire, 'Discourse on Colonialism', p.69.

57   Roger Bastide, 'Variations on Negritude', from *Negritude Essays and Studies*, (A Centennial Publication), Hampton Institute Press, 1967, pp.76–77.

58   Bastide, 'Variations on Negritude'.

CHAPTER THREE

HISTORY AS THE 'HERO' OF THE AFRICAN NOVEL

1

'To make the past present, to bring the distant near.' It seems a modest enough task: it is what we have come to expect of any novelist with a pronounced sense of history: 'to invest', as Macaulay put it, 'with the reality of human flesh and blood beings whom we are too much inclined to consider as personified qualities in an allegory'.[1] In defining the duties of the historical novelist which were once those of the historian, the English essayist uses a language which would surely find immediate emotional responses from those of our writers haunted by the African past and who are trying to develop strategies for 'bringing the distant near'. They must try

> to call up our ancestors before us with the peculiarities of language, manners, and garb, to show us over their houses, to sit at their tables, to rummage their old-fashioned wardrobes, to explain the uses of their ponderous furniture.[2]

This is a task that very few of our writers have seemed ready or capable of performing; and when they have tried very few have performed it with as much success as the Nigerian novelist, Chinua Achebe, who has made day-to-day Ibo life a vivid experience for readers who have never set foot in West Africa. Part of the relative success of the West African novelist can be attributed to the fact that the traditional 'past' is not really that 'distant': it is still very much alive. But surely there is much that has also vanished; certain patterns of daily life and forms of belief in societies which were then effectively sealed off from many contacts with the outside world, social forms and patterns of behaviour which can now only be reconstructed through an intensive effort of a creative imagining.

If African literature can be said to divide itself according to its two main preoccupations to which I have assigned the classificatory terms 'tasks' and 'masks', the balance has for too long, it seems to me, remained firmly fixed in favour of the 'mask' school; but if we are not to see African society as merely static, or rather as a 'mask' which is perennially being turned and examined in detail by our novelists; if we are also to see African society as a living organism, a society constantly in motion, always plunged in conflict and contradiction, we surely need the novelist as much as the professional historian to recover for us the essential meaning from the 'supple confusions' of history and to guide us with a firmer hand than we have been accustomed to through history's 'cunning passages'.

Nevertheless, fiction writers we now have who, if not exactly historical novelists in the sense that Macaulay meant, do possess a large historical sense. Among these, but by no means the only ones, are Peter Abrahams from South Africa, Ngugi (James) wa Thiong'o in Kenya, Sembene Ousmane in Senegal and Yambo Ouologuem in Mali. To my mind, these are just a few of our writers whose works have sometimes dramatised moments in history when events have seemed to loom larger than any individuals; they are novelists who have followed with keen interest the political movements, the social and economic conflicts, which have decisively shaped some recent African history; and these writers have sought not only to represent but also to explain the meaning of the initial confrontation between Africa and Europe and some of its permanent consequences.

The novels I propose to discuss under the present heading, therefore, though not at all alike in treatment or design, have certain features in common. One of these is an acute vision of history as a collective working out of a people's destiny which perpetually haunts us with the infinite range of possibilities, the meaning of which requires constant elaboration and without which the novels are felt to be lacking in their combustive fuels, and are even thought to be defective or incomplete. Indeed, in a novel like Ngugi's *A Grain of Wheat*, so strong is this historical sense, so pervasive the influence of the Mau Mau uprising, that by comparison the characters seem to me not as important: it is possible to argue that history itself, as it unfolded in the Kenya struggle for freedom and independence, becomes the true 'hero' of the novel.

That is not to say that in the novels I have chosen to discuss individual character as such has no special importance, but it is not so much the working out of any single life that gives significance to these works. On the contrary, it is the collective fate shared out among members of the community that provides the novels with their single most important source of energy. Sometimes, as in the case of Sembene Ousmane's *God's Bits of Wood* (*Les bouts de bois de Dieu*), these writers are concerned only with a single dramatic event which is seen as a significant stage in the development of a certain African society; sometimes, as in Chinua Achebe's two novels, *Things Fall Apart* and *Arrow of God*, the writer is concerned mainly with the rendering and elaboration of a certain cultural ethos which might explain his people's attitudes to events of central importance in the development of African society; or more ambitiously, as Yambo Ouologuem has recently attempted, a whole cycle of a people's history is sketched out, filled in, re-examined, paraphrased and mythologised, compressing centuries into the space of a single novel.

From Peter Abrahams' attempts to depict the story of the Great Trek in the South Africa of the 1830s and Sembene Ousmane's largely successful fictionalisation of a 1947−8 railway strike on the Dakar − Niger line, through Ngugi's efforts to portray individuals caught up in the Mau Mau struggle in Kenya, to Ouologuem's epic reconstruction of the rise and fall of the Mali Empire, we shall have covered sufficient ground to be able to recognise a variety of techniques and approaches to the treatment of history in the African novel.

However, it is important to note that we are here dealing not with pure historical facts, if there is ever such a thing, but with fact transformed into myth; out of the raw materials of history the novelists construct for us 'fictions';

in so doing they create patterns of meaning out of a jumble of meaningless chaos. All the same, important as this function is of the novelist as a recorder and vivifier of tradition, modern African writers no less than their European contemporaries, would probably find Macaulay's formula somewhat old-fashioned and less exciting if it were to mean no more than a set of rules for constructing a costume novel. Indeed, dramatising history in the way that Achebe, Ngugi, Abrahams and others have done is, it seems to me, only a step toward an even deeper and darker confrontation with the historical forces at work. At its most audaciously inventive, mischievous form, this latter aspect can be seen to advantage in Ouologuem's outrageous poetisation of the history of the Mali Empire; it is the kind of approach to history with which readers of James Joyce's novels will be particularly familiar; the obsessive but highly coloured view of Irish history as a form of tragi-comedy in which the Irish are simultaneously victims of British imperialism as well as casualties of self-inflicted wounds; above all, we see in Joyce the nervous apprehension of the historical as always mysteriously present and contemporaneous, though he is always mixing it with the bitter commemorative rehearsal of the narratives of its victims.

To speak of 'victims' in this context immediately suggests a view of history as a conspiracy of malevolent forces in the presence of which individuals have no choice but to suffer their collective fate in ways unexpectedly cruel and fortuitously degrading. Indeed, such an interpretation has an obvious hold on many Africans: the history of Africa and the Africans, it is said, is one of iron, blood, and tears. So far as African writers are concerned, whether openly admitted or merely implied, there seems to exist at the core of their imaginative works a deeply held belief that Africans have been dealt a cruel hand by fate; that they have been victims in a very special way. Enslaved, harassed, and brutalised, the 'nigger-trash' of Ouologuem's novels might agree with Stephen Dedalus' view of history as a 'nightmare from which I am trying to awake'.

2

Chinua Achebe's two novels of Ibo village life (*Things Fall Apart* and *Arrow of God*) provide fine examples of the good uses to which the African past can be put by an imaginative writer acting both as an inventor of 'fictions' and a recorder of 'social history'. Though Achebe is not an 'historical novelist' in any ordinary sense of that word, Gerald Moore is right, it seems to me, to call attention to the historical dimension in Achebe's fiction.[3] Moore pays tribute to Achebe's 'piety' toward the past and sees in the novelist's passion for reconstructing Ibo village life a necessary 'act of restitution' the result of which is both 'a piece of social history' as well as 'offering ground for some degree of cultural continuity'.

> Thus his first novel, *Things Fall Apart*, has made a deeper impression upon the literary sensibility of Africa than all the valued labours of historians and archaeologists put together.[4]

This is praise indeed but it is by no means excessive or unjustified praise.

We have the novels themselves to substantiate these claims. Nor does it seem from what we know of the author's stated intentions that Achebe is unaware of what he meant to achieve by his labours; he has stated unequivocally that he considers the restoration of African 'dignity' and 'self-respect' as his, as well as what ought to be every African writer's responsibility.[5] According to Achebe a more fundamental theme than the 'politics of 1964' is that reclamation of the past which surely can only come to us through novels as social history:

> This theme put quite simply — is that African people did not hear of culture for the first time from Europeans; that their societies were not mindless but frequently had a philosophy of great depth and value and beauty, that they had poetry, and, above all, they had dignity. It is this dignity that many African people all but lost during the colonial period and it is this that they must now regain.[6]

From Achebe's point of view nothing can happen to a people which is worse than a loss of dignity and self-respect. Accordingly, part of a writer's duty in Africa is helping his people, former colonial subjects, to regain their lost dignity. And here we must note that the terms which Achebe is using puts the emphasis firmly, if by implication, on the historical dimension: a novelist must explain 'what happened' and must show his people 'what they lost'; but being a creative writer himself Achebe insists that a novelist must do this 'by showing in human terms what happened to them', by which he means through a social reconstruction of the past in novels which deal with recognisable people in recognisable human situations.

In this Achebe has already blazed a trail large enough to be followed by other writers: due to his painstaking fidelity in the representation of Ibo life his writing achieves the exact precision of the documentary; and yet the narrative is always illuminated at strategic points by the writer's skill in the creation of character, by his success in so ordering his materials that a dramatic interplay between character and situation is achieved which lifts even a so-called 'anthropological novel' like *Things Fall Apart* way above the documentary humdrumness of everyday truth. After all, however devoted to the past, a novelist is not merely an auditor of his people's past habits and traditions; he is also a creator of 'fictions', a fabulist beguiling us with half-truths and saucy 'inventions'. He does more: he illuminates that inner life in his characters without which the novel is flat and without much interest.

Here we are doing no more than recognise certain features in Achebe's approach to the past, his skill and precision in the documentation of that traditional African past; of greater interest to us, however, should be his treatment of two interrelated themes of fundamental, if not decisive, historical importance for the African society. The two themes form a backdrop to the action of his two novels about traditional Ibo life, *Things Fall Apart* and *Arrow of God*. Indeed, it is when Achebe explores the inner dynamics of the Ibo society as it comes increasingly under the external pressures of the twin movements of European colonialism and christianisation that he involves us more directly in matters of historical considerations as well as of interpretation.

What Achebe offers us in the two novels is a briefly encapsulated version of the nature of colonialism in Africa, its strategies, its effects on traditional society, and, in the face of this near total physical as well as psychological annexation of the African, the reactions of the indigenous population. Although, with his customary discretion, Achebe confines himself to a small Ibo clan rather than generalise about the whole of Africa, it is clear that the picture he gives us here of both colonialism and Christianity at work is intended to act as a paradigm for the whole of Africa.

In *Things Fall Apart* we are first given a view of an African society (Umuofia, Banta, Abame) with its daily ritual of work and play, its religious rites and its own internal administration; until the second half of the novel this is as nearly self-sufficient a world, as hermetically self-enclosed, as we are ever likely to know of that traditional African society which existed before the first white man came to Africa. Nevertheless, however harmonious and perfectly balanced this society was it seems that it had already reached its point of exhaustion long before the white man came to give it the final push toward collapse. In this respect, I agree with John Povey when he speaks of 'an internal disintegration' which was merely 'sped' on by external and foreign pressures.[7]

Although rooted in an understandable moral rationality*, some of the cruelties of African society had deteriorated so uncomfortably into reflexive gestures of accidental crime and mechanical punishment that an internal revolution or change brought about by external forces had become an inevitable certainty. The 'loss of continuity with the past'[8] may have been tragic but no amount of sentimental woe should be allowed to gloss over this point. To take an example: much more than the sacrificial killing of the boy, Ikemefuna, which is an obvious case of a morally sanctioned cruelty, Okonkwo's automatic exile as a result of an accidental shooting of a boy at Ezeudu's funeral is yet another instance of the ossification of tradition:

> The only course open to Okonkwo was to flee from the clan. It was a crime against the earth goddess to kill a clansman, and a man who committed it must flee from the land. The crime was of two kinds, male and female. Okonkwo had committed the female, because it had been inadvertent. He could return to the clan after seven years.[9]

Okonkwo's compound is then stormed by a crowd of men dressed in warrior garb; his houses are set on fire, his barn destroyed, his animals killed; but the men doing this 'had no hatred in their hearts against Okonkwo. His greatest friend, Obierika, was among them.'[10] As Obierika later puts it: 'Why should a man suffer so grievously for an offence he had committed inadvertently?'[11]

Equally, it is well worth noting that it is the *osu*, the village outcasts — those who according to tradition 'could neither marry nor be married by the free-born', those who had to live in a special area and could neither attend an

---

* In his book *Theories of Primitive Religions* (OUP, 1965) E.E. Evans-Pritchard has criticised the French anthropologist, Levy-Bruhl's views on 'primitive' thought in the following manner: 'Levy-Bruhl is . . . wrong in supposing that there is necessarily a contradiction between an objective causal explanation and a mystical one. It is not so. The two kinds of explanation can be, as indeed they are, held together, the one supplementing the other; and they are not therefore exclusive.'

assembly nor take a title in the clan — who finally form the backbone of the converts to the new religion.

Though in many respects ambiguous figures, both Okonkwo, the hero of *Things Fall Apart*, and Ezeulu, the hero-priest of *Arrow of God*, are similar in at least this respect, that they embody more fully than any of the other characters the rigid value-system of this society at different points of growth and decline. Achebe makes much of the fact that their tragedy arises, in part, out of their personal psychology; however, it is fairly clear, I think, that legalistically speaking, both Okonkwo and Ezeulu are acting within the letter of the moral law as they have known it; their personal psychology is nothing if not a reflection of the social order within which they operate. Their fanaticism only helps to cast into sharper relief what already exists independent of their own moral aberrations.

Okonkwo's relationship with his family and kinsmen forms the core of the novel from which the action radiates outward until it illuminates everything surrounding the village life of Umuofia. Beyond Umuofia is of course the slowly approaching world of white men and their administrative apparatuses. It is precisely because Achebe does not let that outside world, the reality of which must have remained for the villagers only a fantastical and improbable rumour, intrude upon his characters until nearly the very end of the novel that we are made to feel with even more disruptive violence the impact of the arrival of the first white men in the village. Their arrival forms the climax of the action; the beginning of the end both in the novel and the society about which the novel is written. Needless to say this arrival, though it is accompanied, inauspiciously enough, by the martyring of the first white man, followed by wholesale retribution against the village, is announced by Achebe in a narrative surprisingly free of melodramatic excitement; the tempo of the novel hardly ever varies; if anything Achebe errs on the side of restraint. This is how Obierika, Okonkwo's friend, tells of the arrival of the white man at the adjoining village of Mbanta:

> The arrival of the missionaries had caused a considerable stir in the village of Mbanta. There were six of them and one was a white man. Every man and woman came out to see the white man. Stories about these strange men had grown since one of them had been killed in Abame and his iron horse tied to the sacred silk-cotton tree. And so everybody came to see the white man. It was the time of the year when everybody was at home. The harvest was over.
>
> When they had all gathered, the white man began to speak to them. He spoke through an interpreter who was an Ibo man, though his dialect was different and harsh to the ears of Mbanta. Many people laughed at his dialect and the way he used words strangely. Instead of saying 'myself' he always said 'my buttocks'. But he was a man of commanding presence and the clansmen listened to him. He said he was one of them, as they could see from his colour and his language. The other four black men were also their brothers, although one of them did not speak Ibo. The white man was also their brother because they were all sons of God. And he told them about this new God, the Creator of all the world and all the men and women. He told them that they worshipped false gods, gods of wood and stone. A deep

murmur went through the crowd when he said this. He told them that the true God lived on high and that all men when they died went before Him for judgment. Evil men and all the heathen who in their blindness bowed to wood and stone were thrown into a fire that burned like palm-oil. But good men who worshipped the true God lived for ever in His happy kingdom. 'We have been sent by this great God to ask you to leave your wicked ways and false gods and turn to Him so that you may be saved when you die,' he said. [12]

The tragedy which accompanies the encounter between black and white, between Europeans and Africans, is rooted not just in differing social-economic systems but in a mutual incomprehension as to what either system stands for, what its norms might mean. For instance, the Christian missionaries who form the vanguard of imperial administrative power approach their task with an overweening simplicity bordering on criminal negligence; it is as if they alone have ever heard of God:

'If we leave our gods and follow your god,' asked another man, 'who will protect us from the anger of our neglected gods and ancestors?'
'Your gods are not alive and cannot do you any harm,' replied the white man. 'They are pieces of wood and stone.' When this was interpreted to the men of Mbanta they broke into derisive laughter. [13]

In the last reckoning it is, of course, economic and political power which give legitimacy to any social or religious system. The African gods lose out to the new God of the Christians precisely because they had already outlived their usefulness and had become a power not for social progress, but only for conservatism. Since Achebe has up to now rigorously refused to situate himself inside the novel or to pass judgement on any aspect of village life, except by the most circumspect of implications, it is by introducing another social system, another scale of moral values, that the defects in the traditional African society can be exposed or assessed. The defection of Okonkwo's first son, Nwoye, to the other side constitutes for the Christians not only an important gain in its own right, it also helps to underline an interesting irony which will be more than hinted at in *Arrow of God*, when Ezeulu's favourite son commits a sacrilegious act in the name of Christianity.

Superficially, it might be thought that the Christian missionaries achieve their victory over diehard traditionalists because they possess a superior form of logical explanation of how the world *is*: but Achebe quickly, and rightly, warns us against such a fallacy of interpretation. The Christian concept of the Trinity, for example, is no more 'rational' than the African worship of the various deities whom the missionaries contemptuously dismiss as 'pieces of wood and stones'. Christianity wins out because Christianity probes and exploits real weakness in the old social order which has begun to crumble internally from its own contradictions: Achebe makes this obvious in a passage explaining Nwoye's conversion:

It was not the mad logic of the Trinity that captivated him. He did not understand it. It was the poetry of the new religion, something felt in the marrow. The hymn about brothers who sat in darkness and in fear seemed to answer a vague and persistent question that haunted his young soul — the question of the twins crying in the bush and the question of Ikemefuna who was killed. He felt a relief within as the hymn poured into his parched soul. The words of the hymn were like the drops of frozen rain melting on the dry palate of the panting earth.[14]

The African gods become meaningless the moment they fail to dislodge the Christians from the land. The struggle for 'rationality' is merely a struggle for power. It is at once the most comic as well as the most touchingly tragic episode in the book: when, certain of the divine doom which must befall those who try to set up house in the 'Evil Forest', with a cynical generosity which is endearingly cunning in its purposes the Mbanta clansmen offer part of this land to the Christians to build their Church. They then wait cheerfully for their destruction:

They did not really want them in their clan, and so they made them that offer which nobody in his right senses would accept.[15]

Needless to say, by the end of the seventh week, which is the time it must take for the gods to punish the offenders, the Christians are still very much part of the landscape, with no visible harm come to them.

This then is the beginning of the end for the old social order and the emergence of a new one. Two novels later, in *Arrow of God*, Achebe will merely resume the story where it ended; only now the British colonial administration, which in *Things Fall Apart* was still in its rudimentary form, in *Arrow of God* is now in full political muscle, brooking no opposition from the clans. The thrust into the interior and the subjugation, not only of the bush but also of the tribes, is symbolised by the road-building programme carried out by Wright, with the help of what amounts to a 'forced labour' gang. Now sorely divided, feeling the pressure from outside, the villages are increasingly engaging in dangerous rivalry which leaves them depleted of energy and incapable of resisting effectively British imperial power. The enmity between Ezeulu, the Chief Priest of Ulu, and Ezidemili, the priest of Idemili, is itself merely a reflection of this internal instability due to increasing competition between various centres of power in the traditional community, which leaves the society weak and some would say 'ripe' for a 'take-over' bid by an outside power. As Ezeulu, Umuora's chief Priest, a man of unusual intellectual and analytical powers, puts it:

We went to war against Okperi who are our blood brothers over a piece of land which did not belong to us and you blame the white man for stepping in. Have you not heard that when two brothers fight a stranger reaps their harvest?[16]

As before, the Christian religion plays a crucial part in the annexation of Iboland and the spiritual resources of the people, leaving the whole of society helpless and weak, without any weapons with which to fight back. As we have seen in *Things Fall Apart*, the new religion was keen to exploit every spiritual vacuum left by traditional religion. For example, when in order to punish his clansmen for having allowed the British administration to detain him, Ezeulu decides, in accordance with tradition, not to declare the New Yam Feast until the last yam has been eaten, it is the followers of the new faith who reap the benefits of the disaster that befalls the villages of Umuoro. 'There was one man who saw the mounting crisis in Umuoro as a blessing and opportunity sent by God. His name was John Jaja Goodcountry, Catechist of St Mark's C.M.S. Church, Umuaro.' Goodcountry's solution is devastatingly simple. The Chief Priest of Ulu will not sanction the harvesting of the Yam crop which is now rotting in the ground, leading to an economic disaster which is beginning to strain the loyalties of even the devoutest traditionalists: Goodcountry has an inspiration:

> His plan was quite simple. The New Yam Festival was the attempt of the misguided heathen to show gratitude to God, the giver of all good things. They must be saved from their error which was now threatening to ruin them. They must be told that whoever made his thank-offering to God could harvest his crops without fear of Ulu.[17]

Arrow of God is a complex novel, with a complex meaning; but it is essentially both a continuation and a completion of a project begun in *Things Fall Apart*. It brings to the surface an underlying trend in Achebe's 'traditional' novels, which is a continuous attempt to recreate the African past as a living drama in which we can appreciate much that was noble and worthy of respect, while recognising some of its weakest features; it is also an attempt to paraphrase the history of the colonial mission in Africa. This history is as complex as Achebe's novel, its interpretations just as varied, but the essential message in *Arrow of God* emerges quite early in a debate between Moses Unachukwu and his fellow clansmen. The novel harks back to an earlier time in *Things Fall Apart*.

> Before any of you here was old enough to tie a cloth between the legs I saw with my own eyes what the white men did to Abame. Then I knew there was no escape. As daylight chases away darkness so will the white man drive away all our customs.[18]

Three paragraphs later Unachukwu sums up:

> Yes, we are talking about the white man's road. But when the roof and walls of a house fall in, the ceiling is not left standing. The white man, the new religion, the soldiers, the new road — they are all part of the same thing. The white man has a gun, a matchet, a bow and carries fire in his mouth. He does not fight with one weapon alone.[19]

It is this unified vision of the combined effects of the internal and external pressures on African traditional society which is the driving force of these two novels. In *Arrow of God* the handling of the colonial theme has become distinctly more brittle, less chary; the malice, rather rare in Achebe, lies just below the surface of a narrative which threatens repeatedly to break out into fully-fledged satire, especially in the Winterbottom sections of the novel. Yet, in an almost paradoxical way, just because its debt to actual historical interpretation is so nakedly obvious. I find Achebe's attempt to portray the system of 'indirect rule', with the aid of large stretches of imaginary documentation, less than satisfactory; the passages have too often the feel of having been discussed in the university seminars on African history: slightly hackneyed from past handling, they lack that wild imaginative inventiveness such as is to be found in the confrontation between Christian missionaries and African traditionalists in *Things Fall Apart*. The colonial 'types', too, seemed to be cut to order, too much indebted to a long tradition of fictional creations from Joyce Cary to Graham Greene.

To say all this is not to minimise Achebe's achievement in a complex task, which is the dramatisation of African history in such a way that we can extract meaning from it without losing sight of the living drama in which real men and women were involved. Achebe has sometimes been criticised, quite unfairly, it seems to me, for his version of this 'history'.[20] It is sometimes said that this judgement of both the British colonial administration and the activities of Christian missionaries is unnecessarily harsh and frequently a distortion of what were after all benign intentions. This is hardly borne out by any careful reading of the novels. As we have seen, in both *Things Fall Apart* and *Arrow of God* there is a constant shift in the amount of blame assigned to either of the two sides in the confrontation. Achebe is more of a 'realist' in his treatment of African history than some rigorously trained historians. Certainly, it would be difficult to quarrel with Margaret Laurence's conclusion that

> Achebe in *Arrow of God* follows the course of history with accuracy, and at the same time manages to confirm that fiction is a great deal more true than fact.[21]

3

In *A Grain of Wheat* and *God's Bits of Wood* Ngugi wa Thiong'o and Sembene Ousmane have respectively devoted their considerable powers for formal organisation to the reconstruction of a slice of contemporary African history, to the examination of a single event, a single monumental occurrence, which has shaped decisively the lives of everyone in the community.

In the case of Ngugi, it is the struggle for political independence in Kenya and the scars left upon those who participated in or were the victims of the terror, which engages his interest. In Ousmane's case it is the 1947–8 railway workers' strike on the Dakar–Niger line and the effect this strike has upon the community, especially the workers and their dependents as they face the hardships of a protracted war against a ruthless management, which forms the subject-matter of the novel.

Ngugi and Ousmane are nothing if not political animals; in the case of Ousmane, perhaps as a result of differences in social climates, this is more immediately apparent than in the case of Ngugi. Ousmane from French-speaking Senegal, a one-time docker in Marseilles and a former trade unionist of some standing, uses a more Marxian framework in his work which very definitely owes something to the French intellectual tradition of committed literature. Ousmane's novel looks back to Malraux's *La Condition Humaine*, a book mentioned by Tiemoko, one of Ousmane's characters, as offering some guidance to the conduct of the strike. Ngugi, on the other hand, is indebted to the traditional English novel (including the works of Chinua Achebe), a tradition which, whatever its vicissitudes, has never been very much concerned with intellectual ideas whether of the Left or the Right.

Ngugi's novel, *A Grain of Wheat*, is clearly concerned as much with the 'psychological consequences' as with 'the theme of a people living and acting within the Mau Mau period itself'.[22] The role of each of the main characters is examined, his or her claims to recognition assessed, and very few of these individuals, it would seem, have not faltered somewhere or betrayed someone. There are certainly examples of heroism but there are also instances of treachery and cowardice.

Indeed, the novel is built around a series of ever-widening concentric circles of guilt and betrayal: from the most obvious case of Karanja who once flirted with the freedom movement but later turned administrative chief for his area, rounding up Mau Mau suspects for the British; to Gikonyo who broke down during his detention at Yala camp and confessed the oath he had taken; to Mumbi, Gikonyo's wife, who in an incredible display of gratitude at the news that her husband is to be released from detention, yields to Karanja's sexual advances and later bears him an illegitimate son: they all, one by one, betray someone. Even the whites, it seems, have a mania for treachery of one kind or another. Friendships, confidences, wives, mistresses, even servants, are cheerfully betrayed. However, at the centre of the novel lies a bigger betrayal and larger irony, which is the final revelation that Mugo, the man chosen to lead the Uhuru celebrations, was himself an arch-traitor − the man who betrayed to the British authorities Kihika, the hanged hero of the forest fighters. From one staggering irony to the next, in a gradual unfolding of the plot as suspenseful as a thriller, Mugo is led to the final confession of his guilt on the very platform from which he had been expected to render homage to the memory of his friend, the martyred Kihika. On the last page of this skilfully constructed novel, Mumbi might have been talking for the entire community when she tells the husband she betrayed while he was in detention:

> People try to rub out things, but they cannot. Things are not so easy. What has passed between us is too much to be passed over in a sentence. We need to talk, to open our hearts to one another, examine them, and then together plan the future we want . . .[23]

With the possible exception of Kihika, this novel has no heroes. In one of his wryest moments Ngugi writes of a village meeting addressed by ex-detainees: 'The rhetorical tone was seized by the detainees who rose to speak. They talked of suffering under the white man and illustrated this with episodes which revealed their deep love of Kenya.' The novel is throughout haunted with this feeling of discrepancy between false rhetoric and what actually happened when men were tried by fire. This is perhaps the crucial difference between *A Grain of Wheat* and *God's Bits of Wood*.

Ousmane's novel celebrates the collective strength of the workers on strike while Ngugi refuses to concede more than a drab, dreary dignity to his characters. It might be thought strange that a self-confessed 'socialist' novelist should build a novel around a group of traitors, each one only more or less culpable than the others; it might be thought that Ngugi has left himself curiously open to the charge of celebrating 'negative' heroes, ostensible failures; however, Ngugi does not minimise the heroic role of those who sacrificed a great deal so that Kenya might one day be free. *A Grain of Wheat* has the further advantage of avoiding the impression, which is very strong in *Petals of Blood*, that Marxist categories have been falsely imposed upon the character or the development of the plot. As George Lukacs himself, the arch-priest of 'socialist realism', has argued:

> No writer is a true realist — or even a truly good writer, if he can direct the evolution of his own characters at will.[24]

In contrast, Ousmane's characters do not easily avoid the impression of being subtly manipulated in order to carry out an illustrative programme especially designed by the author. The novel's didactive purpose is everywhere made plain; the characters speak only to reveal the nature of their commitment to class or economic interests. Whereas, Ngugi depicts the anti-colonial struggle in Kenya as having been dominated by nationalist sentiment, Ousmane's re-creation of the Niger — Dakar rail strike is given a wholly Marxist interpretation. The French directors, especially Dejean, Victor and Isnard, represent the exploitative capitalist class standing in direct conflict to the interests of the workers led by Bakayoko, Doudou, Lahbib and others. During a negotiation with management which turns into a heated confrontation, Dejean, a former Vichy Government official, who always wore a 'thin, red ribbon of the Legion of Honour' on the lapel, accuses Lahbib of insulting a 'great nation and a great people' — France. Lahbib's reply puts the entire conflict within a Marxist framework: 'Monsieur le directeur,' Lahbib said, 'you do not represent a nation or a people here, but simply a class. We represent another class, whose interests are not the same as yours.'[25] That the nature of this conflict is one of class rather than of nationalities, is given sharper emphasis by Bakayoko's contemptuous dismissal of the black deputies in the National Assembly, one of whom, it is suggested, might perhaps act as mediator:

> 'Our deputies,' he said, with an ironic smile which stretched his mouth to the line of the scar that split his face. 'Our deputies. Do you know what we think of them? To us, their mandate is simply a license to profiteer . . . There are some of them who, before their election, did not even own a second pair of pants. Now they have apartments, villas, automobiles, bank accounts, and they own stock in companies like this one.'[26]

Both Ngugi and Ousmane are keen to indicate their allegiances, subtly or more openly, in the opening class war in modern African politics. Ngugi can be very subtle in the way he does this: it is worth noting, for example, that *A Grain of Wheat* is set in a rural area and its characters are almost totally cut off from Nairobi and its shoddy, commercial world of glamourised thrills. In Chapter 14 of this novel Ngugi opens with the sentence:

> Kenya regained her Uhuru from the British on 12 December 1963. A minute before midnight, lights were put out at the Nairobi Stadium so that people from all over the country and the world who had gathered there for the midnight ceremony were swallowed by the darkness. In the dark, the Union Jack was quickly lowered.

A banal statement of fact: this is history. But in the second paragraph Ngugi is already distancing both himself as well as the people whose lives he is trying to record, from the glamour and highlights of Nairobi stadium: 'In our village,' Ngugi writes, 'and despite the drizzling rain, men and women and children, it seemed, had emptied themselves into the streets where *they sang and danced in the mud*.' (Italics mine.)

Ousmane, too, will have none of the false glamour. In *God's Bits of Wood* the more militant workers are mostly self-made men, including an obvious intellectual like Bakayoko, who take from books only what is useful for the struggle. A message from Bakayoko to one of the strike leaders in Dakar begins: 'Tell Abdoulaye that nothing is more damaging to our cause than a worker who plays at being an intellectual and patronizes his own comrades.'[27] Except for N'Deye Touti and Beaugosse none of Ousmane's characters seems to have spent much time at school, let alone gone to university; and significantly it is N'Deye Touti and Beaugosse, both young and addicted to Western life-styles, who are portrayed in the novel as showing acute signs of alienation. Whenever their academic achievements or their recently acquired social manners are mentioned, Ousmane permits himself a degree of mischievous satire rarely shown in the description of the other characters in the book. Instead of being in their favour even good points are sometimes made to tell against them.

On page 56, for instance, we are told: 'In the midst of a generally unpleasant world he [Beaugosse] was extremely pleasant to look at', as if this very pleasantness of look is in itself an act of betrayal against fellow-workers. Beaugosse's very 'stylishness' is held up as a mark against him. 'His first contacts with the other workers', we are told, 'had been difficult because of his passion for clothes.'[28] That, his diploma from a trade school, and his love for speaking French, are clearly meant to set him aside from the other workers as a possible 'phoney'. A little further on the point is driven home with a characteristically malevolent humour: 'Beaugosse put on a pair of trousers of a light fabric, cut in the baggy, Turkish fashion, and studied the holes in his socks sadly, muttering to himself in French.'[29]

In a novel which is distinguished as much by its unflagging energy as by its intermittent flashes of humour and wit, Sembene Ousmane seems to enjoy himself to an uncommon degree at the expense of young Beaugosse who, despite his trade diploma, could not even hold his own in sexual competition with the older but more radical trade union leader, Bakayoko. In the end, unable to win N'Deye Touti's love away from Bakayoko, Beaugosse deserts the strike movement in a typically opportunistic fashion.

As for the girl, N'Deyi Touti, though extremely attractive — 'her most striking features . . . were her eyes — and her full, finely drawn mouth' — she lives in a kind of 'separate world', 'a universe in which her own people had no place'. Before the strike, she had gone to the teachers' training school, and though the girl fights valiantly at times to regain her identity, she is ill-equipped to do so by a colonial education which enables her to know far more about Europe than she did about Africa. 'She had never read a book by an African author: she was quite sure they could teach her nothing.'[30]

When unexpectedly N'Deye is obliged to watch a documentary film about Pygmies in a local cinema, she is filled with insupportable shame: 'She had felt as if she were being hurled backward, and down to the level of these dwarfs, and had an insane desire to run out of the theatre, crying aloud, "No! No! These are not the real Africans".'[31] However, despite the implied adverse judgement on N'Deye Touti's moral and spiritual confusion, Ousmane does not altogether succeed in convincing us of the utter worthlessness of the girl. It is finally with compassion that we regard her tortured, self-conscious quest for true identity and fulfilment. She herself is not unaware of her own shortcomings and seems to pay more attention to Bakayoko's criticism of her than to Beaugosse's bashful admiration. 'You say, I've read too many books,' she tells Beaugosse, 'and Bakayoko says I don't read enough, and the books I do read are bad ones!'[32] And yet, in the end, through a participation in the struggle and by identifying herself with her people, N'Deye Touti does acquire a measure of personal dignity.

Ousmane's and Ngugi's novels have further similarities in the pervasive influence exerted by their two heroes — Bakayoko and Kihika — who for long periods of the action vacate the centre of the stage, in the case of Kihika never to reappear except as a point of focus for the memory of others. Bakayoko is the intelligent, dedicated trade unionist who seems to hold the movement together as much by the force of his personality as by the scrupulous correctness of his ideological position: 'Not the sort of person who goes unnoticed,' N'Deye recalls. Whenever the others are in doubt it is to Bakayoko they appeal for advice. Both Kihika and Bakayoko retain intangible qualities of mystery and charisma which make others feel peculiarly dependent upon their guidance and leadership. Frequently mentioned but very infrequently encountered, the mystery around the two protagonists is increased, not diminished, by their simultaneous vacancy and tenancy of the centre of the narrative.

Rather surprisingly, Ousmane's range of characters is wider, his characterisation more varied and strikingly more resourceful, than you would suppose from someone whose formulation of character is so rigidly designed to meet the demands of political category. Part of Ousmane's technique is to let his characters be defined by the situation in which they are obliged to act. Nothing is better handled, for example, than the cameo scene in which Mame Sofi contrives to obtain water on credit from the water carrier after water and food have been cut off from families of the striking workers. As well as possessing an abundance of cunning and humour, the exchange with the water-carrier reveals Mame Sofi as a woman of considerable resourcefulness and toughness:

> 'Do you believe in God?' Her expression gave not the slightest hint of
> trickery.
> 'Who, me?' the man stammered, disconcerted by this unexpected question.
> 'Yes, you.'
> '*Ouai*, of course, I believe in God.'
> *Al Hamdou lilah*,' Mame Sofi said, as if the answer had relieved her of a
> great burden. Then she added, 'I owe you five pieces, of five francs each.'
> '*Ouai, Koni!*' The exclamation seemed to burst from the dumbfounded
> man. 'But, woman! I didn't say that I would sell you my water on credit!'
> 'That is true – you did not say it, but I must owe you for this water just the
> same. I live in this house, so you will have no trouble finding me. And if, for
> some reason, I do not pay you in this world, then I shall pay you in the other,
> before I can hope to enter Paradise.'[33]

It is not only the depiction of the workers' struggle but the richness and
variety of the characterisation which give this novel its peculiar power and mus-
cularity. Nevertheless, when everything is said and done, the workers' struggle,
the total organisation of men and women moved by a single collective impulse
for justice and equity, is what gives this book its true epic quality. The strike: its
absorbing and overwhelming nature, the all-consuming battle which for long
months begins to embrace and to engulf everyone in the community, from the
smallest baby trampled under the boots of soldiers to an old woman knocked to
her death by waterhoses; the long march of women on Dakar and the exacting
skills of the trade unionists as they take on an immensely powerful, Govern-
ment-backed company: it is this complex, titanic struggle which emerges as the
true hero of the novel, just as the Mau Mau movement is the true hero of
Ngugi's novel. It is through common action that the men and women of Thies,
Dakar and Bamako discover their true consciousness: 'When the smoke from
the trains no longer drifted above the savanna, they realised that an age had
ended.'[34]

The characters have a collective rather than an individual hold upon our
imagination which is intended to emphasise the strength of their shared responsibility and, equally, to diminish the moral significance of any single character.
When the fire engines are brought out to quell a women's demonstration we are
told that 'the massed pressure of hundreds of bodies was stronger than any
pumps'.[35] Near the beginning of the novel Doudou wants to know how many
strikers have been wounded or killed and Gaye unfolds a piece of paper and
begins listing their names: 'The dead? There is Badara, the smelter, and . . .'
Doudou peremptorily interrupts: 'No, Gaye, no names.'[36] The meaning is clear
enough; in Ousmane's view no individual should assume an importance greater
than the whole, and the workers' power is realised only in the collective. The
description of the of the strikes at the beginning of the novel makes this explicit
enough:

> The faces seemed to have lost all traces of personality. As if some giant eraser
> had rubbed out their individual traits they had taken on a common mask,

anonymous mask of a crowd.[37]

However, it is when Ousmane is reflecting on the nature and meaning of the strike, when he is meditating upon its historical purpose, that he commands our attention to the contribution he is trying to make to the current discussion of African developmental ideology. Despite men's temporary enslavement to it, technology, which is symbolised by the railway line, has the same energising effect which was recognised by D.H.Lawrence in his Mexican novel,[38] though treated by him in his characteristically negative fashion. 'Bolshevists', said Lawrence, 'somehow, seem to be born on the railway.' He went on:

Wherever the iron rails run, and passangers are hauled back and forth in the railway coaches, there the spirit of rootlessness, of transitoriness, of first and second class in separate compartments, of envy and malice, and of iron and demonish panting engines, seems to bring forth the logical children of materialiasm, the bolshevists.[38]

Lawrence understood only too well the effects of industrialisation upon the peasants and, no doubt, feared the consequences, for he recognised the class war which would ensue between those who occupied the 'first' and those who occupied 'the second class' compartments. Far from condemning this development, Ousmane welcomes it; and far from decrying the railroad simply as an agent of spoliation and dehumanisation, Ousmane celebrates it as an agent of man's liberation from Nature which he must control to his own advantage. When trains no longer run the strikers gather 'like rejected lovers' at nearby stations; they 'squat down in the shade of a sand hill, their eyes fixed on the two endless parallels, following them out until they joined and lost themselves in the bush'.[39]

The passage has the elementary poetry of men confronting nature with a consciousness of new possibilities for themselves and society; and we are offered here a Marxian vision of boundless hope for the future in which the new technology is harnessed for the benefit of society, and men and natural resources are transformed into a new relationship. 'Even in the midst of their confusion', Sembene writes of the striking men, 'they were conscious that the machine was the source of their common welfare.'[40]

Something was being born inside them, as if the past and the future were coupling to breed a new kind of man, and it seemed to them that the wind was whispering a phrase they had often heard from Bakayoko: 'The kind of man we were is dead, and our only hope for a new life lies in the machine, which knows neither a language nor a race.'[41]

Both Ngugi and Ousmane are committed to change as a matter of political principle; their subject-matter is politics — more precisely, characters in the process of creating their own history. In this respect, I find myself in dispute with my distinguished country-woman and novelist, Nadine Gordimer, who writes in her pamphlet on African writing that no African writer 'gives any clear-cut indication of the political ideology within which they envisage the

African future'.[42] In the same pamphlet Miss Gordimer more appropriately complains that she has not come across 'more than one African novel dealing concretely and specifically with political aspects of the colonial struggle of which one could say that the treatment was equal to the potential theme'.[43]

The terms in which this judgement is presented make it very difficult to deal with it: however, one of the novels which, though commended by Gordimer, is finally excluded from this category of 'the colonial struggle' is Ngugi's *A Grain of Wheat*, a novel which, as I have already said, deals not only 'with the subtleties of the psychological consequences of Mau Mau in the post-independence period' but also deals specifically with the preparation and prosecution of that struggle. The fact that these episodes are offered to us in a series of flashbacks, as fragments of memory, does not make them any the less a proper substance of the novel than if they had been allowed to command a more central position in the narrative. Taken together they build up a complete picture of the process by which Kenya was transformed from a colonial possession into an independent African state.

To state the case in somewhat more general terms, then, Ngugi and Ousmane are interested in 'history' as a revelation of a continuously unfolding human consciousness in characters who are engaged in changing society or the circumstances of their lives. If we go back to Achebe's portrayal of the conflict between African traditional society and European colonialism, we sense there an underlying pathos which finds its most poignant expression in Ezeulu's perception that the new social order spells 'the collapse and ruin of everything'.[44] The necessity for change is hinted at; there is a rueful recognition that 'these are not the times we used to know and we must meet them as they come or be rolled in the dust';[45] but all the same, the characteristic tone of Achebe's two novels is one of plaintive elegy and bitter regret at the passing away of a way of life. This is not the feeling we get from reading *A Grain of Wheat* or *God's Bits of Wood*. To be sure, neither of these two novels deals in any substantial way with the African past; nevertheless, Ousmane does portray traditionalist characters in conflict with the younger, more progressive generation which is clamouring for change; and we are left in no doubt on whose side Ousmane is. Niakoro's horror at the news of the impending trial of Diara, the ticket collector who breaks ranks with the strikers, is a good example of how Ousmane shifts our sympathy away from the old traditionalists to the younger radicals. For example, the terms Old Niakoro uses in her argument against the public trial are simply too absurd: 'But think of it!' she cries. 'To allow the honour of such a good man to be dragged through the mud − a man of such a good family! These children will never have white hairs − our world is falling apart.'[46]

These two novelists, Ngugi and Ousmane, are forward-looking in many important respects. There is in their works a noticeable absence of nostalgia for the past. And, although, as I have suggested, Ngugi's novel is a study in failure; it is not, I suggest, a study in resignation. In Mumbi's final words we may detect Ngugi's purpose in reconstructing this historical phase in his country's evolution which is to 'examine' the past in order 'together to plan the future we want'.[47]

4

It may be wondered what, except inventive licence, can permit a critic to see hidden connections between novels like Peter Abrahams's *Wild Conquest* and *A Wreath for Udomo* on the one hand and Yambo Ouologuem's *Bound to Violence* on the other. After all, Abrahams's conventionality of form is much closer to the simple narrative approach followed in the novels of Ngugi and Achebe than to the curious amalgam of techniques — African *griot* tradition, Mohammedan recitatives and the extreme narrative modes of European experimentalism — so impressively assembled in Ouologuem's novel.

However, beneath the obvious divergence in technique is to be found an unexpected unity of vision which ought to command our otherwise distracted attention. Abrahams's and Ouologuem's views of current African politics, and perhaps of African history, have certain features in common. The cheerful cynicism of the one and the romantic despair of the other are merely the outcome of a similar conviction about the African past, which is seen as having been largely enveloped in a mist of needless ignorance, superstition and bestial lust for blood in the pursuit of power.

Toward the end of *Wild Conquest*, Abrahams' novel about the Great Trek, Mzilikazi's and Gubuza's twin judgements of their own people are also, unquestionably, Abrahams's most consistent view of African history. The collision between the world of the Jansens as they make a bid to escape from the confinement of British rule in the old Cape, and the world of the Matabele at the glorious zenith of their power, is what the novel attempts to portray. Forced to give up their slaves and their conquered lands, the Boers choose to move away from the relative comfort and safety of the Cape Colony into the interior of the country, thereby setting into motion some of the forces which have helped to shape contemporary South African society. To this day nothing can equal the evocative power of the Great Trek for resuscitating the old passions in the hearts of present-day descendants of the Boer trekkers: the imagined epic quality of that tortuous journey in primitive ox-wagons into the interior of the country, the murderous ambushes and savage skirmishes with countless African tribes are what for many white South Africans endow the Great Trek with its truly Promethean quality. In Abrahams' novel, as we know, this voyage into the hitherto little-known interior, unknown to the Boers that is, culminates in a full-scale battle between the Boers and the Matabele.

As with the Ibo society of Chinua Achebe's novels, Abrahams hints at the internal decadence of the Matabele before their fall: the bloody domestic feuds, the internecine wrangling, the endless executions and the crushing oppression of the vassal states, create weaknesses within African society which finally bring about its fall. The sacking of the city of Kunana and the summary execution of some forty-one people suspected of witchcraft are just two instances in which the Matabele society reveals itself to have an insatiable appetite for bloodshed. As Mzilikazi says of the Matabele, 'We are cursed by a bloodlust.'[48] A little later, in what seems a cry torn from the heart, he repeats this judgement: 'Oh, but their bloodlust!' To which Gubuza responds with the brief and despairing rejoinder: 'And the darkness of their minds!'[49] Michael Wade is right when he insists in his study of Abrahams' work that 'the picture of African society he gives in his description of the Matabele is one of cruelty, corruption, bloodthirstiness and arbitrary and sudden death'.[50]

For Ouologuem, too, as reflected in this tragic, sometimes comic, study of a mythical African empire of Nakem, the African past is a singular chain of disasters. It is a horrendous procession of errors and crimes endlessly repeated, in which the present appears only as a mirror of past injustice, with a future that is grimly uncertain. The only victims are the ordinary people, the 'nigger-trash' upon whose exploitation is built, first the Saif dynasty, then the colonial empire of the French; after the departure of the French these common folk will, no doubt, become yet again instruments of self-enrichment by the new class of the African bourgeoisie.

With this uncompromisingly cynical picture of African political evolution as a vicious circle of violence and counter-violence, of rape, murder, enslave-ment and self-debasement, Ouologuem sets out to destroy the myth of a grandiose, peaceful African civilisation which he wryly suggests to have been invented by a starry-eyed German anthropologist, Shrobenius – a notion which Ouologuem dismisses blithely as 'stamped with the genius of lunacy'. A myth-maker and, like a good German scholar, a man addicted to metaphysics (he was determined to find metaphysical meaning in everything, even in the shape of the palaver tree'), Shrobenius romanticises outrageously about the African past. Of the Nakem empire he has written: 'It was only when white imperialism infiltrated the country with its colonial violence and materialism that this highly civilized people fell abruptly into a state of savagery . . .'[51]

This paradisal notion of Africa before the Fall, Ouologuem impatiently puts aside; instead he gives us a picture of 'hunger, sickness, and privation', of bloodlust and greed when 'under the lash of necessity a father sold his son, a brother his brother'; the countless wars and pointless brutality when 'paralysed with pain, the castrated husband, his thighs sticky with blood, looked helpless as his wives . . . became the harlots of the victorious village'.[52] The religion 'vomited' by the clergy of Nakem had become a 'deliberately confused mum-bling about human dignity, a learned mystification' which, having lost its mystical content, became a mere instrument of power.[53]

Ouologuem will stop at nothing in order to darken a picture already too black to be credible. There is an element of playful mischief in all this. 'Canni-balism', he tells us at one stage, 'was one of the darkest features of that spectral Africa over which hung the malefic shadow of Saif-al-Haram.' This is an Africa of pestilence and unbridled sexuality ('Transfigured and half delirious, con-scious of nothing but their possession of each other, of their profound penetra-tion, they lay enlaced, saturated with the mingling of their bodies . . .') and its sordidness conflicts directly with the favoured notion of a once pristine inno-cence. When the whites arrive they are no better; they 'pillage, loot, destroy everything in their path'. The rape of Awa by Chevalier, a French colonial administrator, with the aid of two setter dogs which rip off her clothes, tear off her 'loincloth and shift without scratching her skin', is one of those baroque delights which can transform a passage plagiarised from somewhere else[54] into something that only Ouologuem could have fully assimilated into this multi-faceted novel. His picture of Africa is not only dark but the prospects for the future are full of gloomy forebodings about many despotic Saifs 'forever reborn to history beneath the hot ashes of more than thirty African republics'.[55] This is a grim picture, with more than a touch of cruel, if hilarious, insanity about it. As Bishop Henry, 'the hunchback priest obsessed by the tragedy of the Blacks', preferred to put it: 'The crux of the matter is violence, vibrant in its unconditional submission to the will to power.'[56]

The disparity in feeling between the novels of Peter Abrahams and Yambo Ouologuem's fictive history lies, I suggest, not so much in the discrepancy of attitude to African society as it does in the handling of language as a medium for expressing this attitude. Very often Abrahams' prose, even in a novel as contemporary as *A Wreath for Udomo*, seems to lack any vibrancy or energy: seems, in fact, very frequently to collapse into the dead, cliché'd language of *Woman's Own*. Phrases such as 'sun-kissed valley' and the 'whispering voice of time' are not merely artificial but are indicative of a deeper crisis which may finally be located in the vacuous blandness of Peter Abrahams' bourgeois liberal ethic which in *Wild Conquest*, at any rate, is further underlined by his failure to arbitrate properly between legitimate African interests and the illegitimate claims to plunder by a white settler minority.

Ouologuem, on the other hand, has assimilated his extremely pessimistic vision of African history to a language that continually matches it in its poetic radicalism, combining strong dramatic rhythms with dazzling surrealist imagery. We may be inclined to reject the extravagant arbitrariness of this view of African history; we may be tempted to dismiss his interpretation of this history as a species of intentionally provocative, if sometimes witty, attempts at burlesque, but the language itself, because of its rich inner resources, achieves for the book an exactness of tone which finally compels our assent to its vision because of a proper fusion between language and feeling.

Paradoxically, Peter Abrahams is a far more competent craftsman than many African novelists whom I nevertheless find more satisfying than him; this satisfaction has something to do with the novelist's power to communicate sensations of having lived the life he represents; satire, distance or even technical incoherence can sometimes conceal a personal sense of loyalty and outrage which a writer is struggling to express. Abrahams often fails at this deeper level of personal commitment. Despite the evident sincerity and in spite of some of its obvious virtues, *Wild Conquest* retains a curiously synthetic atmosphere which is wholly lacking from the pages of *Bound to Violence*, and this notwithstanding some well-documented charges against Ouologuem's lifting of vast stretches of prose from heterogenous sources.[57]

Abrahams' distrust for traditional African society, sometimes ambiguously stated, is only occasionally relieved, as in *Wild Conquest*, by concessions to its exotic grandeur or, as in *Mine Boy*, by the granting of a naive nobility to a figure like Xuma. Frequently, the picture Abrahams wishes us to accept is of a traditional Africa steeped in ignorance which is only compounded by useless magic. Apparently, this belief in the power of magic retains its grip on even a modern, pragmatic politician like Udomo; for when he hears the drums thundering, '*Udomo traitor Udomo die*,' it is not merely the fear of the assassins and their long knives that breaks Udomo's nerves, it is the feeling of magic in the air communicated by the talking drums. 'The drums were getting at him, too!'[58]

When Beier suggested that Abrahams had succumbed to the white man's myth of the 'primitive Negro' he was surely right and Wade's defence of the novelist remains unconvincing.[59] The fact that Abrahams is coloured and dislikes apartheid does not, unfortunately, acquit him of Beier's accusation; nor does the quote about the undemocratic nature of tribal society, which is even more damaging in its crass ignorance of African anthropology, do anything to support Wade's view of the matter. For Abrahams tribalism and witchcraft are the main obstacles to modernism and development; but the harshness of his vision of tribal society, often based on lack of familiarity with African tradition, is so unmitigated that one can scarcely recall in his work any instances, as in Ngugi and Achebe, in which the debt owed to this past by contemporary African society is acknowledged and recorded.

How far Abrahams has allowed his special phobia to interfere with his sense of proportion can be seen clearly in the total disintegration of his novel *A Wreath for Udomo* in its final chapters. A book that follows closely the fortunes of some African colonial exiles in Britain, with a commitment to overturning the colonial set-up when they return home, the main figures in the narrative are closely modelled on actual personalities like Kwame Nkrumah, Jomo Kenyatta, and George Padmore, all of whom Abrahams knew during their exile in Britain. In its earlier sections the novel does well enough; but later, when the action shifts to Africa, there is a clear evidence of arm-twisting to achieve certain ends which are not foreshadowed at the beginning of the novel. Abrahams' endorsement of Udomo's betrayal of Mhendi and his cautious approval of Udomo's alliance with an unnamed racist White state, rather like the South African republic in exchange for development aid, and Abrahams' total condemnation of Selina, a tribal woman who had masterminded Udomo's accession to power, are some of the most curious aspects of this work.

After such an odious betrayal of Mhendi a reader might suspect that Selina and Adebhoy had some justification for having Udomo assassinated. Indeed, in their willingness to put the resources of the Party at Mhendi's disposal, hiding him when he is on the run, Selina and Adebhoy seem more Pan-Africanist than tribalist. Rather surprisingly, however, Abrahams' sympathies are for Udomo, whose attempts at self-justification reeks of the language of opportunism. Udomo's views would, no doubt, find a certain amount of favour with those Western intellectuals who consider a certain political 'pragmatism' the hallmark of sophistication, as they also, no doubt, reflect Abrahams' own views on how to cope with the problems of nation-building; but nothing justifies Abrahams' attempts to engage our sympathies on behalf of his hero by a last-minute sleight of hand. For instance, in a letter we are entitled to regard as expressing many of Abrahams' own sentiments, Paul Mabi writes to Udomo's former girl friend in London, explaining about Udomo's murder:

> The papers, if you read them, will tell you his body was found hacked to pieces. I don't think they'll ever find the man or men who did it. The tribal curtain of silence will be down, and I know just how complete it can be. But the real killers, even if they didn't strike the blows, are our laughing friend Adebhoy and a terrible tribal woman called Selina who controlled the party when I was out there.

You can guess the reason for his murder. They wanted to go back to the days of tribal glory.[60]

This charge is nowhere satisfactorily substantiated by events in the novel itself. On the contrary, Udomo seems to be the main traitor, betraying freedom-fighters to the white regime, and generally behaving with unwarranted arrogance and aloofness toward those who helped him climb to power.

Whereas in Ouologuem's novel traditionalists are treated as reckless knaves, secretly cunning even as they allow themselves to be bought and sold by a succession of alien masters and exploiters, Abrahams' tribal chieftains are nothing more than fools, men so unaware of the real meaning of power that a twin-engine aeroplane bringing Udomo in from the capital is enough to impress them to such an extent that they are prepared to relinquish their authority at a stroke.

However cynical and patronising toward the 'inborn imbecility' of the fanatical crowds, Ouologuem's burlesque performance has at least some connection with the larger historical reality; it is a grotesquely exaggerated picture of what in its essential aspects was a true state of affairs: African kingdoms spurned on by greed and lust for new wealth, pillaging each other's cities, raiding enemy settlements for slaves and selling each other for whatever returns they could get. Again, it is the intensity of his vision, the extreme form of its poetisation, which endows Ouologuem's novel with its peculiar integrity. Ouologuem seems determined to incarnate Nietzsche's literary sentiments that 'aphorisms should be peaks — and those who are addressed, tall and lofty. The air thin and pure, danger near, and the spirit full of gay sarcasm . . .'

5

South Africa already has a considerable number of historical novels written in African languages. Some of these, like Thomas Mofolo's *Chaka*, have already been translated into European languages; others, like R.R.R. Dhlomo's biographical novels of the Zulu kings, from Chaka to Cetshwayo, have not yet been translated. I have not discussed vernacular novels because I am not competent to discuss similar works by vernacular authors in other parts of the continent. Also I have felt that some of these novels are too much indebted to the historical record and very little inspired by the creative urge to interpret and to illuminate. This may be too arbitrary a view. However, I hope that in discussing even a few of these novels I have indicated the range of attitudes to African history revealed by African novelists and the variety of techniques they employ in carrying out their enterprise.

REFERENCES

1   Thomas Babington Macaulay, *Critical and Historical Essays*, Dent, London, 1961, p.1.
2   *Ibid.*
3   Gerald Moore, *The Chosen Tongue*, Longman, London, 1969, p.151.
4   *Ibid.*
5   See 'The Role of the Writer in a New Nation' by Chinua Achebe, included in *African Writers on African Writing*, ed. by G. D. Killman, Heinemann, London, 1973, p.8.

6   Achebe, 'The Role of the Writer'.
7   John Povey, 'The Novels of Chinua Achebe', included in *Introduction to Nigerian Literature*, ed. by Bruce King, University of Lagos/Evans, London, 1971, p.109.
8   *Ibid.*, p.109.
9   Chinua Achebe, *Things Fall Apart*, Heinemann, 1958, p.111.
10 *Ibid.*, p.111.
11 *Ibid.*, p.111.
12 *Ibid.*, p.129–30.
13 *Ibid.*, p.131.
14 *Ibid* p.132.
15 *Ibid.*, p.133.
16 Chinua Achebe, *Arrow of God*, Heinemann, 1964, p.162.
17 *Ibid.*, p.269.
18 *Ibid.*, p.105.
19 *Ibid.*, p.105.
20 See Austin J. Shelton's article: 'The Offended *Chi* in Achebe's Novels', *Transition*, iii, 13 (1964).
21 Margaret Laurence, *Long Drums and Cannons*, Macmillan, London, 1968, p.113.
22 Nadine Gordimer *The Black Interpreters*, Spro-Cas/Ravan, Johannesburg, 1973, p.14.
23 James Ngugi, *A Grain of Wheat*, Heinemann, 1967, p.280.
24 Georg Lukacs, *Studies in European Realism*, Merlin Press, London, 1972, p.11.
25 Sembene Ousmane, *God's Bits of Wood*, Heinemann, 1970, p.250.
26 *Ibid.*
27 *Ibid.*, p.102.
28 *Ibid.*, p.56.
29 *Ibid.*, p.57.
30 *Ibid.*, p.84–5.
31 *Ibid.*, p.84.
32 *Ibid.*, p.90.
33 *Ibid.*, p.81.
34 *Ibid.*, p.52.
35 *Ibid.*, p.170.
36 *Ibid.*, p.43.
37 *Ibid.*, p.20.
38 D. H. Lawrence, *The Plumed Serpent*, Penguin, London, 1950, p.121.
39 Ousmane, *God's Bits of Wood*, p.109.
40 *Ibid.*
41 *Ibid.*
42 Nadine Gordimer, *The Black Interpreters*, p.44.
43 *Ibid.*, p.14.
44 Achebe, *Arrow of God*, p.286.
45 *Ibid.*, p.260.
46 Ousmane, *God's Bits of Wood*, p.124.
47 Ngugi, *A Grain of Wheat*, p.124.
48 Peter Abrahams, *Wild Conquest*, Faber, 1951, p.257.
49 *Ibid.*, p.258.
50 Michael Wade, *Peter Abrahams*, Evans, London, 1972, p.77.
51 Yambo Ouologuem, *Bound to Violence*, Harcourt Brace, Jovanovich, New York, 1971, p.94 (and Heinemann, London, 1971).
52 *Ibid.*, p.15.
53 *Ibid.*, p.23.
54 Robert McDonald, 'Bound to Violence: A Case of Plagiarism' published in *Transition*, viii, 41, (1972).
55 Ouologuem, *Bound to Violence*, p.182.
56 *Ibid.*, p.173.
57 McDonald, 'Bound to Violence'.
58 Peter Abrahams, *A Wreath for Udomo*, Faber, 1965, p.304.
59 Wade, *Peter Abrahams*, p.150.
60 Abrahams, *A Wreath for Udomo*, p.308.

CHAPTER FOUR

THE NEW AFRICAN NOVEL: A SEARCH FOR MODERNISM.

1

The African novel in the European languages is sometimes damned for its double ancestry which is both African and European. The bastard child of many cultures and genres, the accumulator of many styles and traditions, the modern African novel, it is said, cannot properly reflect African reality. As we have pointed out in chapter 1, by virtue of its use of European languages alone some have gone so far as to deny it the legitimate right to even be called 'African'.

While there is a certain amount of truth in these charges it may equally be argued in its favour that the very diversity of the African novel, the variety of the languages in which it is written, reflect more accurately than anything else the realities of modern Africa; that what is sometimes seen as the embarrassing mixture of styles and traditions is often a source of strength and vitality, not a cause of weakness and diminution of insight. What may now turn out to be the new centre of focus for discussion is not whether Africans ought to have written in English, French and Portuguese, which is now a matter of history; but what kind of direction the African novel has been taking since the publication of Amos Tutuola's *The Palm-Wine Drinkard* in 1952 and the appearance of Camara Laye's *L'enfant noir* in 1953, to take two arbitrary but convenient dates.

With the exception of Laye's *Le regard du roi* (1954) which in its applica-tion of Kafkan techniques to black/white relations in an African environment seemed to look forward to an imminent period of fuller experimentation, the African novels which followed one another into print in the next decade belonged to the classical tradition of the novel, at least as Africa has received it from Europe, with its fidelity to linear plots and character-development and the fairly straightforward descriptions of setting as a backdrop to action. Because of his intelligent use of certain linguistic resources from the Ibo language, Chinua Achebe more than anyone else has helped to extend and to supplement this tradition, thereby setting an example which has influenced many younger writers of whom Ngugi wa Thiong'o may be said to have been the most obvious disciple, at least, until the publication in 1977 of his novel, *Petals of Blood*.

It now seems clear, however, that since the middle of the 1960s a cleavage has been developing in African fiction between the continuers of this central tradition and what we may call, for lack of a better word, the 'experimentalists' and manipulators of form who insist on bringing to our immediate attention not only the queer content of their novels but wish us to notice in particular the manner of their execution. In the earlier traditional novel style is used to conceal art in favour of content; in the later novels style deliberately and provocatively calls attention to itself and becomes the object of its own contemplation. Indeed, it has sometimes been argued that what distinguishes *modernism* in art is not so much the oddity of the subject-matter as the deliberate focusing of our attention on technique as interesting in itself, so that, instead of the object which it is supposed to represent, artistic form itself now becomes its own subject-matter. Such a definition is, of course, too extreme to apply without qualification to the specifically African conditions. But if we disregard, for the moment, the 'art for art's sake' implication inherent in such a formulation, we shall soon find that this definition does, in fact, contain a key element in the kind of distinction we are trying to make: the fact that in opposition to, say, the almost classical serenity of Chinua Achebe's narrative style, which may be said to represent the sort of 'art which conceals art', the novelists whom I shall group under the 'modernist' label are constantly calling our attention not just to the events being narrated but to the essential duplicity of form itself, to the strained artificiality of language, to the uncertainty of the ground which modern art tries to inhabit. That the 'modernist' writer should choose this unstable ground upon which to build his house is, so to speak, the very essence of what we now think of as the 'modernist temper', its final irony and its artifice.

If we take half a dozen or so African novels, beginning with Camara Laye's *Le regard du roi* (*The Radiance of the King*), Gabriel Okara's *The Voice* (1964), Wole Soyinka's *The Interpreters* (1965), Ayi Kwei Armah's *The Beautyful Ones Are Not Yet Born* (1968), Kofi Awoonor's *This Earth, My Brother* (1971), Ngugi wa Thiong'o's *Petals of Blood* (1977) or more astonishing than any of these, Yambo Ouologuem's *La devoir de violence* (*Bound to Violence*) (1968), it is fairly obvious that a 'modernist' movement is now taking shape in Africa which may create links with modernist movements in other parts of the world, chiefly in Europe, in North and South America. Nevertheless, to see what is now occurring in African fiction merely as an extension of a development occurring somewhere else is seriously to misjudge the nature of the African phenomenon, its roots and its ideological compulsions. For one thing the modernist movement in Africa faces both ways at once; it faces forward to the latest innovations in fiction as well as backward to the roots of African tradition. Indeed, some of the experiments being carried out in African fiction owe nothing to European and American examples, but achieve their queer effects by returning us to African traditional sources and by exploiting certain properties of native languages. Yambo Ouologuem's narrative style owes far more to African and Islamic recitative traditions than to any examples Europe could offer. Gabriel Okara, on the other hand, has tried to achieve his effects by transferring certain peculiarities of the Ijaw language into written English forms. Above all, whatever their obsession with form, African novelists are still deeply committed to the simple act of telling 'a story'.

There are two main reasons for this preoccupation: firstly, the oral tradition of story-telling is still very much alive in African societies and there is genuine joy and satisfaction to be derived from telling a story well. Secondly, and more important, African authors still have a major story to tell. The modern African state, so lately the plaything of colonial powers, is a relatively new creation, the conditions of its emergence from colonial occupation to full independent status so compelling a theme, that few African writers can resist the call to celebrate in their novels, so momentous an event..In their careful reconstruction of the precolonial past, in their vivid chronicling of the struggle against colonialism, the works of modern African writers constitute, almost without exception, the most valuable documentation of the vicissitudes of African society at major points of crisis. Surprisingly, for such a colossal undertaking a quiet discreet realism usually suffices. This is not to say that traditional fiction is less difficult to write, simply that it is not concerned so much with innovation as it is with telling a story. Indeed, in its commitment to simple clear-cut narrative objectives, this kind of fiction may even be said to be more responsible than an eternal quest for spurious stylistic excitement.

2

This search for style which, it is hoped, would lay bare the new strains and tensions in African society is what, in fact, defines the work of novelists like Soyinka, Ouologuem, Armah, Awoonor and others; and there is more at stake here than a mere struggle with language; more at stake than a mere 'search for style' for its own sake. In novels like *The Interpreters, This Earth, My Brother* or *The Beautyful Ones Are Not Yet Born* we see, in fact, the objectification of the growing split between the literary intellectuals and the ruling bureaucracies in Africa; and by 'literary intellectuals' I do not simply mean the so-called 'men of letters' but all those intellectuals, easily distinguishable from scientists or administrative cadres, whose function is to explain, disseminate or represent through images, the essential nature of society to its own members. Naturally enough, to the extent that literature both projects an image and provides a criticism of this society in microcosm, writers are only the most effective spokesmen of the group. In the words of Colin Mercer, the ultimate function of these intellectuals 'is to cement and bind and make coherent the contradictory elements of the social formation in order to establish a consensus, a hegemony at all levels'.[1]

Obviously where writers, or 'cultural' intellectuals in general are prevented from acting as a cement and bind of the 'contradictory elements' in society they appear to the rulers to be an additional burden, a greatly disruptive force, alienated and discontented, which poses an immediate threat to the established order itself. In this context it is not difficult to see why Ngugi wa Thiong'o of Kenya should have been detained by his own government for merely writing and producing a play critical of the ruling elite. Thus we can safely conclude that the current shift toward 'modernist' techniques in modern African fiction, though sometimes disguised as mere quest for stylistic excitement and innovation, is in reality something more than this; we are obliged to note that this shift in style is occurring against a background of chronic instability in African society; that the basis of a close organic relationship between the individual and the rest of the community is being seriously undermined by new economic and social forces; that anxiety, alienation, and the emergence of an anguished pessimistic vision, so forcefully projected in Kofi Awoonor's *This Earth, My*

Brother, a novel which actually ends in suicide, are indices of widespread dislocation and loss of equilibirium in modern African society.

3

It is something of a paradox that the first traces of the modernist movement in
Nigeria should be found in the work, not of a sophisticated university graduate
(made familiar with the latest innovations in European fiction by long hours of
study and seminarial discussions), but in the work of Amos Tutuola, a simple
story-teller with very little formal education; but a writer, nevertheless, whose
'thronged, grisly' tales, to quote Dylan Thomas' description of *The Palm-Wine
Drinkard*, have attracted wide attention in Europe and other parts of the
world.

In a more systematic way than I could ever hope to match, Professor A.
Afolayan has applied the tools of linguistic analysis[2] to show how much of
Tutuola's stylistic 'vigour and freshness' owes not only to his unconscious translation of certain features of the Yoruba language into English, but to reworkings of Yoruba tales from the oral tradition into his modern narratives. Such an
analysis suggests two things. First, that the plots of Tutuola's tales are to a large
extent still communal property, drawn from the common heritage of the oral
tradition. Secondly, that those features of style which have exercised the most
dramatic impact on English readers, 'sensitive', as Gerald Moore once put it, 'to
all that has become jaded and feeble in our language', may be the result not of
Tutuola's conscious revolt against linguistic propriety but the result of a collision, fortunate or unfortunate, between two languages, the acquired standard
school English and the 'deep grammar' of Tutuola's native Yoruba language.

Lest such an analysis should minimise Tutuola's own creative contribution, it can never be stated too strongly that no slide-rule measurements can
ever exhaust the description of a writer's work, its magic and its singularity.
Even when it is admitted that the plots of Tutuola's novels are little more than
the reworkings of traditional materials, there remains a large element of
choice, of selection, of collation and conformation; in particular, the choice of
particular words, whether their source be the Yoruba language or the fund of
standard English vocabulary he has at his command, produces the kind of
stylistic effects which we have come to associate with Tutuola's work. What
lures us again and again to this Yoruba writer, and what finally makes him a
cohabitant with many other writers of the surrealist tradition, is his lurid,
lunatic imagination, the shameless, improbable exaggerations, his mad, dis-
continuous narratives held together by a logic of such extreme fragility that
believing in them would plunge one into further madness; this and the
unimpeded gathering together of material objects belonging to the traditional
economy – cowries, palm trees, kolas, yams, and palm oils – into a weird
adjacency and admixture with those that are part and parcel of the flotsam and
jetsam of modern society – pounds, petrol drums, bombs, orchestras and
debt collectors – create an effect in Tutuola's work which stimulates a wink-
ing recognition among modernist writers everywhere. We can also note in
passing the naive predilection for tabulation, examples of which abound in
The Palm-Wine Drinkard, a tendency which was also pronounced in Defoe at

the outset of realism in English fiction:

> Now by that time and before we entered inside the white tree, we had 'sold
> our death' to somebody at the door for the sum of £70:18:6d and 'lent our
> fear' to somebody at the door as well on interest of £3:10:0d per month, so we
> did not care about death and we did not fear again.[3]

Unarguably Tutuola is a problematic figure in modern African literature;
he faces both ways at once: backward toward the oral tradition and forward
toward the non-naturalistic styles of the modernist, chiefly surrealism. Along
side Tutuola's experiments with language we can place the work of another
Nigerian writer, Gabriel Okara, who uses roughly the same technique in his
novel, *The Voice*, of translating Ijaw syntax into English, though Okara's
method is more deliberate and carefully worked out: its deliberateness also
constitutes its artificiality. Where the technique succeeds it often reminds us of
the queer effects produced by American Jewish writers, primarily Isaac
Belshevis Singer, who translates directly from Yiddish, but also Bellow,
Malamud and other Jewish writers who, standing in close proximity to the
Yiddish tradition and its associated habits of speech, often achieve certain
comic effects by incorporating these linguistic peculiarities into standard
American English. However, Okara's experiment finally breaks down into
complete incoherence: his experiment fails precisely because it remains just
that, an experiment; the language is not as integrated into ordinary Nigerian
English as Amos Tutuola's worst excesses always seem to be; the strained, rare-
fied air of the laboratory lingers over lines like these:

> . . . Me know nothing? Because I went not to school I have no bile, I have no
> head? Me know nothing? Then answer me this. Your hair was black black
> be, then it became white like a white cloth and now it is black black be more
> than blackness. The root, what is it? You keep quiet. Answer me. I know
> nothing, you say.[4]

There is very little to say about this sort of thing. However, Okara is also an
excellent poet; his struggles with language are those of a poet trying to force
English to commit itself to newer and stranger habits of thoughts. However
removed from common speech, this sort of *mata-language* creates its own
specific universe, sometimes bleak, sometimes erotic, sometimes merely poeti-
cised. Here at its full stretch, with its peculiarity of syntax, of sentences which
end inevitably with a verb, the language has a startling freshness which almost
justifies the more egregious failures of the experiment.

> It was the day's ending and Okolo by a window stood. Okolo stood looking at
> the sun behind the tree tops falling. The river was flowing, reflecting the
> finishing sun, like a dying away memory. It was like an idol's face, no one
> knowing what is behind. Okolo at the palm trees looked. They were like
> women with hair hanging down, dancing, possessed. Egrets, like white
> flower petals strung slackly across the river, swaying up and down, were
> returning home. And, on the river, canoes were crawling home with bent

backs and tired hands, paddling. A girl with only a cloth tied around her waist and the half-ripe mango breasts, paddled, driving her paddle into the river with a sweet inside.[5]

Up to now we have paid special attention to the style of the two writers, not to the content of their work; we have pointed out some similarities in their handling of language, but there the link between Tutuola and Okara is terminated: it is ended precisely at that point where the search for style becomes incomprehensible without a proper description of the expanding social consciousness which makes such a search necessary. There is an element of chance in Tutuola's choice of style, even blindness, which suggests lack of full consciousness; more significantly his narratives are rooted in the world of the African folk-tale and legend, elements of which have become indigestible and therefore can no longer be assimilated in their original form into the modern sensibility. The world of the African folk tale and legend is a world of myths developed in order to embody human needs and goals and, making them, in the words of Diana Laurenson, 'vehicles for symbolic figures and common predicaments' which are then handed down from generation to generation.[6] The modern novel on the other hand demands a more differentiated handling of particular experiences. Tutuola, it must be said, has destroyed forever the purity and innocence of the African folk tale. Simply by *working* upon the raw materials of myth, which is what his type of literary production involves, by breaking this material down into its various segments and reconstituting them into a newly articulated form, Tutuola has contrived to give us something new, freshly minted. What he has not done — and this is not necessarily meant as a reproach — is to use this reconstituted article to enable us to grasp the movement and contradictions of modern African society. This failure or refusal to emerge fully from the milieu of the African 'fairy tale', whatever other elements we may find in his work, immediately calls into question Tutuola's status as one of the representative figures within the current 'modernist' movement in Africa. After all, extreme self-consciousness is one of the movement's key attributes.

4

Camara Laye and Gabriel Okara, two novelists who can be said to stand closest to Tutuola's world of mythological constructs can also be shown to have distanced themselves sufficiently from this magical universe by casting their stories in the form of political allegory and religious parable which both reinterpret and continuously subvert the innocence of the 'folk-tale'. Such a world, they continually nudge us, does not exist. Seen in this way even their use of the supernatural is simply a re-enacting of our own human world in symbolical terms; but a human world, all the same.

There is a sense in which Camara Laye's novel, *The Radiance of the King* (*Le regard du roi*), like Kafka's *The Castle* before it, which is both its model and its true prototype, can legitimately be described as an extended dream, a form of meditation on religious themes and a kind of reverie, provided, of course, we keep in mind Freud's penetrating comment on these mattters: 'Do you not know that all the transgressions and excesses of which we dream at night are daily committed in real life by waking men!'

The content of our dreams as mere exposés, or rather as expositions of our hidden wishes and desires, as an inestimable and timely illumination of what lurks in the depths of our unconscious, is recognised in the novel by Clarence himself, its white hero. The author tells us: 'But then everything had become clear, everything had become violently and cruelly clear. Clarence was now perfectly aware that he had been dreaming; but he could also see now *that his dream was true*.'[7] (Italics mine.) The dream-like technique of the novel is obvious in the most surrealistic scenes of the book; it is evident in the constant shifts from the *terra firma* of realistic representation to the spell-bound world of entranced vision in which 'armchairs and their occupants' disappear 'as if by enchantment', in which old women copulate with snakes, and the Christlike figure of the boy-king, the object of Clarence's quest, 'seemed in a curious way to be moving forward into the open sky'.[8] Clarence's cry: 'I'm dreaming, but I'm going to wake up soon', is the same cry out of the modern nightmare from which Joyce suggested we dare not awake, a nightmare rendered headily potent by the magic wand of modern fictional techniques. Modern fiction, according to David Lodge, 'is much concerned with consciousness, and also subconscious or unconscious workings of the human mind. Hence the structure of external 'objective' events essential to narrative art in traditional poetics is diminished in scope and scale, or presented selectively and obliquely, in order to make room for introspection, analysis, reflection and reverie'.[9] Nothing, I suggest, could be truer of Camara Laye's narrative technique which is a continuous process of condensation, displacement, and symbolisation in the actual reproduction of dream material. Here is Clarence contemplating the African boy-king who seems to be an apposition in a dream, whose features have the plasticity of an African carving:

> Clarence was afraid to pursue the thought: it was the sort of smile which one sees on the faces of idols − remote, enigmatic − and which is composed perhaps as much of disdain as of benevolence; the reflection of an inner life, no doubt, but − what sort of inner life? Perhaps of that very life which lies beyond death . . . 'Can that be the sort of life I have come here to find?'[10]

It is possible, of course, to wish that Laye were less obviously indebted to Kafka's *The Castle*, to the extent of including a pair of roguish boys in his story not at all unlike the assistants of Kafka's novel. The pair are forever leading Clarence astray whenever the mood for playing pranks overwhelms them; but the borrowing sums sometimes justified; it would also be impossible to deny the richness of Camara Laye's own invention. The fecund and deleterious atmosphere of the tropics with which Laye has shamelessly invested this novel makes it as alien to the icy snows of the north European *Castle* as the grotesque, fiendish sensuality of *The Radiance of the King* makes even the frankest sexuality of Kafka's novel seem pallid by comparison. But Laye's novel is more than this: in the plight of Clarence, its debased and humiliated hero, who gambles and loses all his money; who, stripped of his clothes and whatever European authority he still possesses, is driven out of his hotel room, the butt of many jokes and cruel pranks until at the end of the book he is reduced to what the novel calls a 'great cock', servicing the *naba's* women; the book provides us with the clearest metaphor for the uncheckable decline of European colonialism and White power in Africa. Of course, the religious theme, which is embodied in the hero's search for authentic experience, is just as strong and just as relevant. Clarence's journey south is not only a movement away from the cold north and the cold impersonality of European civilisation, it is also a blind, impulsive journey by a sleepwalker toward the interior of the tropics, which is only a symbolic journey toward the interior of the self and true knowledge; and this knowledge is gained after constant submission to degrading but ultimately liberating sensual experience. Before he can acquire any valuable experience Clarence is required to divest himself of his assumed mantle of power. As the beggar who acts as his guide tells Clarence:

> There *are* paths. If you can't see them — and why should you see them? — you've only got your own eyes to blame. A white man can't see everything: and he has no need to see everything either, because this land is not a white man's land.[11]

There is a much more real conjuncture between Tutuola's world of African myth and Camara Laye's whimsical creation of a mystical Africa than there is between Tutuola's world of myth and Okara's bleak construction of an allegorical African state. Okara's novel does signal a real break with the spiritualised world of *The Palm-Wine Drinkard* in order to plunge deliberately within the actual material circumstances of contemporary African society. Okolo, the hero of *The Voice*, said to be in search of 'it', is clearly cut in the cloth of the problematic Lukacsian hero in search of 'authentic values'. Instead of the integrated world of the traditional economy, with its communal solidarity, its tradition of reciprocal aid and mutual co-operation, the capitalist mode of production inaugurates a new era of class divisions or merely accentuates those social divisions already present in precolonial African society — indeed, imbues them with a newer and deadlier content. Alienation, estrangement, an acute sense of anxiety are the immediate result of this lack of organic unity between the individual and the community, between the individual and the world. Okolo, the hero of *The Voice* confronts the world constantly as *other* and hostile to him: when he is overpowered and thrown to the ground by the messengers of Chief Izongo, his implacable adversary, Okolo feels 'clawed by a thousand hands, the hands of the world'. Temporarily free from his pursuers, Okolo makes a bid to escape, and again the feet that run after him are said to be 'the caring-nothing feet of the world'. This is a world of existential nausea, bleak, corrupt, deformed and lacking decency and security; the very language in which it is inscribed seems equally distorted, the language of the new *angst*. Alone, embattled, cut adrift from the world and society, Okolo is the first truly anguished hero of the new African fiction; he is forever swimming in a dark existential void where 'grim faces like the dark mysterious forest afire with flies' haunt him like figures in a nightmare; his very education, instead of fitting him for service in his community, isolates him, provokes hostility and suspicion:

Okolo started his search when he came out of school and returned home to his people. When he returned home to his people, words of the coming thing, rumours of the coming thing, were in the air flying like birds, swimming like fishes in the river. But Okolo did not join them in their joy because what *was there was no longer there and things had no more roots.*[12] (Italics mine.)

This, of course, is precisely what the new African novel is constantly reminding us: that things have no more roots; that a new instability and incoherence are threatening African communities. But though Okolo's estrangement from society is nearly total he doggedly continues his search for 'it': what 'it' is exactly we are never told because, as the hero explains 'names bring divisions and divisions, strife. So let it be without a name.' This reticence about describing the actual site where the social struggles are supposed to be taking place tells us an awful lot about what some African writers, either through class affiliation or through lack of proper analytical tools, feel unable to face up to: mainly that a new era of struggle is opening up between the new ruling elites and the rest of the population over which this ruling elite exercises power and control. African writers have tended to see the contest as existing on a single level; the terrain of the civilian/military bureaucracy versus a frustrated but impotent intelligentsia.

But there is much more than this involved here as *The Voice* recognises and makes explicit. From his conversation with Tebeowei, it is clear that Okolo is in revolt against the new materialist society in which 'everybody's inside is now filled with money, cars and concrete houses and money being scattered all around'.[13] This theme is reiterated after Okolo's frustrating encounter with the white man, during which he meditates on the nature of corruption. As he puts it: 'Nothing has any more meaning but the shadow-devouring trinity of gold, iron, concrete.'[14] If part of the purpose of criticism is to make visible what remains implicit in the text it seems not unreasonable to conclude that what Okara has given us in this short allegory of a man's search for 'authentic values' is a critique of capitalist formation in the new African society; but the perspective from which the criticism is mounted is backward-looking, reactionary and finally self-defeating because the hero seeks to resurrect or refurbish a system of traditional values which is clearly beyond recuperation. Unless allied to a revolutionary potential existing within the mass of the population such a swimming against the tide can only end in nihilistic gesture or pseudo-religiosity. It is in this sense that I agree with J.P. O'Flinn's conclusion when he asserts that Okara is aware here of the size of the crisis:

. . . in ways that, for example, those members of the political elite shortly to be assassinated or imprisoned were not, and in this sense his novel represents a real extension of the consciousness of his social group. And yet in other ways he is unable to pass beyond the limits of that group-consciousness and hence is as unable as the political elite he rightly attacks to find solutions to the problem he has posed. Thus, he regards the people as an undifferentiated and ignorant mass, 'the knowing-nothing footsteps, the bad footsteps', scarcely human at all — sometimes, as the text suggests, more like a pack of dogs or a colony of ants. This disdain for the people means that they are seen, along with the political elite, as part of the problem rather than its potential solution, and, granted this perspective, the novel is forced to pose a different kind of elitism as the only hope for the future. [15]

5

Such a criticism can be extended, of course, to other important West African writers, chief among whom we can mention the Nigerian novelist and playwright, Wole Soyinka, and, to a lesser extent, the Ghanaian novelist and poet, Kofi Awoonor, writers whose literary works arouse a critical response of a profound respect and admiration for the artistic energy which animates them while leaving us with feelings of strained discomfort and unease at the general sense of hopelessness their vision of society evokes in us. In this connection, some critics would include (though I think with less justification) another Ghanaian writer, Ayi Kwei Armah, whose first novel has sometimes been attacked as too gloomily unjust in its depiction of Ghanaian society, and by one critic, at least, as presenting 'a world in which the sewage pipes of history have exploded and everything is polluted'. [16]

What is important to record here is that all these novelists have provided us with some of the most telling images of corruption and premature decay which presently afflicts post-independent African society, and the alienation and despair of which this corruption and decay are the symptoms. As the Ugandan critic, Shatto Gakwandi has said of Soyinka: 'In his first novel, *The Interpreters*, he captures vividly the decadence and sterility of the contemporary social and political set-up in many African countries.' [17] So have the two Ghanaian novelists, Armah and Awoonor. The result is a common search for the kind of style which can respond adequately to the immense pressures which are felt to be acting upon human character or which are seen to be threatening the community with disintegration; and what we find apart from the extreme image of mutilation, degeneracy, and atrophy, is a self-conscious manipulation of language, sometimes excessively poetic, a sudden turning away from external reflection of reality to internal explorations of individual consciousness which can be said to 'reflect both an artistic criticism of the limits of realism as well as the isolation and uncertainty of the modern intellectual, no longer securely anchored in the bourgeois class'.

That the present literary intellectuals are no longer secure within the ruling class in Africa cannot be doubted and their novels reflect this fact. In all of African fiction no characters are, of course, more isolated or insecure than Amamu, the hero of *This Earth, My Brother*, or more alienated and disorientated than the unnamed hero of Ayi Kwei Armah's *The Beautyful Ones Are Not Yet Born* who, characteristically enough, is called simply 'the Man'. Both writers are products of African and Western universities; both grew up at the time of tremendous promise in Africa when Nkrumah suddenly took Ghana into independence; but they also belong to a generation that later witnessed the country's gradual decline into chaos before the final collapse of the regime. Both writers, therefore, bring a measure of personal bitterness to their meditations on the theme of power and corruption in a modern African state. They bring something else too: the tremendous poetic gifts and familiarity with the combined techniques of European and traditional African narrative modes to a fiction that is constantly surprising as much for the depths of its insights as for its most casual observations. Here is Awoonor's simple, realistic record of a lovers' meeting, with its sense of futile repetition, of routinised attempt at fulfilment, which seems to strike a universal note about the conditions of modern urban life:

> She moved towards the record player. Underneath the table were records. She looked out for his record. She turned the first knob, and the turntable began to turn. It was a popular song those days. One of those sentimental love songs which even serious-minded people like him found soothing. It created the illusion of escape into other worlds, of dim cafes and lovers, of love, physical contact and sensuous pleasures, an illusion which flees the light of day. Its words are about a promised land, about love gained and love lost.[18]

Kofi Awoonor, a former director of the Ghana Film Corporation under the Nkrumah regime and a one-time teacher of African literature at Stony Brook, New York, is in fact a considerable poet in his own right. Until the publication of his first novel, he had seemed content enough to explore the narrow area of the personal lyric based on the important heritage of his Ewe people. As befits a modernist novel, *This Earth, My Brother* is a melting pot of varied ingredients: of actual history, personal memories, anecdotes, a mixture of autobiography and invention, linked together by a style which is a constant blending of different genres and literary techniques, an adroit wedding of European and African narrative procedures. The novel uses what must be acknowledged as a fresh device in the handling of African experience. That is to say, we are given a simple narrative in the third person but every chapter has an alternative one consisting of a more undifferentiated, freer flow of images and memory in the Joycean manner of the stream-of-consciousness; each alternative chapter therefore acts as a commentary on the first and *vice-versa*.

As can be expected from a poet, the language is densely rich, with a great deal of the imagery drawn from African life and places: for example, the reference to 'silk cotton seeds cracking among distant baobab pods like breasts of pubertal virgins'. And this description of an African patriarch has the quiet dignity of African traditional rhetoric: 'He was a tree on which they all leaned, and under whose shade they all took shelter'. The book is also an uncompromising personal testament, full of awkward allusions to the present state of African politics. Because of its scope, encompassing as it does the hero's progress from childhood in an Ewe village, through school, to his wanderings in European countries, and back to Accra to a successful law career, and finally to mental breakdown and death by suicide, the novel achieves genuine epic quality in only about two hundred pages!

Some critics may object that Awoonor achieves this 'spatial effect' at the expense of a well-knit plot and deeper characterisation; they may feel that apart from the hero very few characters are dealt with in any depth; that references to these other characters are most casual and when it suits the author they are unceremoniously discarded: Amamu's wife, for instance, or the numerous girl-friends, black and white, whom the hero befriends, sleeps with and then quickly abandons in his odyssey toward madness and death are never explored from within; what the novel does very well is to reflect the modern African experience at the point of disintegration both of its hero and of the external society. What Awoonor gives us is the fragmentation of a man's grip of reality, together with a kaleidoscopic view of African society as it passes from colonial bondage to freedom and self-determination, and finally — from the hero's point of view at any rate — to a new form of bondage in the hands of its new African masters. As we have suggested, and, as we shall also see in the work of his fellow countryman, Armah, Awoonor's novel is of a type which is beginning to be familiar in the post-independence era in Africa. Its deepest emotions are disgust, anger and despair at the betrayal of the ideals of the newly independent African states. Change, we are strongly made to feel, is no change at all, only an illusion: the history of African societies is a vicious circle of exploitation of the ordinary people, first by one master, then another.

It is no wonder then that such a view of African history often generates a certain amount of cynicism which is the least attractive quality in Awoonor's novel. I distinguish cynicism from a genuine pessimism which is usually a deeper emotion. For instance it must be real pessimism and despair which bring Amamu to a state of madness, and finally death under an Indian almond tree, facing the Atlantic breakers, where he supposes he can see his former childhood sweetheart rising upon the waves 'her breasts bare, her nipples blacker than ever'. This death occurs after Amamu has tried to have his house servant's brother released from jail only to find that he has been murdered, clubbed to death.

But the cynicism is always there, behind the genuine despair, making us aware of the author's cleverness and sophistication, his refusal to be taken in. When a Cuban revolutionary addresses in African comrades on the 'need for dying a little for mother Africa', the hero's comment is a cynical derisory cry: 'O motherland, we pledge to thee our death!' an unworthy emotion which seems to call into question the hero's often proclaimed concern for social justice.

In contrast, Armah's novel, *The Beautyful Ones Are Not Yet Born*, may reflect cynicism in the society about which the novelist is writing but there is no cynicism as such in the writer's own approach to social problems; at all times he is utterly serious and it is this seriousness, his passionate concern with the plight of the people he is writing about — 'those whose desire has nowhere to go' — which keeps the writing alive to its own acute sense of injury and plaintive distress. But to characterise Armah's language this way is also to minimise its essential robustness, its extraordinary toughness: here, for example, is a description of the scummy, wasted women of a modern Accra:

Women, so horribly young, fucked and changed like pants, asking only for blouses and perfume from diplomatic bags and wigs of human hair scraped from which decayed white woman's corpse?[19]

This is a language of disgust. There is nothing feeble or poetically sentimentalised about it; always rooted in the grim tawdry materiality of the world in which the hero daily picks his way, whatever poetry this language evokes derives from the lurid glow of objects which have come under the powerful gaze of a novelist's eye; a novelist, moreover, who knows how to make language work *for* him rather than against him. This is a lesson which even a Soyinka could learn with some profit. Often what Armah is forcing us to observe is ugly, repulsive, ramshackle, mutilated; but his language can describe defeat without yielding to it; its very animosity is its salvation and its animus: rot, slime, decay cling to the prose like the caked dirt Armah so ably describes; the streets that are littered with refuse, bannisters coated with grime, and wombs which have collapsed with overuse; and fused into this general image of a city at the edge of breakdown and death are the sounds and smells which claw inward to the throat. 'Sometimes it is understandable that people spit so much, when all around decaying things push inward and mix all the body's juices with the taste of rot.'[20] One supposes that this phenomenological kind of piecemeal description of the organic world owes a lot of its glowing vivacity to readings of existentialist writers for which Armah has already been severely rebuked by a fellow-novelist,* but another obvious influence is Dickens whose novels Armah read at Harvard; yet neither Dickens nor Sartre, of course, could supply the very strong sense of locality which *The Beautyful Ones* displays on every page.

That *The Beautyful Ones* is a 'modernist' novel at the extremist reach of consciousness we need not doubt; its harrowing intensity, its disconsolate introspection, its deployment of imagery showing us the world at near breakpoint, as it were, a society 'sick unto death', accord well with Alan Swingewood's definition of the anguished modern novel as depicting 'isolated man pitted against other men, against society, sometimes engaged in a hopeless quest for his identity or in self-conscious exploration of the act of writing itself'.[21] The nameless Everyman hero of Armah's novel is indeed such an individual, stubbornly clinging to the last fragment of his fractured personality; scrupulously honest in his work, spurning the ever-present lure of the bribe in public service, he is also shrewd enough to recognise that he too is one of the 'walking dead'. His own passivity in the face of the threatening collapse, both in his private and the public life, is what condemns him to the terrible anonymity in which the novel abandons him on the last page, with 'the never-ending knowledge that this aching emptiness would be all that the remainder of his own life could offer him'. By comparison his wife's grotesque lusts for money and possession are conveyed with an exemplary passion for the epitomising phrase: 'When you shook Estella Koomson's hand, was not the perfume that stayed on yours a pleasing thing?'[22]

Armah's novel is so carefully constructed around certain images and symbols, the road, the sea, the sewage system in which Koomson and the Man are obliged to make their last escape before the final cleansing in the sea, that it

---

* Armah's command of language and imagery is of a very high order indeed. But this is a sick book. Sick, not with the sickness of Ghana but with the sickness of the *human condition*. The hero, pale and passive and nameless — a creation in the best manner of existentialist writing, wanders through the story in an anguished sleep, neck-deep in despair and human excrement of which we see rather a lot in the book' (from 'Africa and Her Writers' in *Morning Yet On Creation* (Essays) by Chinua Achebe (Heinemann, London, 1975, p.25.)

can so easily lend itself to the worst type of 'symbol-hunting'. This would be a mistake because symbols in this novel are never gratuitously used. Excrement, the prevailing stench of filth and corruption which have done so much to alienate even those of Armah's readers with the strongest stomachs, are ostensibly used to reinforce the central meaning of the book. Admittedly few novels are as capable of provoking so much disgust as the few pages of the scene in which Koomson, the corrupt ex-trade union leader turned politician, is forced to make his escape through a lavatory hole after a military coup:

'Help me push the can aside,' he said.
Together they shifted it to one side. The touch of the can had something altogether unexpected about it. It was cold, but not at all wet or slippery. It felt instead as if a multitude of little individual drops had been drying on the can for ages, but had never quite arrived at a totally dry crispness. When the can itself was shifted, a new smell evaporated upward into the faces above the hole. It was rather mild, the smell of something like dead mud. A very large cockroach, its colour a shiny, deep brown, flew out from under the can, hit Koomson's white shirt front and fell heavily on top of the box seat before crawling away into a crack down the side.[23]

Some critics have also noted the central importance of the symbol of the road in the organisation of the book's pattern: the fact, for instance, that the novel opens with the description of a bus bringing passengers into the city, the symbol of a society and the common plight of its citizens: 'Its confused rattle had given place to an endless spastic shudder, as if its pieces were held together by too much rust ever to feel completely apart.' And, after the military coup the novel concludes with a brief description of 'a small bus, looking very new and neat in its green paint' being waved through a police road block after the driver's payment of the mandatory bribe: the paint, we are made to feel, is new but nothing else apparently has changed. Nevertheless, what finally endows this novel with its peculiar symbolic force is not simply the self-conscious marshalling about of symbols but the accumulation of realistic detail about a modern African state in which change is seen, some will say too cynically, as being entirely illusory. Typical of how Armah goes about selecting the most telling detail in order to drive his unpalatable message home is this description of Accra's commercial centre seen by the man with the aid of the feeble illumination of the street lamps in the misty light of dawn:

The GNTC, of course, was regarded as a new thing, but only the name had really changed with Independence. The shop had always been there, and in the old days it had belonged to a rich Greek and was known by his name, A.G. LEVENTIS. So in a way the thing was new. Yet the stories that were sometimes heard about it were not stories of something young and vigorous, but the same old stories of money changing hands and throats getting moistened and palms getting greased. Only this time if the old stories aroused any anger, there was nowhere for it to go. The sons of the nation were now in charge, after all.[24]

As we have seen from Achebe's rather reprovingly school-masterish remarks, *The Beautyful Ones* is a novel which from the moment of its publication has divided and continues to divide the critics. There are those, like Achebe, who concede that this is a powerful first novel, with an admirable command of language, but who also see in it a falsification of African reality in order to serve foreign artistic gods. In support of this position we have the remarks of the Ugandan critic, Shatto Arthur Gakwandi, who protests that 'the senses of the reader are vigorously assaulted to the point of being numbed by the persistent imagery of decay, putrefaction and death'.[25] Gakwandi's commentary on the novel is a bewildering mixture of perceptive observation and obtuse prejudice which seems, at times, to be merely a question of ideological bias, as when he demurely complains that: 'The novel dismisses the black elite as slaves of the colonial boss and their only ambition to take over the privileges of their former masters.'[26] I dare say many will find nothing essentially wrong with such a picture of the modern elite in Africa.

In the opposite camp there are those critics, among whom I count myself, who see in this novel, despite its minor weaknesses, the arrival of a major talent on the African scene. It may be that Armah's latest fiction has not entirely justified this judgment. Dathorne's characterisation of *The Beautyful Ones* as a 'great milestone', his assertion that it is 'individualised in style and language, radical in thought'[27] seems to me wholly justified. As for its status as a 'radical novel' *The Beautyful Ones Are Not Yet Born* seems to me to be in the best 'protest tradition', with a message that is wider and more profound in its significance than is usually the case in many novels of this kind. The reason why despite the novelist's refusal to offer any easy solutions, this still seems such a 'radical book' is because of the general perspective from which the novel is written. There is a rage here which is harnessed to the yet unrealised power of ordinary men and women, to the conviction that 'famished men need not stay famished', and that beauty is 'in the waking of the powerless'.[28] In this respect, Armah differs from Kofi Awoonor, and even more radically, from Wole Soyinka, two novelists whose critique of post-independent African societies, however powerfully mounted and however eloquently expressed, seems focused entirely on the predicament of the intellectual elite.

6

The bitter ferocity with which Soyinka attacks the incompetent hacks who run the universities, the civil service and the newspapers in *The Interpreters*, the vitriolic send-up of figures like Dr Ayo Faseyi of the University Teaching Hospital, the savage raillery against Professor Oguazor and the teaching Establishment, and the gleeful lampoon of Chief Winsala and Sir Derinola of the *Independent Viewpoint*, reflect a genuine sense of outrage by an intelligentsia which is baffled by its defeats, frustrated by its impotence, and embittered at being so successfully outmanoevred by what this intelligentsia considers to be a powerful if bumbling civil/military bureaucracy. 'The treatment of the intellectual class in many African novels', Gakwandi says, 'often reveals an underlying assumption that it is their historic mission to rule their fellow countrymen.'[29] Another critic writes: 'What appears in Soyinka's work as a

continuing anger is his dislike of the limited and stultified mission-school outlook, his hatred of corrupt politics, and his sardonic attitude toward the prim
status-seeking within the universities.'[30]

This undoubtedly is Soyinka's greatest strength as a writer; his relentless
attack on the tragic abuse of power by the present ruling elites in Africa; but
important as this criticism is, it is not one that is mounted from any radical
standpoint; on the contrary, its symbiotic alliance with the present sources of
power becomes clearer with each reading of Soyinka's fiction and other important works. For Soyinka never questions the whole social and economic edifice
upon which rests the power of the present ruling classes; he complains only of
the misuse of that power. His attack on the ruling elites is not based on any
demand for radical transformation of African society; indeed, his social criticism is attached to the same modes of thought as those Soyinka attacks. What
Soyinka wishes to see is a replacement of a group of vulgar philistines with a
more polished, more discriminating group of young pretenders. Again and
again *The Interpreters* shows us how vulgar, degraded and incompetent the
present rulers of important sectors of African society are compared to the
better-educated, more sophisticated group of younger claimants to power. To
suppose that this constant criticism, the frequency and the rage with which it is
mounted, has nothing to do with Soyinka's own class affiliations is to be
extremely naive.

The group of young intellectuals who collectively provide Soyinka's novel
with its title of *The Interpreters* have a great deal in common. All of them are
university graduates, all of them are members of the professional elite: they
include Sagoe, a journalist, Egbo, a foreign office functionary, Bandele, a
university teacher of art, Sekoni, an engineer and sculptor, Kola, a painter,
and Lassunwon, a political lawyer. The only woman member of the group is
Dehinwa, whose only role seems to be to minister to Sagoe's needs. Friendship
apart, the group is further knit together by the fact that they are all sitting for a
huge canvas Kola is painting of the pantheon of the local gods for which the
'interpreters' act as models and through which they gradually define their own
identities. For the rest of the time, whatever else they are supposed to be
engaged in, the 'interpreters' do very little of it in this novel. They go to night-
clubs, they drink, they attend parties, they make love to women; they also
meditate a great deal on their role in society. They write and they paint, we
suppose, but when they are not doing any of these things they are more than
likely to be lengthily attacking the sterility and philistinism with which they are
unhappily surrounded. As such not only are 'the interpreters' members of a
privileged elite, an obvious extension of a social group which occupies a place of
strategic importance for the articulation of ideology in African society, they are
also meant to be standard-bearers for a new 'modernist' culture within which
the relations of the traditional to the new values can be defined and clarified.
However, their failure to even raise the right questions, let alone to participate
in ameliorative action, casts them in the role of noisy dilettantes. Talk is all they
do!

The true character of the 'interpreters' can be grasped from the manner of
Sagoe's response to a challenge by a minor politician he has met at a party. This
is how Sagoe himself relates the story to the members of the group:

'And the man says to me, you young men are always criticising. You only criticise destructively, why don't you put up some concrete proposal, some scheme for improving the country in any way, and then you will see whether we take it up or not' . . . 'I told him, you should do something about the sewage system, it is disgraceful that at this stage, night-soil men are still lugging shitpails around the capital. And in any case, why shouldn't the stuff be utilised? Look at the arid wastes of the North, I said. You should rail the stuff to the North and fertilise the Sardauna's territory. More land under cultivation, less unemployment.'[31]

This quotation makes obvious what is the least attractive feature of 'the interpreters': their intellectual snobbery. The only impressive exception to the rule is Sekoni; a gentle, humorous Muslim from the North, who seems driven by boundless passion and energy to serve his society but is thwarted at every step by corrupt time-serving officials. A qualified engineer, he is forced to twiddle his thumbs in the Ministry office, signing vouchers for 'bicycle allowances'; when he rebels against his enforced idleness his superiors think him possibly mad: 'He obviously needs a transfer. He's one of the keen ones.' He is thereafter banished to some out-of-the-way place 'where you may work with your hands until your back blisters'. Indomitable, ceaselessly creative, Sekoni crowns his exile by building a small experimental power station; but even this achievement is nullified by the corrupt machinations of the chairman whose company ('registered in the name of his two-month-old niece') is under contract to supply electric power. An expatriate 'expert' is hired to condemn the power station as unsafe. This last act drives Sekoni into a mental breakdown, but recovering he turns to sculpture and for his first effort produces a veritable masterpiece:

Sekoni began sculpting almost as soon as he returned. His first carving, a frenzied act of wood, he called 'The Wrestler'. He had not asked Bandele or anyone to sit for him, but the fact and the form of the central figure, a protagonist in pilgrim's robes, was unmistakably Bandele. Taut sinews, nearly agonising in excess tension, a bunched python caught at the instant of easing out, the balance of strangulation before release, it was all elasticity and strain. And the rest, like the act of his creation which took him an entire month and over, was frenzy and desperation, as if time stood in his way.[32]

Time is indeed standing in his way for Sekoni soon dies in a car crash, 'showers of laminated glass around him, his beard one fastness of blood and wet earth'. Sekoni is a noble creation, the only one in the group who impresses us with his integrity, humanity and abundant humour: 'his one aberration in a life of painful sincerity'. Nicknamed 'the Sheik' because of his Muslim upbringing he has defied the father to marry a Christian girl, an act of rebellion which results in his being cast out from the family. His favourite symbol is the bridge because it faces backwards and forwards, to the past and the future; in Sekoni the warring religions and traditions are finally synthesized and harmonised.

Egbo, too, is a man in search of a single identity which would bring into clear focus the two aspects of his heritage, the inherited sensibilities of Yoruba culture and the values of a modern industrial state; but though associated in

Kola's canvas with the Yoruba god Ogun the explorer, warrior and creator, and though, he is the reluctant heir to the Osa throne which is soon to fall vacant, Egbo is unable to make a choice between tradition and modernism. This inability to choose can also be seen in his being simultaneously attracted to the pagan love goddess, Simi, who initiates him into the ways of sensual love, and a university student whom he deflowers on the bank of the River Ogun, before washing her virginal blood in the waters of the sacred river.

Like his creator, Egbo shows an ambivalence toward modernity. He is half drawn to the idea of helping his grandfather maintain his fiefdom against the might of the modern state, thereby helping to shore up tradition against the threatening onslaughts of modernism; but finally he settles for the empty meaningless chores of the Foreign Office. Asked by Bandele if he thought the group has either the will or the ability to fight against the gradual erosion of traditional values, Egbo angrily sums up: 'No. Too busy, although I've never discovered doing what. And that is what I constantly ask — doing what?'[33]

Soyinka has always shown excessive interest in religious experience of one kind or another, which is, of course, his business. What is our business, though, as critics is determining to what extent these religious themes are integrated into the structure of the novel and to what extent they are merely the flounce and trimmings or something more important if more mundane. My own view is that dramatic as these episodes are — for Soyinka is nothing else if not a good dramatist — and in spite of the knowing exegeses which the insertion of such material into a novel always encourages among some critics — the quasi-religious antics of Lazarus and Noah illuminate very little in the novel. In fact, I fail to see what the 'interpreters' could learn either about themselves or about the mysteries of existence from the kind of gibberish nonsense spoken by Lazarus in his apostolic church. These scenes are simply tableaux which add nothing revelatory except a spurious drama to a novel already structurally a mess. Thematically these episodes are not even as fully integrated in the novel as Egbo's mystical experiences and his efforts to rediscover the sources of Yoruba tradition. What Soyinka does well is to capture the comic opera flavour of proceedings like the two funerals of Sir Derinola and the elder of Lazarus' church. They are superbly done because though Soyinka hints at some religious symbolism he maintains his distance and keeps up admirably well the burlesque atmosphere; at least, he keeps *us* entertained.

In the end, though, what makes this a remarkable novel despite its many faults, is the impassioned, frenzied hatred, conveyed in the most caustic language Soyinka is able to muster, for the phoney unauthenticated lives led by members of the new ruling elite; it is remarkable for the truly buoyant rage against the intellectual sterility and moral vacuity such lives usually signify. With their bogus charm and hidden malice, with their desperate echo of other accents and inflections, the voices at Professor Oguazor's party begin to sound more and more like a bad foreign movie played at the wrong speed. These counterfeit gestures, accompanied by empty meaningless ritual, are enacted against a background of appalling artificiality and bad taste, the very tomb of warm feeling and native originality:

From the ceiling hung citrous clusters on invisible wires. A glaze for the warmth of life and succulence told the story, they were the same as the artificial apples. There were fancy beach-hat flowerpots on the wall, ivy clung from these along a picture rail, all plastic, and the ceiling was covered in plastic lichen. Sagoe had passed, he now noticed, under a special exhibition group of one orange, two pears, and a fan of bananas straight from European wax-works. [34]

In the end there is one question we are left to ask: how is it possible for the group of the young 'interpreters' to separate themselves from this shoddy, pretentious existence? It cannot be by being well-educated because Ayo Faseyi who is held up as a walking example of servile philistinism is also a well-educated man. The 'interpreters' are certainly not interested in politics which they consider to be the very tomb of self-respect. So in what does their salvation consist? How are they differentiated from the rest of the community of the damned? The only answer that the novel is able to provide us with is: Good Taste! But however satisfying Art and Good Taste may be as a consolation they are not unfortunately the kind of solution that a novelist can give to questions such as we have asked without any feeling of discomfiture. Indeed the solution which the novel proposes indicates clearly the inherent weakness in the social criticism of many of the writers of the 'modernist' movement in Africa — what O'Flinn calls the 'pseudo-radical elite' — which makes them unable to move 'beyond the spit in the eye of the nearest establishment figure with which Soyinka closes *The Interpreters*'. [35] Ngugi is even more specific in his criticism:

> Confronted with the impotence of the elite, the corruption of those steering the ship of State and those looking after its organs of justice, Wole Soyinka does not know where to turn. Often the characters held up for our admiration are (apart from the artists) cynics, or sheer tribal reactionaries like Baroka . . . Soyinka's good man is the uncorrupted individual: his liberal humanism leads him to admire an individual's lone act of courage, and thus often he ignores the creative struggle of the masses. The ordinary people, workers and peasants, in his plays remain passive watchers on the shore or pitiful comedians on the road. [36]

Soyinka is usually thought of as a 'radical' writer. This view was even more strengthened by his public performance at the Afro-Scandinavian Writers' Conference in Stockholm in 1967. He is certainly a vigorous critic of contemporary African society, of the shallow philistinism of the new ruling classes, the sort so cruelly satirised in his poem 'And the Other Immigrant' and later in this novel, *The Interpreters*. As we have already pointed out the central feature of the 'modernist' movement is its struggle with language, the effort to invent a style in the larger sense of the word, which would accommodate the new dislocations and instabilities in contemporary African society. Soyinka's struggle with language is fiercer, more debilitating, precisely because the contradictions he is trying to resolve have reached a newer and more complex level of formation, and the tensions and anguish which he continually points up have to do with the anguish and tensions of a *particular* class or group in African society — the petit bourgeois intellectual group which is tied up an invisible umbilical cord to the present ruling class. Even when his criticism is presented in the form of comic satire the increasingly bitter tone with which Soyinka denounces the self-seeking but incompetent bureaucrat, from the religious figure of Kadiye in *The Swamp Dwellers* — the nearest, by the way, Soyinka has ever got to an outright condemnation of the mystification of religious practice — to Professor Oguazor and the farcical figure of Chief Winsala in *The Interpreters*, indicates a depth of disgust by a member of a group which sees itself as the natural aristocracy of the newly independent states but lacks the means with which to fulfil that role. It is by focusing on the stock Soyinka figure — the scapegoat, the redeemer or healer — that we can see reflected in them all the hopes and peculiar frustrations of this emasculated intellegentsia. This group has one slippery foothold in the centres of actual power and another in the teeming world of petty crooks, prostitutes, and urban workers just below it. Only by making the conscious decision to move beyond the predicament of this special group to an identification with the fate and fortunes of the broad mass of the population can the modern writer in Africa escape the suicidal mood of complete isolation and nihilism. Ngugi wa Thiong'o, the Kenyan novelist and dramatist, is one writer who has made that transition.

Powerful works of literature usually break out of some great national trauma or personal obsession: the Mau Mau freedom struggle with its attendant sacrifices, its triumphs and betrayals, has become Ngugi's own personal preoccupation. His first published novel, *Weep Not, Child* (1964), and his third, *A Grain of Wheat* (1967) are prolonged meditations on the theme of national struggle, the courage, sacrifices and loyalties it requires and, not surprisingly, some of the opportunism and failure of nerve which are brought to the surface by such momentous events.

Indeed, *A Grain of Wheat*, which seems to me a much better novel in its structural balances and tensions than his latest work, *Petals of Blood* (1977), has sometimes been criticised for not being 'ideologically correct' by some socialist commentators who are depressed by a novel which has only traitors for its heroes: in Ngugi's defence it must be said that many readers may see this as a more or less valid metaphor for the disappointed hopes of those in Kenya who expected more from their leaders. *Petals of Blood* is not so much a novel as an attempt to think aloud about the problems of modern Kenya: the sharp contrast between the city and the countryside, between the 'ill-gotten' wealth of the new African middle-class and the worsening plight of the unemployed workers and peasants.

Ngugi's novel has four important characters whose lives interlock as they attempt to find a place for themselves in the new Kenya society, and realising that none has been made for them. In order to live they either have to sell themselves to the new 'power-brokers' in the land or fight; and the novel is about how each tries to find a solution to the dilemma: Wanja, who has the capacity to give love but ends by prostituting herself in order to make a good life for herself; Abdul, a petty trader, who lives perpetually on the verge of bankruptcy; Karega, who constitutes the most revolutionary hope for the powerless and the dispossessed, is a school teacher who turns to militant trade unionism as he gradually acquires consciousness; and, finally, Munira, the school teacher who turns to the mystification of religion as a way of resolving the contradictions in his society. Sometimes the novel veers very sharply, as many such novels tend to do, toward the fable, albeit a socialist fable, with capitalists carrying such unlikely names as 'Sir Swallow Bloodall'.

I think Ngugi's latest fiction fails because the author is so conscious of not having written a 'socialist novel' before, that he gives up concrete observation which is the correct starting point of all true materialists, in favour of a fable-cum-satire-cum-realist fiction in order to illustrate class formations in modern Kenya. To do this he is impelled to create characters who are so unreal as to invalidate a great deal of what Ngugi sets out to prove. For example, to make us believe in the fiendishness of capitalism does not require Ngugi to make Sir Swallow Bloodall speak such undiluted nonsense as when he is praising 'golf and cricket (for) creating a climate of stability and mutual goodwill so necessary for investment'.[37] In the same way, to be on the side of the people does not mean creating African peasants who know the socialist implications of the Vietnam war, who talk of their ability to work as their 'labour power'.

There are some fine touches in *Petals of Blood*, as in the scene in which Wanja, now a rich brothel-madam, is keeping a rendezvous with Karega, an old acquaintance (or lover) who has become an important trade union leader. Asked why she still maintains the old hut although she now owns a palatial mansion Wanja replies: 'I don't want to forget old Ilmorog. I never shall forget how we lived before the Trans-Africa Road cleaved Ilmorog into two halves.'[38]

The line not only rings true because all over the world there are many prostitutes and members of the *nouveau riche* who feel that way about their background, but because the statement also illustrates the heart-rending contradictions that people who prostitute themselves have to live through. It is a small example of how well Ngugi can dramatise these contradictions when he becomes more concrete and is prepared to delve into his characters.

What becomes clear in *Petals of Blood* is a major shift in Ngugi's work, ideological in nature, from the earlier emphasis on nationalism and race questions to a class analysis of society. In *The River Between*, for instance, Ngugi was concerned with the conflict between tradition and modernism, a trite theme in modern African literature, with a rather over-heated love affair to give the story its glossy 'Romeo and Juliet' finish. His short story, 'The Village Priest', contained in *Secret Lives*, is an attempt to dramatise this conflict by pitting a Christian convert with a wily medicine man who causes the rain to fall after a long drought, thus proving the old gods are still more powerful than the new.

In *Petals of Blood* the perspective shifts from concerns with nationalism and cultural identity to the overriding question of class conflict and internal exploitation. When Wanja says to Karega, 'You used to argue that the past was important for today', the trade union leader answer:

. . . We must not preserve our past as a museum; rather, we must study it critically, without illusions, and see what lessons we can draw from it — no. Maybe I used to do it: but I don't want to continue worshipping in the temples of a past without tarmac roads, without electric cookers, a world dominated by slavery to nature.'[39]

In conclusion we must repeat what we have already stated, that the 'modernism' of some of these novels consists not so much in making a radical break with the traditional form of the novel, but in discovering and endorsing a new mood of disillusionment running through many segments of the African society at the moment. This is quite apparent in a book like *Petals of Blood* which is in many ways a traditional novel, technically less forward-looking than, say, *A Grain of Wheat*, but whose mood and content brings it into significant alignment with novels grouped under the 'modernist' rubric. The second point to reiterate is that some of the works most critical of the present distortions in African society do no more than provide us with an image through which to grasp and make sense of the current contradictions, but the writers themselves have been unable to suggest, even in fictional terms, the direction in which we should be moving. The third point, related to the second, is the fact that the mood of nihilism and pessimism which affects some of the 'modernist' fiction is in itself the measure of the alienation of these literary intellectuals from the ordinary people; so that with some significant exceptions, their despair is not to be taken as necessarily that of the mass of the population but is to be located specifically in the small group of the intellectual elite which is secure neither within the ruling class nor among the mass of the people. This is not to suggest that it is necessarily the function of writers to provide in their works solutions which have not yet been found in the actual social practice of living men and women; what I am suggesting is that, apart from some cases where a naturally melancholic temperament is already a factor, writers whose works are created from the perspective of the struggle of the people for social justice will always have an inner buoyancy and hope denied the writer who feels himself entirely isolated from the people.

REFERENCES

1   Colin Mercer, 'Culture and Ideology', in *Red Letters*, 8.
2   A. Afolayan, 'Language and Sources of Amos Tutuola', in C. Heywood (ed.) *Perspectives on African Literature*, Heinemann, London, 1971
3   Amos Tutuola, *The Palm-Wine Drinkard*, Faber, London, 1952, p.67.
4   Gabriel Okara, *The Voice*, André Deutsch, London, 1964, p.12.
5   *Ibid.*, p.13.
6   Diana Laurenson, 'The Writer and Society', in Diana T. Laurenson and Alan Swingewood (eds.), *The Sociology of Literature*, MacGibbon & Kee, London, 1971, p.94.
7   Camara Laye, *The Radiance of the King*, Fontana Books, Collins, London, 1965, p.202.
8   *Ibid.*, p.36.
9   David Lodge in M. Bradbury and J. McFarlane (eds.) *The Language of Modernist Fiction: Metaphor and Metonymy in Modernism*, Penguin, 1976, p.481.
10   Laye, *The Radiance of the King*, p.22.
11   *Ibid.*, p.96
12   Okara, *The Voice*, pp.9−10.
13   *Ibid.*, p.48.
14   *Ibid.*, p.103.
15   J.P. O'Flinn, 'Towards a Sociology of the Nigerian Novel', *African Literature Today*, 7, Heinemann, 1975, p.47.
16   Shatto Arthur Gakwandi, *The Novel and Contemporary Experience in Africa*, Heinemann, 1977, p.87.
17   *Ibid.*, p.66.

18   Kofi Awoonor, *This Earth, My Brother*, Doubleday, New York, 1971, p.68.
19   Ayi Kwei Armah, *The Beautyful Ones Are Not Yet Born*, Heinemann, 1968, p.105.
20   *Ibid.*, p.47.
21   Laurenson and Swingewood, (eds.), *The Sociology of Literature*, p.214.
22   Armah, *The Beautyful Ones*, p.51.
23   *Ibid.*, pp.196−7
24   *Ibid.*, p.111.
25   Gakwandi, *The Novel and Contemporary Experience in Africa*, p.87.
26   *Ibid.*, p.91
27   O.R. Dathorne, *The Black Mind*, University of Minnesota Press, 1974, p.195.
28   Armah, *The Beautyful Ones*, p.100.
29   Gakwandi, *The Novel and Contemporary Experience in Africa*, p.72.
30   Margaret Laurence, *Long Drums and Cannons*, Macmillan, 1968, p.74.
31   Wole Soyinka, *The Interpreters*, André Deutsch, London, 1965, pp.238−9.
32   *Ibid.*, pp.99−100.
33   *Ibid.*, p.13.
34   *Ibid.*, p.140.
35   O'Flinn, Towards a Sociology of the Nigerian Novel', p.48.
36   Ngugi wa Thiong'o, *Homecoming* (Essays), Heinemann, London, 1972, p.65.
37   Ngugi wa Thiong'o, *Petals of Blood*, Heinemann, 1977, p.314.
38   *Ibid.*, p.323.
39   *Ibid.*

CHAPTER FIVE

SOUTHERN AFRICA: PROTEST AND COMMITMENT

1

If the majority of African novelists, poets and dramatists seem eager to explore traditional African values; and if the intention is to see how these values might determine the shape of contemporary African life, with very few exceptions the literature of Southern Africa is wholly concerned with the theme of struggle and conflict – conflict between the white conquerors and the conquered blacks, between white masters and black servitors, between the village and the city. In particular, if South African literature seems unable to contemplate any kind of human action without first attempting to locate it within a precise social framework of racial conflict it is merely because very often colour differences provide the ultimate symbols which stand for those larger antagonisms which Southern African writers have always considered it their proper business to explain.

Consequently, whether written by white or by blacks the literature of Southern Africa is committed to the notion that certain 'tasks' are the legitimate function of socially responsible writers. Protest, commitment, explanation: South African readers and critics expect these qualities of their authors; sometimes, as I myself have occasionally insisted, critics claim to expect more from Southern African writers than a mere rendering of 'the surface meaning of the scene', but the nature of this expectation is itself controlled by what is perceived to be the proper relationship between literature and commitment, between truth and art.

From its writers the nation, including the organs of state oppression, has always expected not so much art as confidential reports about the condition of society, its health or lack of it, its ability to survive. For instance, it is not very difficult to imagine the South African Prime Minister privately poring over the latest controversial work of fiction or poetry not so much to be entertained or ennobled as in order to find out what the local 'Reds' and 'trouble-makers', using the convenient medium of print, put down as his chances for survival. Strangely enough, the majority of South African writers have always written, as it were, in direct response to such hopes or needs. Consequently, one way or another, whether liberal or illiberal, South African literature has always been a literature of protest and social commitment in whose mirror the nation hopes to catch glimpses of its face even if only to later reject or denounce what it sees there as an outrage or falsification.

In Doris Lessing's first novel, *The Grass is Singing*, a book, incidentally, which grows in importance as time passes, Tony Marston's gradual perception of the nature of the conflict between masters and servants in Rhodesian society enables him, a relative newcomer from England, to understand that the killing of a white woman by an African servant is not necessarily such a simple matter as to be unravelled once and for all by the mere discovery of the motive or the murder weapon:

> He knew now, at least, that what had been fought out in the room they had just left was nothing to do with murder as such. The murder, in itself, was nothing. The struggle that had been decided in a few brief words – or rather, in the silences between the words—had had nothing to do with the surface meaning of the scene. He would understand it all a good deal better in a few months, when he had 'become used to the country'. And then he would do his best to forget the knowledge, for to live with the colour bar in all its nuances and implications means closing one's mind to many things, if one intends to remain an accepted member of society. But, in the interval, there would be a few brief moments when he would see the thing clearly, and understand that it was 'white civilization' fighting to defend itself that had been implicit in the attitude of Charlie Slatter and the Sergeant, 'white civilization' which will never, never admit that a white person, and most particularly, a white woman, can have a human relationship, whether for good or for evil, with a black person.[1]

This brief passage tells us a great deal, not only about the strange strategies of moral survival on the other side of the racial divide, but encapsulates for the reader the demands made on South African writers by their art as much as by life in general. Forced to rely less on whimsy and fantasy than on the terrible actualities of that unending war between the 'conquerors' and 'conquered', South African writers try, as Tony Marston must try, to 'see the thing clearly'. This seeing clearly attunes everyone concerned, writers and public alike, to the small echoes of the unspoken, to the 'silences between the words'; and it is in the nature of the commitment that our wishes feel the need to explain to the reader how the 'war' is shaping up between the hordes of dispossessed blacks and the local representatives of that 'white civilization'.

Of course, Marston's recognition that once the knowledge is extracted from the experience of living in the country he must 'do his best to forget that knowledge' has desperate implications for South African artists; for it is precisely in the ambivalence underlined by Marston's insights – the need to 'see the thing clearly' and then to 'forget' that we come to some understanding why South African writers and artists frequently come into conflict with the state. The novelists, dramatists and poets remind the public constantly what the public wishes to forget. Black writers in particular, feel an urgent sense of obligation to expose the wounds and to make the 'knowledge' public; but such an attempt by black writers only creates for the other side huge anxieties and discomfort.

Among white authors, those denounced most frequently, Gordimer, Paton, Jacobson, Breytenbach, are also the ones who remind the white public more frequently of the 'many things' to which the white public has closed its mind. It is for this reason that despite a massive propaganda campaign which proclaims them to be new leaders of the South African *avant garde*, the group of Afrikaans writers known as the 'Sestigers' have remained on the whole curiously irrelevant, even faintly comic. These vast stretches of mannered, surrealistic descriptions, the formidable limitations of the *nouveau roman* in which racial conflict is absent and murder is a metaphysical game, strike us as implausible, unreal, even deliberately fraudulent. Where, one wishes to know, is the sjambok and the gun and the stolen sexual confidences on a private beach at night, the whole ghastly comedy of the laboured heart transplants and the accelerating rate of malnutrition and infant mortality?

2

Nadine Gordimer, the South African novelist, has made the claim that prose writing by black South African writers in the 1950s and the early 1960s 'was some of the best on the continent'.[2] As she points out, nearly all those seminal black writers went into exile in the 1960s, and their works are now banned.

> The lopping-off of a young indigenous tradition − as distinct from the central tradition of the European language the black writer uses − has had a stunting effect on prose writing. No fiction of any real quality has been written since then by a black writer still living in South Africa.[3]

Nadine Gordimer notes in particular the deleterious effects of censorship on so explicit a medium as prose. The black writer will not touch controversial subjects except those already made too familiar, in the hope of attracting less attention from the over-sensitive censor and the police. 'Such stories as there are, for example, repulp the clichés of the apartheid situation − the illicit drinking den, the black-white love affair − that have been so thoroughly blunted by over-use in literature.'[4] There can be no question that so far as the internal situation is concerned, Nadine Gordimer is right about the general sterility of black South African fiction; she was, of course, determined to draw a distinction between fiction and the astonishing but wholly understandable, if sudden, flourishing of black poetry inside South Africa. However, even with regard to prose, the appearance since the middle 1960s of new novelists like Bessie Head, Enver Carim and D.M. Zwelonke, though admittedly living in exile, demands, it seems to me, a re-statement of positions and, if necessary, an abandoning of others. The whole critical approach to writing by black South Africans has in recent years unnecessarily hardened into a received doctrine which in time can only prevent a proper response to works of literature whose energies are political. These tendencies, I now realise, could only have been encouraged by the hard tone I assumed in a much-quoted essay on fiction by Black South Africans.[5] Since then I have been dismayed to see parts of that essay occasionally wheeled out to support critical positions which it was no intention of mine to uphold.

For example, I was surprised to read in a foreword of a book allegedly devoted to 'socio-political thought in African literature', that South African literature had been excluded 'on the basis that it is predominantly protest literature, as Lewis Nkosi and Ezekiel Mphahlele point out'.[6] My complaints about black South African literature in the past have had nothing to do with the mere fact that it is protest. How well, and how significantly it utters that protest, has been my main preoccupation. But even Gerald Moore, someone who rarely loses his critical faculties has persisted in talking about what he calls the 'DRUM' style of writing, as if writers ever from a collective entity. Having trapped himself within his categories, and forgetting the examples of the liberating influence of the cinema and jazz on such American writers as John Dos Passos, Ralph Ellison and Norman Mailer, Moore supposes that 'the strong direct influence of jazz and the cinema' upon South African prose has been wholly pernicious.

There may be grounds for disagreements here; but when Moore reproduces a specimen of writing which he considers superior to the 'crude energy' of South African writing[7] he merely displays a personal prejudice in favour of a certain type of society, which is not yet sufficiently industrialised. Such a society he calls 'unhurried' and seems to think that any 'unhurried prose which matches the slow pace of such traditional communities is far superior to the 'jazzy' fast-paced writing which comes out of the industrialised South. And yet one can think of any number of stories by La Guma, Can Themba, or even Richard Rive, not a particularly favourite writer of mine, which would be far superior in shape and execution to the inadequate trivialities of Ama Aidoo's story.

While it is true that the range and depth of South African fiction has often seemed too narrow and limited, it is also truer still that much of this literature is more ably written and much more substantial in its achievements than a great deal of the 'masks' and 'kola nut' school of writing which is unhappily pouring out of the presses at an unprecedented rate and is so frequently applauded by European critics in search of the exotic.

The question of a usable tradition still lies at the heart of the problem of South African literature. This problem is not, by any means, unique to the country, but in South Africa what has often been the plight of all literatures created out of 'unformed societies' begins to assume grave proportions. The question is not whether Xhosa, Zulu or Sotho cultures exist, from which a writer might derive sustenance in the same way that a Soyinka might draw inspiration from Yoruba lore or Achebe from the Ibo one; it is simply that the black South African writer is engaged in a contest the nature of which gravely limits his ability to make use of the indigenous tradition.

In other parts of Africa the conditions of independence have enabled the writer to turn back to the past in a more leisurely exploration of his precolonial heritage. In South Africa the pressure of the future is so enormous that looking backwards seems a luxury. The present exerts its own pressures which seem vast, immanent, all-consuming. All the elements which have fertilised the African novel elsewhere, the proverb, myth, legend and all the other linguistic procedures which give their own peculiar stamp to social relationships in a traditional African setting appear as a kind of distraction in the urban environment of South Africa. Here, the writer seems to require something more potent if also more ephemeral: 'a powerful suction draws your awareness to something even more garish and clanking,'[8] as Enver Carim, our newest, most lyrical prose writer has put it.

It has been stated many times, that South African literature is intensely urban, written out of the chaos of urban life, with all its peculiar insecurities and rootlessness. What has not often been pointed out is that not only the blacks but the whites themselves have been radically transformed by this environment, by the immense weight of their mission to rule over others in per- petuity: 'This jealousy of the world they've wrought with ball bearings and alarm clocks, this metallic wisdom, has engineered a mutation in these people themselves.'[9] As Conrad so acutely recognised at the turn of the century: 'The conquest of the earth, which mostly means the taking it away from those who have a different complexion or slightly flatter noses than ourselves is not a pretty thing when you look into it too much.'[10] Like Conrad, Enver Carim has some grisly insights into the dialectical relationship between the conqueror and the conquered; and it is this relationship between the white rulers and their black subjects, the resultant corruption of one and the dehumanisation of the other, which absorbs and exhausts the energies of the South African writer. The black writers' gruff impatience with models from old traditional cultures is due in part to the recognition that such models provide no clues as to how life is to be lived under apartheid conditions where survival is the only test of human intelligence. Without these clues, tribal morality, the grace and dignity of African traditional life, the severe ethical restraints such a way of life imposes, seem for the embattled city-dweller to have only an empty pietistic appeal.

Dikobe's novel, *The Marabi Dance*, whose combination of bad taste, clumsy construction and wooden characterisation must seem, at least, to exceed anything we have yet encountered in African writing, is oddly instruc- tive in mapping out that bleak landscape of city chaos out of which issue some brave works by South African writers. The novel also provides glimpses of that three-cornered war between rural and urban moralities, with apartheid consti- tuting a dismal graveyard for both. Most of all, what we learn from the novel is the lack of continuity between tribal and city institutions, the almost mutual incomprehension between these two ways of life. Nowhere else in Africa is this disruption so complete.

Not only is the racial struggle an intense and bitter one but upon its out- come depends the final shape of the South African society. That is to say, until a solution is found to the political problem, we are not really entitled to speak of a South African 'culture' just as we may, but are not entitled to speak of a South African 'nation'. On the contrary, what we find in South Africa is a group of contending nationalities but no proper 'nation' able to confer autho- rity to its artists. The energies required to enable a writer during a process of creation to maintain a proper perspective on his material, which is to say, to 'see clearly' the society he is writing about, are quite formidable. The writer is like someone with a telescopic lens trained on a target which is constantly moving on. The result is either moral shapelessness or hysteria which turns the novel, not into an instrument of order but a vehicle of resourceless terror and panic.

In Dikobe's novel, Martha's protest at being asked to marry a young man from the countryside may seem unreasonable and one inspired by very shallow motives; but the desperation is recognisable, indeed shared by many black South African girls in similar situations. However, it is the series of impertinent injunctions and moral exhortations, drawn from a communal life barely comprehensible to the girl, which drives Dikobe's heroine into final isolation:

'Ma, I was born in town,' Martha tells her importunate mother. 'I don't know the laws of the people at home* and Sephai is not a boy like the town ones. He is what we call 'skapie-sheep'. He won't allow me to go to the Social Centre or bioscope.'[11]

Indeed, in contrasting the country and city moralities, Dikobe's novel suffers from a peculiar indecisiveness as to what, beyond the destruction of the repressive institutions, might constitute real *order*: what could be the source of a new morality. The lives of the characters are traced: episodes are told; but the intention remains obscure. However, one thing is clear: the old traditional morality, together with its ethical and artistic forms, cannot be the answer. Against the bewildering and complex pressures of urban living, best described as 'guerrilla warfare', the representatives of the old tribal order are depressingly ineffectual. Significantly, the only hope of a way out of this moral chaos is conceived in political terms; for instance, in Rev. Ndlovu's establishment of a black nationalist church, which combines in its evangelical message, spiritual as well as political redemption. The ending may seem a trifle sentimental; but here, finally, in the bosom of a religious order founded by a former petty crook and embezzler turned religious leader, Martha, the heroine, and George Sibeko, her lover, are blissfully if implausibly united in matrimony.

Being urban, above all, being South Africans, acutely aware of the need for political solutions, most black writers tend to be indifferent to traditional narrative forms and motifs. Outside vernacular literature, only one poet so far bothers to explore the oral tradition of *praise-poetry*.[12] South African writers find it more congenial to borrow their models from American literature, primarily that of black Americans. Peter Abrahams' autobiography, *Tell Freedom*, records an instance in which the debt owed by a black South African writer to black American writing has been publicly and movingly acknowledged. There are other examples, such as in the work of the South African poet, Keorapetse Kgositsile, in which the language and idiom of black American verse has been so wholly assimilated that Kgositsile's verse could, and often is, included in black American anthologies without any noticeable violation of the criteria for inclusion.

We must also, I suppose, pay some close attention to music because of its pervasive influence upon the South African sensibility, and the way musical movement attempts to assimilate the external chaos in order to control what are very nearly conditions conducive to public madness, conditions whose existence threaten the very core of the human personality. It is no accident, for instance, that a highly developed form of jazz, the music most capable of carrying out such a programme, has become as much a part of urban African culture as the more native forms. Enver Carim's memoir of a jazz concert in Johannesburg hints at some of the reasons for the hold which jazz exerts upon the emotional life of the black South Africans. During a jazz performance 'human energy' collides

. . . against its own fervent hope, reverberating with booms and twangs,

---

* In South Africa a generation of city dwellers often talks of the countryside from where its parents came as 'home'.

thudding and gasping, conceding in Bantu cadences that neither assegais nor delirious dreams can stop the engineer's clock . . . Little sound motifs trace, midst the vaster saga, purple zones of distress more immediate, of rent and cash and bread, of scheming guile and knowing glances and quick talk that somehow finds a way. The turmoil of township life, its streaks of pus and billowing laughter, policemen and knives and big-hipped girls, passes through the filter of unscored music and enters the heart of those who came to listen.[13]

The language is somewhat purple but where it succeeds it captures with unsurpassed dramatic intensity not only the surge of feeling generated by a jazz concert in Johannesburg but the external conditions which make jazz an intrinsic part of black South African consciousness.

Indeed, whatever rhetorical excesses such a passage may exhibit, it is impossible to see how any critic wholly lacking in sympathy for jazz music can give a just estimate of it as prose; for what the passage seeks to achieve in prose is what the jazz musicians are attempting to accomplish on the stage. Alienation, the war against the diminution of pleasure, which ultimately implies diminution of personality, the quest for orgiastic forms of self-expression against the warm pressures of a suffocating bureaucracy: these are some of the elements which distinguish black South African writing from both its local white counterpart and that of black Africa in the north.

Tracing influences is generally a risky business; all the same, it would be difficult to find anywhere a literature which has exerted more influence on black South African writing than that of black Americans, and, occasionally, white American authors. Evidently, both in terms of racial composition and social conflict, as in the brute challenge presented to society by modern industrialism, something in the nature of the American writer's response to forces which seem all but uncontrollable, evokes sympathetic recognition from black South Africans. Except for the Elizabethan period, the English civil war, and some individual works from the Romantic Period and the odd novel by an unruly writer such as D.H. Lawrence, English literature has not held the same wide appeal for black South Africans as it has done for Africans immediately to the North, especially West Africans. Indeed, it is impossible to conceive of any black South African composing comic novels in the style of the Nigerian writer, T.M. Aluko; or much nearer home, composing works which resemble those of the Malawian novelist, Legson Kayira, novels which whatever their immaturity, are notable mainly for their open sanity, humour, cheerfulness and measured distance between the author and his characters. South African fiction seems determined to close the gap between the author and his inventions; often the author is his own subject matter, the anguish of his characters essentially his own. This self-dramatisation has led to a spate of memoir and autobiography, but often these elements spill over into fiction, the most recent examples of which are Mphalele's *The Wanderers* or Enver Carim's *Golden City* from which I have already quoted the above passages.

3

In *Golden City*, Enver Carim has, in fact, given us more a memoir than a novel;

the place and people are all too identifiable, but what is surprising is that a black writer so irrevocably estranged from his native city should record its brutality with such a burst of affectionate lyricism. The novel or memoir tells of the author's last few days in Johannesburg, 'making the rounds' of farewell parties, 'kissing and jiving and wondering if it really were possible to stay away from Jozie forever'.[14] During the ensuing partying we are introduced to friends, to girl friends, cons, drug-pushers, entertainers, and we encounter, above all, the city whose love story this is. *Golden City* is a book that recreates with loving fidelity the shadowy life of the black people in the biggest city in South Africa; its manner of doing so is to evoke through expressionistic language all the sensations one is forced to experience in such a life: pain, love, anger, tenderness, the explosive sensuality which is drawn upon as an antidote against the crippling anguish of oppression:

> The brandy burns down my throat and I'm beginning to feel sad. Leaving my city of action, grenadillas, and guavas, leaving girls who ripple as they dance, leaving marabi jazz, familiar streets and balconies; going away from the dialects and languages my ears are so attuned to, the idiom and the humour: stop saying words that are tactile upon the tongue and phrases that free an inner zest, surrender the prestige of permanency and the small glories of being greeted wherever you go, stop being praised by old ladies who knew your father's father and say you look just like him.[15]

And his evocation of individual characters is so immediate, the visual faculty so effortlessly exercised, that people seem to come to life before you as you read: 'I notice how lovely this girl is; large brown eyes and long lashes, the shifting angular planes of her face, the slender nose and the overall, quiet glow of her cocoa skin. There are waves in her black hair, shiny and thick with a bit of Africa.'[16]

If the hero of this novel seems at times too hedonistic, dedicated merely to the accumulation of pleasures and physical sensation, it is necessary to point out that this is also, undoubtedly, a highly moral book: the prose is shot through and through with the dazzling language of moral insight. Life, goodness, value, fulfilment, are the book's major preoccupations; and sensual pleasure is a moral good only to the extent that it creates a tissue which connects one human being with another or brings the individual into a dynamic relationship with the vital sources of being. A Lawrentian dream it is, but it is one that gives the book its moral tone: this heroic effort 'to remain alive and continually receptive'. A dream of sanctification through temporary refuge in the abodes of the flesh. No writer anywhere in South Africa is so constantly aware of the 'density of flesh', of the 'shape and possibilities of the human body' as an instrument of sensual experience. Smoking *dagga* (cannabis) with friends in some dark lane, the author reminds us in another sudden burst of lyricism that 'in a hundred other lanes and yards all over Johannesburg, men are finding it not enough to have charge of their bodies, they want to swamp the mind as well, invest it with a soft curvature'.[17]

Thus, in his second novel, *A Dream Deferred*, Enver Carim's severest condemnation of human character is in the form of a self-judgement by Mrs de

83

Villiers, the wife of a fanatical Afrikaner journalist who yearns for love and fulfilment but is reduced to the indignity of a mute hunger for a twenty year-old instructor at a shooting club. If De Villiers, her husband, is a hypocrite, an ardent supporter of apartheid who equally sees nothing wrong with ravishing young African girls in his domestic service, Mrs De Villiers is a pathetic individual, joyless, cheated, neglected, unable to accomplish even temporarily an illicit sexual liaison with the younger man. She is left only with the feeling of impotence, 'A feeling that nothing associated with her personally would ever be fruitful or warm or passionate.'[18]

One cannot help feeling that this failure is held by the author to be a terrible judgement against Mrs de Villiers herself. Her unsated, scarcely acknowledged lust, is an instance of human frustration and futility which seems even more pitiable when seen against the facility with which the blacks are able to extract some small pleasures from life, however miserable their condition. 'Their overalls are soiled, their boots gaping, there is a distracted air about them; nonetheless I have felt emerge from them collectively a kind of subterranean strength, a music even, of primordial honesty and uncorrupted pride.'[19] The quest for the life-giving force, for the redemptive power of love and sensuality is a continuous process in Carim's work; even the hero's memory of his brother's wife, large with child, moves him into fitful apprehension of the peculiar resonance of human brotherliness and companionship, the pulsating, radiant 'reservoir of love and rapture'.

> And I am filled, too, moved by a paroxysm within me of magnificent possibilities . . . accepting . . . each genuine grief and stifled breath of hope, each moan of pain and resounding cry of accomplishment — with such particles to create a child of cinnamon fragrance, strong of bone and deeply versed in the pleasures of companionship. In turn this child will be a mother, her tissues and spirit bequeathed until the last truncheons are put away in perplexity.[20]

Enver Carim writes like a prodigal son. To the last breath of his nearly breathless narrative he is a spendthrift for whom words are no object: he is a big spender among big spenders who, one hopes, will learn thrift with the passage of time. However, woven into his language, as I said, is a deep moral concern and genuine commitment. Politics as a lived reality is never far away from his considerations. 'A vast waste drags everywhere', we are told. 'The very ground is foul with treachery.' But this is no pessimistic book; in the middle of a piece of meditative prose we are reminded with a shocking abruptness that from the multitudes will soon 'emerge those who will not yield',[21] and that 'for one hour of brilliant magnificence their flames burns bright, the euphoria of unshackled manhood sweeps them forward into combat'.[22]

The poetic excess of that phrase — 'brilliant magnificence' — is typical of a style that sometimes overreaches itself and instead of finding the sublime phrase merely stumbles into verbosity and grandiloquence. All the same, there are occasional outbreaks of linguistic violence, quite appropriate in a narrative dealing with life in South Africa, which recur like brief hailstorms in Carim's memoir. 'There is a rip in the awning and rain comes pelting through.'[23] So that the poetisation of squalor, the deep exultation the narrator feels in his ability to snatch trophies of friendship, human kindness and moral courage from the jaws of defeat, are never allowed to lapse entirely, nor too long and too often, into lush sentimentality without a sudden hardening of tone and an unexpected bunching of muscle. Nevertheless, like a true poet, Carim is never forgetful that, whatever the heartaches, life triumphantly goes on. Even the sounds of an ice-cream vendor's bicycle remind the author of the never-ceasing process of life itself: 'The bells I then heard pealing were only those of an ice-cream vendor on his bicycle, but they were as sonorous as the moment, celebrating the commencement of a new passion.'[24]

In *A Dream Deferred* Carim has written a novel of the future in which revolutionary warfare has come to the cities of South Africa. His subject-matter is therefore politics in a very direct sense. But for us the book's interest lies not in its treatment of revolutionary politics, but in some of the most casual observation it makes about the relationship between black and white in simple human situations: for like Alex La Guma's recent fiction, read strictly as a novel of revolutionary politics, Carim's narrative has about it an air of nervous implausibility; there is something about it, at any rate, which is curiously intangible as if one were reading a piece of science fiction. This atmosphere of contrivance, an air, if one might call it that, of uneasy manufacture, is not only difficult to shake off, it is also difficult to account for. After all, it is not as if the events with which these two authors are dealing have not already happened or could not happen in the future: in the case of La Guma's novel, the creation of an underground 'railroad' for channelling men out of the country in order to undergo guerrilla training; and in the case of Carim's novel, the actual outbreak of urban guerrilla warfare in which white hostages are taken, and, in turn, counter-violence is ruthlessly unleashed by the Government.

To take La Guma first: thirteen years after the appearance of *A Walk in the Night*, and three novels later, he has produced no work, in my opinion, which matches the nearly perfect style of that first book, its accuracy of social observation or economy of language. In both *The Stone Country* and *And A Threefold Cord* there are passages of succinct power, but structural difficulties and an increasing loss of energy begin to show. By the time we get to *In the Fog of the Seasons' End* the deft characterisation which was the most startling feature of *A Walk in the Night* has increasingly given way to clichés in which La Guma struggles valiantly with the portraiture of an underground leader like Elias Tekwane; but despite the mass of details with which he provides us, the man's character remains shadowy and elusive.

As for Beukes, the underground organiser and hero of this novel, he has already appeared in different guises before: as George Adams in *The Stone Country* or Charlie Pauls in *And a Threefold Cord*. He is not an original creation who can be said to take a hold upon our consciousness; nor is he like Bakayoko of Ousmane's novel, a man bristling with ideas. In reading La Guma's latest fiction a formula begins to emerge: minor characters, hustlers, surly frustrated cons and self-deceivers, continuously appear and reappear, orchestrated against men of serious political commitment but who as characters in fiction have lost that initial power to shock which made the frustrations and thwarted life of even a minor character like Willie Boy in his first novel an object of our deepest concern and sympathy. Though *In the Fog of the Seasons' End* is a competent novel by a dedicated Communist writer, the book lacks that enormous sweep, the exhaustively worked out political and intellectual framework, which distinguish Sembene Ousmane's *Les bouts de bois de Dieu*.

All the same, as a novelist of social commitment, La Guma still holds an enviable position in South African literature. With a frequency which few can match he still manages to find the exact mataphor for the cancer which is eating away at the country's entrails. He writes always to expose what he has accurately described as 'the grim face of an executioner hidden behind a holiday mask'. Despite the tendency to repeat himself, he can still come up with a character like Tommy in *In the Fog of the Seasons' End*, both vividly and affectionately drawn, in whom La Guma reveals a sympathetic understanding of the plight of ordinary people. Tommy, always buttoned up in his black dinner suits, and 'forever practising his ballroom steps', 'white teeth grinning like an advertisement for toothpaste', is a child of the sun who lives in the make-believe world 'of sugary saxophones and sighing strings'. But even he cannot entirely escape politics; used as a courier by Beaukes he tries, but does not always succeed, to detach himself from politics because of the risk of arrest and physical violence he senses in that kind of work. Tommy lives only for his music and his ballroom dancing. His conversations are always mixed with snatches from popular music: ' "How about some tea for two, for me for you?" ' he asks Beukes. And sitting down to supper, while working 'at the crackling slab of fish with his fork' he hums *Blue Heaven*.

> Beukes asked, looking at him curiously, 'What the hell, you bloody well sing when you eating, too?'
>
> Tommy said, 'Youse too serious, *ou* Buke, too serious like. Me, I take things *mos* easy all the time.' He filled his mouth with fish and potato and chewed.
>
> 'Too bladdy easy,' Beukes said. 'Too bladdy easy. There's people worrying their brains out in this world and you just take it easy.'
>
> 'Ah, why worry? If you worry you die, if you don't worry you also die,' Tommy said. 'This fish is blerry stale.' He picked a fishbone from his mouth. 'You can't depen' on nobody. Lookit this stale fish, hey? I ask for fresh stockfish. This must have come out of the blerry Ark.'[25]

There are individual scenes, too, like Beukes's meeting with Frances at the fair, which for the accuracy of observation and the precision of the dialogue, cannot easily be bettered. Nevertheless, it is generally true that La Guma has written nothing since the appearance of *A Walk in the Night* which compels a fresh evaluation of his work. He is a competent novelist who after the flashing promise of that first collection of stories seems to have settled for nothing more than an honourable, if dull proficiency.

4

The difficulties which Carim encounters in *A Dream Deferred* are of a different kind from those which plague La Guma. As I see it, La Guma's current predicament is a troubling lack of fresh insight into the developing crisis of South African society. In art commitment is not enough: each time we pick up a new novel about South Africa we expect to know and feel it in our bones that we have been brought into contact with a fresh experience. I suppose that is what accounts for the unusual excitement one derives from reading a new novelist like Enver Carim. There is a singular boldness in his trial and a winning audacity in his failure. In a way, La Guma understands, and perhaps understands *too* well, the limits of what he can do with his material, given his kind of temperament.

Carim understands nothing! Paradoxically, it is this very inexperience that saves him; it is his singular lack of caution which frees his imagination and which endows his enterprise with its essential boldness. Even some of the melodrama which at crucial moments affects the plot of this novel is the consequence of this untrammelled imagination. Carim is not about to be taught the limits of anything. He piles on agony upon agony — murder, rape, looting; a certain amount of voyeurism, even good old-fashioned pornography, are sometimes smuggled in to enliven the plot.

A Dream Deferred is an overheated book. At times Carim seems unable to impose any realistic structure upon the chaos of what he imagines may follow political insurrection in South Africa. The mixture of political violence and strip-cartoon sex threatens to turn the novel into low farce. A perfect example of this is the section of the novel dealing with the seizure of white hostages by black revolutionaries. A bus carrying white passengers is stopped somewhere in a Johannesburg suburb; shooting breaks out; after the hostages have been taken to a nearby house, first the white men, and then the women are ordered to strip. In a kind of tit for tat, as it were, among the white hostages Carim has Marie de Villiers, daughter of the same fanatical Afrikaner journalist, who earlier on in the novel rapes an African maid—coincidentally, a girl friend of one of the revolutionaries. Marie is first shocked at the suggestion that she should take off her clothes in front of black men; but then quite suddenly, in a surprisingly swift change of mood, she enters into the spirit of the thing: 'As if rising to a challenge she hadn't previously understood, Marie's hands moved instinctively to the zip at the side of her skirt. She would not be ashamed . . . She would unveil herself and be proud of her posture and the lines of her form.'[26]

Surely, Carim is 'romancing' here: it is difficult to believe that with guns being fired, one woman already injured, Marie de Villiers should be concerned with 'posture' and 'the lines of her form'. The gravity of tone seems even more misplaced given the nature of the proceedings. A little later in the passage, just in case we have not noticed, Carim insists on telling us: three other girls were stripped 'down to their panties', and 'one of them, a squat girl whose hair was gathered in a bun, was trying to hide her breasts under her folded arms'.[27] Since there is nothing in what has gone on before to indicate the nature of the revolutionaries' sexual appetites, it is more than probable that it is the author who has turned into a voyeur, delighting in the minutest titillating revelations.

Nothing, for example, quite prepares us for the graphic salacity of the rape scene in which Kumalo, with a stump for a hand, employs this stump with grave

87

effectiveness on the girl's nipple. The scene is laid on with much provocative detail; nothing is too unimportant to escape notice as Kumalo, surveying the possible spoils of victory, takes in the scene: 'Her pants', we are told, 'were almost transparent; he could see how they clung and entered the cleft of her buttocks'[28]. Kumalo watches her closely. 'Her hips were barely covered by the frill of cotton'; the broken floor boards upon which Marie stands, and on which she will doubtless be ravished, emphasise 'her frailty'; and finally the sexual impulse already too strong to resist, Kumalo puts his hand between his own legs and strokes 'the thickening flesh'.

'You'll never forget me,' he said. 'Even when I'm dead, you won't forget me.'[29]

Neither can we!

If all of this seems too improbable and reads too much like an overheated sex-thriller, Carim has elsewhere in the book given us some valuable insights into how things are in South Africa, how carefully or carelessly lives are lived there, at how much cost to the individual. Like most perceptive writers who have handled the theme of the relationship between colonial masters and their subjects, Carim very accurately perceives the ambiguous position of white women in a racist society. At times he sees the position of the white woman as lying between oppressor and oppressed.

Oppressors these women are, of course, in the general sense; they have the same power over the black servants as their menfolk; and no amount of buck-passing by some feminist spokeswomen who see this purely as a masculine enterprise, can entirely absolve women of their share of the blame. And yet, recognising equally their special status as an 'oppressed group' within a ruling class, white women sometimes feel themselves to be stranded in a kind of no-man's-land (the pun should be forgiven) in which they are permitted some unusual insights into the nature of the war between the rulers and the ruled.

Marie de Villiers emerges as such a type. Unlike Mary Turner in Doris Lessing's *The Grass is Singing*, who seems to be driven by forces she can scarcely comprehend, Marie de Villiers is permitted a measure of self-recognition which makes her less pathetic than Mary, though in the end Carim is unable to create around her a full-scale tragedy in the way that Doris Lessing has done with Mary.

We first encounter Marie de Villiers at a garage, calmly contemplating Letaka ('calmly' is perhaps not the word) while the latter is changing a motor tyre, the very man, by the way, who will later take her hostage in a guerrilla war. While she watches Letaka, Marie experiences a range of emotions which indicate that she is capable of something more than a shallow perception of what society is doing to the blacks as well as to herself. Letaka, too, is covertly watching her. They are both trapped in the impossible roles. And in that scene in which Marie is both observing and being observed is contained, in a nutshell, the entire story of the relationship between white women and black men in a white racist society:

As she glanced down from the windscreen, Marie caught a glimpse of the

African cleaner half-concealed behind the cylinder of the jack. He had a broom in his hands and he was watching her. His gaze startled her. It was so direct and unexpected that she was momentarily flustered, wondering irrationally if he knew what she'd been thinking. Her instinct was to turn away, to save herself in the chatter of the proprietor, but the proprietor had stepped back and was talking about terminals to one of the mechanics. A fleeting sense of vulnerability overcame her, a heavy dread. Then she regained her composure, tensed herself, and returned the black man's gaze. She looked at him as white women of her country never do. She saw him.[30]

This act of 'seeing' is for the white woman in that situation the most revolutionary act; it is what the society, under normal circumstances, will not permit her: and this act of 'seeing' is, of course, an act of rebellion that is capable of freeing her if she will but permit herself to be freed from the shackles which society has so carefully woven around her. Significantly, Doris Lessing, herself a white woman who grew up under the same circumstances as Marie de Villiers, insists on the radical importance of this act of 'seeing'.

> . . . when a white man in Africa by accident looks into the eyes of a native and sees the human being (which it is his chief preoccupation to avoid), his sense of guilt, which he denies, fumes up in resentment and he brings down the whip.[31]

Indeed, this is the emotion which finally overwhelms Marie de Villiers; as Tony Marston promises to do in the beginning of *The Grass in Singing*, so does Marie de Villiers attempt to blunt her own sensibility — to 'forget the knowledge', to use Marston's phrase, of what she has seen, which curtails any possibility for her own personal liberation. She must deny the flash of recognition of Letaka as a human being capable of arousing a human response from her. However, during the brief moment that she is watching him, she guesses at his age, she notes the sleeves of his denim shirt rolled to his biceps, and feels slightly 'disturbed' by the power in his arms. Dimly, Marie de Villiers perceives in this emotional awareness some dire threat to her own standing as a white person whose self-control has 'wilted'. In order to recover her balance she convinces herself that Letaka is being 'insolent' and begins to see his 'steady gaze' as 'insufferably arrogant'.[32] Marie de Villiers seems to be continuously tugged between the two extremes of sympathy and revulsion. For instance, a little later, when she is looking through the window of the hairdresser's salon, and sees a group of African roadmenders breaking stone in the sun, she is appalled at the gross insensitivity of the white male hairdresser, a new arrival from England, who remarks sneeringly: 'I can't bear to think of the calluses they must have on their hands.'[33]

A sudden anger rose in Marie; she glanced away quickly. Her earlier impression that there was something obscene about him was confirmed, something unclean. The way he wet his pink lips with his tongue and the vaguely sweet odour of his body repelled her.

'They would rather not be in the sun,' she replied, listening to the song.
'What makes you say that?'

'They're singing about us.'

'About us? You must be joking.'

'Yes, you and me, and everybody else allowed in the shade.'

'Fancy that,' the hairdresser murmured. He looked more closely at the sweating bodies, at the baggy trousers tucked into their boots. He made a play of listening, turning his ear to the window.

'I must admit I can't make head or tail of what they're saying. On the other hand, I couldn't care less.'

Marie looked at him: 'You're new to this country, aren't you? From England.'

'As a matter of fact, I am,' he smiled.

'Why didn't you go to Rhodesia? It's full of your kind.'

He was taken aback; but she was obviously waiting for an answer.

'If you must know, it's because I don't think it's the safest place in the world — and the money's not so good either.'[34]

This scene shows clearly the contrast between a sensitive white woman, secretly aware of some immense damage to others that her life is mortgaged to, and the insensitive white male whose responsibility is power and keeping the machinery of oppression in smooth operation. Since the 'white man's burden', the wielding of the whip, must lie mainly on male shoulders, this means that white man cannot afford to relax their vigilance. At all times they must keep their own humanity closely in check; unlike their women they cannot afford these periodic 'attacks of sentimentality'.

The Lieberman sections of the novel are weakest of all. We are given the 'particulars' but no matter how hard we try we have no full grasp of Lieberman's actual relationship with his African comrades in the liberation movement. A Jewish lawyer with a long history of personal involvement in the freedom struggle, Lieberman somehow fails to come alive; he remains a cliché, a cardboard cut-out, who seems constructed out of newspaper clippings containing information about some of the best-known white figures in the South African Left.

This is in itself ironical, even paradoxical, that in creating the characters of a racist white family, the de Villiers for example, Carim has given us a more vivid picture of blighted individual lives than in his depiction of the Liebermans, a more progressive couple. On the whole, as I have already argued, it is the minute observations, the brief flashes of insight, which taken together build up a convincing picture of black and white society in South Africa. Carim's description of the white motorists caught up in a procession of Africans, surrounded, and in danger, but staunchly refusing to acknowledge their obvious predicament, is not only typical of the acuteness of his observations about black and white situations of confrontation, the scene also provides us with the exact paradigm for that myopic, self-induced, amnesiac blind stare in which white South Africa is trapped:

Although they were surrounded, they did their best not to see or hear anything unusual. But the sweat on their brows and under their damp collars was not all from the beating sun. With so much practice and experience they still could not blot out the silent, gnawing sensation of danger. Their eyes were glazed, but they knew . . . And when occasionally it became impossible to avoid the eyes boring into the windscreen, their faces flickered with false smiles, out of place smiles, smiles they thought were exonerating. Yet the sick tension of the moment, the very urgency that pumped froth from their pores, confirmed what they would rather have ignored: exemption would not be cheap. Sooner or later, one day, somehow, they'd have to pay heavily.[35]

5

No such clear insights or interesting observations about South African society at work can easily be found in Ezekiel Mphahlele's first novel, an omnibus of a book into which everything has been packed but very little of it is of any interest or has not already appeared in his splendid autobiography, *Down Second Avenue*. Indeed, Mphahlele's failure in this long-awaited first novel requires a much closer, more detailed analysis, than is possible within the limits of the present chapter.

First we have to look for the kind of criteria by which a work of fiction as elusive as *The Wanderers* ought to be judged. To evaluate this novel properly we are required to rehearse, I think, certain facts about Mphahlele's life both as a private individual and as a public figure. This distasteful necessity is imposed upon us by the nature of Mphahlele's enterprise which insists on making his own life so unreservedly the subject-matter of the novel, himself the unmistakable hero, and his contemporaries and various acquaintances minor figures in a vast supporting cast.

At the age of 56, Mphahlele is one of the best-known figures of modern African literature A life-long teacher, writer and critic, his fame or notoriety, depending on which side you take in the many disputes which have plagued his career since he left South Africa, derive mainly from his position as a fierce critic of *négritude*; and also, to put it more delicately, as the entrepreneur of African culture. In Johannesburg he worked for a while on the controversial monthly magazine, *Drum*, renamed '*Bongo*' in his novel, and writers like the late Can Themba, Bloke Modisane, Casey Motsisi and Arthur Maimane were his contemporaries there. Of his experiences on *Drum* Mphahlele wrote movingly in his autobiography, *Down Second Avenue*:

> Always I felt too deeply to be objective in my reporting and I was subjected to rigorous editorial censoring. That did not pain me so much as the necessity to be in *Drum* when I did not really want to be a journalist. I wanted to teach and I wanted to be a writer. During those thirty months, I had to live two lives. A life of subediting and reporting and fiction editing during the day, and a life of creative writing in the night. Try hard as I might, I couldn't find a comfortable meeting point between the two. My prose was suffering under severe journalistic demands and I was fighting to keep my head steady above it all. I felt like a slow-footed heavy-weight, wanting to be sure of every punch, in a ring which required a disposition to duck and weave and gamble and love the game or quit.[36]

By the end of the 'fifties the pressure building up in South Africa was reaching such intensity that many intellectuals elected for exile; Mphahlele, too, decided to leave. On 6 September 1957, he emigrated from South Africa to teach at a school in Lagos, Nigeria. His autobiography concludes with a vivid description of what it felt like to be a free man after thirty years of living under South African oppression: 'I'm sitting in the spacious garden of a Lagos house as I write this epilogue . . . I'm breathing the new air of freedom . . . I shall soon know what to do with this freedom.'[37]

Even then, however, there was already a hint of future trouble in the air; how to make this newly acquired freedom work for the writer was now the problem; 'Somehow it feels like having just climbed down from a vehicle that has been rocking violently for countless miles,'[38] Mphahlele wrote. Very ominously, he added: 'I am able to write articles on Nigeria in between times, but I haven't settled down to a short story yet. I have been trying to sniff around and find a distinctive smell to guide me.'

Mphahlele's sojourn in Nigeria was not as happy as the first few months had promised. 'Three years in Nigeria,' he was later to write, 'three years of adjustment, and still no solution in sight,'[39] And Mphahlele sadly concluded: 'A hard fact to live with: that once an exile, always one.'[40] He then moved on to Paris where he was appointed director of the African section of the Congress for Cultural Freedom. Mphahlele was an energetic worker. He organised and took part in many conferences on African culture and literature. At this time he also became engaged in many wearying disputations with the leading figures in the Negritude Movement of which Léopold Senghor and Alioune Diop were and still are its chief exponents. A particularly bitter exchange took place at Dakar between Mphahlele and W. Jeanpierre, a black American, during the proceedings of the conference on 'African Literature and the University Curriculum'. The black American vigorously defended negritude as 'historically justifiable' and spoke of a 'strategy which seeks to neutralise this militancy or to lull the African mind to sleep'. In a long and angry counter-attack Mphahlele concluded his defence of his own position by declaring that 'literature and art are too big for negritude, and it had better be left as a historical phase'.[41]

The latter half of the 1960s found Mphahlele back in Africa, this time in Kenya where he set up the Chemchemi Artists and Writers' Club; but here, too, his stay was short-lived. Mphahlele might have been right about negritude. It did nothing, after all, to cement relations between an exiled black South African and his African brothers; on the contrary, wherever Mphahlele attempted to sink roots, he found it difficult to adjust to local conditions. He began to look farther south, nearer home, and ended teaching at the University of Zambia. Here, too, life was difficult; some Zambian government policies toward South African exiles opened old wounds in the homeless nomad, and in protest Mphahlele resigned his post, packed his bags and left for the United States where he became associate professor at the University of Denver. Finally, in 1977 he returned to South Africa and accepted a position at the University of the Witwatersrand, Johannesburg. His disillusionment with African states seems complete.

A new theme in Mphahlele's life begins to take a clear, and terrifyingly definitive shape: exile, wandering, rootlessness. It is a theme that will be taken up in *The Wanderers*. The voyage toward exile begins in early childhood. First, as a child of two unhappy parents, farmed out at an early age to live with a maternal grandmother outside Pretoria; later as a student traversing the land from the Reef to the Natal Province in search of an education; and later still, an adult moving from South Africa to West Africa; from Africa to France, and from France back to Africa; finally from Africa to the United States; Mphahlele seemed for a time the very embodiment of the twentieth-century exile, doomed to wander over the face of the earth, unconnected to culture or place: 'once an exile, always one'.

All this time, still nursing wounds inflicted a long time ago, Mphahlele was also fighting a private, internal war with himself as a writer. He was trying, and as time went on trying with increasing desperation, to finish a novel; as he later came to admit, it was becoming progressively more difficult to recreate in his work the feel of South African society with any sufficient conviction, solidity, vigour and sureness. These are the facts we are forced to bear in mind as we confront *The Wanderers*, a novel written not by a novice but by a man whose experience both as a critic and a man is considerable.

While still in South Africa Mphahlele had published a collection of five stories under the title *Man Must Live* which *Trek*, a literary journal, praised for not giving us 'economic or political theories about human beings, but real people giving and taking, hurting and sacrificing,' while the left-wing *Guardian* complained that 'the author of these stories has had the gods of his fathers exorcised by missionaries. He has forgotten that he is an African.'[42] How Mphahlele has come to regard these early pieces can be gathered from his reluctance to see them reprinted. 'It was a clumsy piece of writing,' he has said.[43] And writing in his autobiography he confessed: 'I can never summon enough courage to read again a line from any of the stories that were published in 1947 under the title *Man Must Live*.'[44] Some later stories were more competent and in 1960 he published a collection of these under the title, *The Living and the Dead*, and another volume, *In Corner B*, was published by the East African Publishing House in 1967. *The Wanderers* is Mphahlele's first extended work of fiction.

Asked about this novel in 1968 Mphahlele described it as 'set in three countries, South Africa, West Africa and East Africa' and characterised it as 'fictional in most cases'.[45] To those acquainted with the experiences recounted in the book and to those who can recognise some of the personages of this narrative, however maliciously caricatured, Mphahlele's characterisation of the novel as 'fictional in most cases' would seem a bit odd, but perhaps understandably cautious. However, it cannot be the whole truth. 'It's only autobiographical in the sense of movement from one region to another,'[46] Mphahlele has said. On the contrary, the novel is packed with incidents from real life, with only slight variations introduced to give them a dubious fictional disguise. In the same way, some incidents which might have happened to other individuals are here woven into the life of the hero; there are also the minor twists and turns of plot which can be said to be the author's invention; but on the whole the book not only closely reproduces some of the material already published in Mphahlele's autobiography but extends this material by including sections about Mphahlele's life in West and East Africa: the petty quarrels, the bitter conflicts, the anecdotes about old friends and newer acquaintances are here given a new lease of life: what it is all for, what creative purpose is behind it all, it is difficult to say! Mphahlele seems to have given up the cool objectivity of his short stories for a prolonged bout of self-justification and self-worship which do nothing to enhance the quality of this turgidly voluminous prose-work. Indeed, his constant demands upon us to see the hero as a man of superior qualities produces exactly the opposite effect. Finally, in the author's hands this novel turns into the deadest tomb of self-love.

Here is a description of an interview between Timi Tabane, the hero of the novel, and Miss Graves of the University of Takora, in the African state of Iboyoru, where the former is applying for a teaching job, an incident, by the way, which has its counterpart in real life. After denigrating Timi's thesis, the patronising Miss Graves woundingly extends her unwanted sympathy to the candidate: 'Of course, I realise that you've done all your university studies as an external student and in a country where black people are underprivileged and cannot have good libraries.'[47] Later, Timi relates this incident to Emil, a German of Austrian origin, who strikingly resembles his old friend, Ulli Beier:

> I say to her, I say, 'Now look here, Miss Graves, it took me a total of ten years from the year I began my B.A. through the Honours and to the M.A. But that's because I had breaks in between. All the same I had access to the library of Milner Park University, which is an English school that offers borrowing facilities for all external students, black or white. My thesis took me two years and was examined by two other heads of the English department in two universities in addition to the head of my department. Why do you think they would all give me a distinction for a rotten thesis — out of sheer patronage of a black skin? You've got to be joking, Miss Graves. For your information, my examiners have all at one time or another taught for short periods at your English universities.'[48]

The inclusion of this incident illustrates not only the querulous tone of this novel but the poverty of its method as an attempt to illuminate a life already excellently rendered in the autobiography, *Down Second Avenue*. Though we can recognise the individuals upon whose lives these characters are modelled, they do not as characters in a work of fiction strike us as possessing any real solidity; they are the people about whom we are told much, but of whom we have no real clue in the end as to what their true nature is. We can find nothing here, no personality or event, whose existence bears the authority of a creative animus, nor is there the transmutation of banal fact into the terrifying mystery of a creative fiction, which alone can endow a work of art with its innate identity.

There is nothing wrong with autobiographical novels as long as the lives of the people involved are recast in a new and vivid light in such a way as to reveal some imaginative purpose or central design, the core of an idea or obsession by which the various fragments are given a new shape and meaning. Kofi Awoonor's novel, *This Earth, My Brother*, is a good example of this type of fiction. Mphahlele, on the other hand, works and reworks the details of his life all to no apparent or significant purpose. Whereas Carim's *Golden City*, despite its disguise as fiction, soon discloses its true identity as a 'memoir' about place and people, Mphahlele's hybrid work, at once novel and straight autobiography, leaves either form recalcitrantly unassimilated into its own form of disguise: being neither fiction nor autobiography, the book spreads around itself a thick smokescreen in which even the names of various African countries are changed and Johannesburg now bears the improbable name of 'Tirong'. And yet, in some oddly perverse way, we are clearly intended to identify the main characters of the narrative, for the veil behind which they operate is so deliberately thinned out that we feel all the more strongly the intolerable urgings of the novel upon us to recognise these people not only for *who* they were in real life but for *what* they stood.

Mphahlele appears here as 'Timi', the author-narrator, the late Can Themba as 'Pan', Bloke Modisane as 'Blackie' and Casey Motsisi as 'Lazy'. In contrast to Timi, the hero of the novel − if we might call him that in a novel in which proper action is absent − the other characters lack significance. They only appear to demonstrate the discriminating, moral intelligence of the author-narrator, his utmost seriousness and integrity as an artist. This is not, therefore, an instance when we can say with D.H. Lawrence 'trust the tale' and not the artist; quite frankly, in this case, we can trust nothing, neither the 'tale' nor the 'artist'. The 'I' of the narrator is so closely bound up with that of the author as to be inseparable.

The novel has two narrators. Timi, a staff writer on *Bongo* monthly magazine, first tells the story of his life in South Africa, about his frustrations as a journalist with serious literary pretensions, forced to eke out a living by writing vapid, trivial stories for his journal; later, his white liberal editor, Steve Cartwright, takes up the story and retells it from his own perspective, but the two perspectives are really one. Cartwright's own reflections on the South African situation, on the activities of the journal he edits and those who work in it, only reinforce Timi's perceptions of his own moral worth and the moral worthlessness of nearly everyone else. Above all, they reinforce Timi's sense of his own potential as a lonely figure, borne down by the weight of his own integrity and literary ambition in a profession in which everyone else is content to grind out ephemeral journalistic trash. Timi is a good man, a sensitive man, with impeccable tastes and standards; he does not drink much, when he tackles a journalistic assignment, it is always with the utmost gravity and sense of his own responsibility that he approaches the job. For example, here is Cartwright reflecting on Timi's handling of a difficult assignment:

> First class job he did of that Naledi story. Surprised himself, too. Even Pan praised it. Never really liked to be a journalist. Had a superior attitude towards journalists in general. Felt he was prostituting himself. So I kept him off social events altogether. We had our tiffs. He was too heavy-footed for the effervescent spirits of the *Bongo* crew, to say nothing about those of the Sunday *African Sun* lot. I knew they made quips about him in his absence, called him mockingly *son of the people*, or 'T' for teacher.[49]

Without any interposition of irony, Timi is given to frequent self-congratulations; even when he is hard on himself we are not really fooled; we know

Timi thinks himself a fine chap and a capital fellow. So does everyone else, apparently, who has any claim to moral insight. Cartwright, especially, who once felt nothing but exasperation in his dealings with Timi, belatedly discovers the fellow's intrinsic qualities.

> At first I felt he had no right to impose himself on us if he didn't really want to be a journalist. Exasperated me to have goad him, to crank up his enthusiasm for him. I couldn't bear his sullen moods, his conceit. Later I felt differently. Not simply because he was too bloody good a writer to be wasted.[50]

This is the most astonishing, most prolonged, labour of self-love and self-praise we have yet encountered in any African novel, certainly more astonishing and perversely arch for being in a book which is so directly the account of the life of its author, who then stands behind his characters, subtly coercing them into expressing unconditional admiration for the hero's assumed qualities as a man and a writer. By comparison, his fellow staff writers are a drunken, whoring lot, willingly prostituting themselves for the transient glamour of popular journalism. Pan, especially, a character who in every respect most resembles the late Can Themba, at one time *Drum's* associate editor, obviously arouses in Timi a mixture of stringent rancour and deepest insecurity; in the South African sections of the book he is singled out for an especial kind of male-volent caricature. His ruthless, journalistic tactics are mentioned, his corrupted ideals are painstakingly noted, his brilliance and superior intellectual abilities only grudgingly ackowledged; several times his drunkenness is insisted upon, his troublesome ulcers made the object of much squalid sneering. 'Pan had another attack of ulcers,' Timi gloats. 'They were becoming too frequent. But he was unable to keep off drink.'[51] Cartwright, too, is compelled to note Pan's inordinate love of the bottle: 'Funny — isn't it! A man with the journalistic acumen and mind like Pan is his own enemy — booze and ulcers et cetera.'[51]

Another well-known South African writer turns up in this novel as 'Blackie', a refugee now living in London, a fellow whose rooms in South Africa were 'well-furnished', who played records of Mozart and Beethoven, and brought home 'contraband in the form of a white girl'.[53] This particular individual, having left South Africa as a refugee like Timi, has 'suddenly developed rabid nationalist sentiments'; he says he hates white people but has white female admirers. 'He enjoyed recounting bedroom experiences with them; told his stories with a sense of triumph.'[54]

Having decided that life in South Africa has become intolerable, Timi Tabane escapes across the border and travels to West Africa where he takes a teaching post. What Timi finds in the educational system of Iboyoru is not satisfactory. 'Often he became impatient with orthodox, stick-in-the-mud ideas.'[55] Timi and his wife, Karabo, struggle with their new life, they observe local customs and behaviour, go to parties and visit friends. They also have trouble with servants in much the same way as the new rising African middle class that Timi Tabane hates so much:

The first servant smoked opium and was dazed much of the time. He had to go. Another, Moses, was stubborn no matter how kindly Timi spoke to him.[56]

They also have trouble with their son, Felang; as his school report notes: 'Felang shows intelligence and ability, but does not apply himself.'[57] When they move to Lao-Kiku in East Africa Felang carries this rebellion further by running away from home to join the freedom fighters in Southern Africa; there (is this perhaps a case of symbolic infanticide?) the boy is killed in action.

At various points during this narrative, Timi is visited by his old *Bongo* editor, Steve Cartwright, now working for a London newspaper. An intellectual and a powerful journalist, Cartwright's impending marriage to a black South African woman, a domestic servant from the countryside with only a Standard 6 education, strikes one as implausible; perhaps she is more extraordinary than we are allowed to gather from the pages of this book; but Mphahlele's heavy leaden prose, its dreary inability to evoke either a sense of place or the immediacy of a love relationship, does nothing to help.

Indeed, part of the failure of this book is rooted in the failure of language which I first noted in Mphahlele's earlier work. I wrote then:

In the past what had always put me off Ezekiel Mphahlele's writing was a certain dullness of tone, much like the ponderous speech of a dull-witted person, so that it was often difficult to pursue the story to its ending. The gems were often embedded in a thick mud of cliché and lustreless writing.[58]

It would be fair to say that *The Wanderers* has plenty of 'thick mud' but few 'gems' to be found embedded in it. In this first novel the immutability of Mphahlele's defeat is cast in a language, at once dry, brittle and sterile, with a dialogue that is uniformly heavy and awkward in syntax, whoever happens to be talking. In fact, all the characters talk very much alike, that is to say, like Timi; which means that the dialogue is so constructed as to sound as if each character were reading their lines from a script by Mphahlele.

In themselves these failures are disappointing but ought not to be irremediable. What is more disturbing than these deficiencies of language is the feeling one gets with each reading of this book that at the centre of the novel is a hopeless collapse of artistic will, a moral decline in the overall perspective, that is worrying in a writer of Mphahlele's experience. It may very well be that this over-reliance on real life incidents, the result of an immense effort to achieve an atmosphere of authenticity where memory and invention cannot do the job, is the first sign that the author is having severe problems. The second indicator, but closely related to the first, is the constant shift from one narrator's voice to another; with such frequent changes in the narrator we are, of course, now thoroughly familiar as one of the techniques which have become available to the modern novelist; but these occasional shifts of voice are usually intended to provide us with a new perspective on the events being narrated, sometimes enabling us to see the hero in a different light from his own false pretensions and illusions. The result is usually a nicely balanced irony between our perceptions of the qualities of the leading character and the hero's own self-perceptions. As I have already shown, this is not the case in this novel.

There are other problems which create doubt about the whole nature of the enterprise. Since the personalities written about in the book, however grossly caricatured and unfairly treated, are recognisable to any South African reader who moved in the same milieu as the author, it is difficult to know just how to evaluate them as people in a work of fiction. The difficulty is compounded by the feeling we get quite early on in the novel that the author is out to settle scores with rivals and to vindicate himself at the expense of contemporaries whose personalities he did not like, whose careers he held in contempt, whose work he found trivial compared to his own. The strategy seems designed to massage an ego that swells visibly with every self-manipulation.

As the novel moves on from South Africa to West Africa and from West Africa to East Africa, it becomes fatally obvious that Mphahlele is attempting to paint for us, as he himself had admitted, 'a panoramic view' of a continent awakening from the stupor of colonialism, still unsure which direction to go; but since there are no strongly defined characters, only names and a chaos of incidents, the book remains curiously shapeless and unfocused. In the end there are deaths – of Felang and Steve Cartwright – but no tragedy!

In many ways, this is a distressing book whose malice may be unintentional but whose value as a work of a creative imagination is equally small. Mphahlele's criticism of South African society, even more pertinently his just criticism of the newly-independent African states, is mitigated by the failure of the book as a work of art. Wherever Timi goes in his wretched exile his inability to identify with any society condemns him to a terrible marginality; and toward the end of the novel, listening to the noise of independence celebrations in Lao-Kiku, Timi's final question, 'Why does that music sound so plaintive?' carries a terrible irony for himself and for his own kind of dilemma. 'Where's the roar of triumph?' Timi asks, as well he might.

6

If Mphahlele fails in this novel to tell us any more about South Africa than he had already told us in his autobiography, he is not himself unaware of the problem that the South African race question raises for a writer of fiction. As early as 1959 he wrote in his autobiography:

> The main weakness in South African writers is that they are hyper-conscious of the race problem in their country. They are so obsessed with the subject of race and colour that when they set about writing creatively they imagine that the plot they are going to devise, the characters they are going to create and the setting they are going to exploit, must subserve an important message or important discovery they think they have made in race relations.[59]

A natural enough desire, one would have thought; but Mphahlele's strategy of dealing with the problem in a number of stories he published in the late 'fifties and the early 'sixties was not to ignore the race problem altogether, but to attack it obliquely. In a fiction which relies mostly on situation at the expense of character, Mphahlele made the study of character an important element in his fiction: as a result of some of the work he was doing within the short story form, it seemed possible to hope that he might lead the way in the direction of a maturer fusion between literature as social criticism and literature as an intellectual and artistic manipulation of form. On the evidence of his first novel, we are compelled to look elsewhere for the solution.

Luckily, we do not have very far to look: after Enver Carim, we have in Bessie Head, another mulatto writer from South Africa, one of the most exciting new voices to have emerged from Black South Africa in the middle 'sixties. Like her predecessors — Ezekiel Mphahlele, Bloke Modisane, the late Can Themba, Mazisi Kunene — to mention only a few names, she, too, chose to go into exile; but the nature of Bessie Head's exile was made more or less tolerable by her choice to move to Botswana, just across the border, which was close enough to the country of her birth not to seem like exile.

If not culturally, at least economically, Botswana, where Bessie Head has been resident since the early 'sixties is virtually a province of South Africa, a state of affairs which the inhabitants of the country must have many occasions to rue, and yet the direct and obsessive atmosphere of black and white confrontation is mercifully absent from the country's social commerce. Nevertheless, Bessie Head still writes out of a psychology formed by the South African background; she writes a prose that is sometimes dense and cluttered by fear of injury, sometimes pure and carefully poised in its own moral certainties. But Bessie Head works always from the inside to the external, from the exploration of individual character to the depiction of a larger social scene. Without making equal claims for her as novelist, I think she has the same ability that William Walsh recognised in V.S. Naipaul, which is to create characters who are 'seen from within so that they possess intrinsic, spontaneous vitality, and from without, so that they are located in time and place and in a context of value and feeling.'[60]

Just how misleading insistence on a *Drum* 'school' of writers can be, if it means a 'common style' more than a common stimulation, can at once be appreciated after even the most casual reading of Bessie Head's novels. She, too, was a writer on *Drum's* sister Sunday newspaper, *Post*, but her development as a writer, her temperament as a woman and as an artist, are uniquely her own. She has none of the showy glitter that the fast-paced life of Johannesburg can impose on the prose style of someone like Carim; none of the quickness of mind that is so evident in the writing of Can Themba, nor has she the same rigorous political commitment of a writer like La Guma; indeed, for most of the time Bessie Head seems politically ignorant. She has only this moral fluency of an intelligent, intensely lonely individual, worrying about the problems of belonging, of close interpersonal relationships, of love, value, and humanity.

After some short pieces which began appearing in *The New African* and such journals as *The New Statesman*, all of them distinguished by an almost painfully fragile poetic sensibility, Bessie Head published her first full-length novel, *When Rain Clouds Gather* in 1969. Even when some of the novel's shortcomings are fully acknowledged, this is by all accounts a creditable first performance by an unknown novelist. In Britain the novel was unhesitatingly acclaimed by the reviewers; but ironically enough, in the specialist journals of African culture and social criticism there was very little mention of it. To this day Bessie Head remains virtually unknown in certain African literary circles.

This bleak, attentive study of a small community of a mere four hundred people, situated in a dusty, arid Botswana village, a people struggling to improve its agricultural techniques in food production but mercilessly torn by petty conflict and self-seeking ambition, contains an admirable range of characters. There is Makhaya Maseko, the black South African exile in 'search of a peace of mind', his white counterpart, Gilbert Balfour, the expatriate Englishman who struggles heroically to organise the self-help co-operative farms on a scientific basis; Sekoto, the benevolent local chief, who loved 'fast cars, good food, and pretty girls . . . and gave the impression of waddling like a duck when he walked'; there is Matenge, his wickedly malevolent brother 'with his long, gloomy, melancholy, suspicious face and his ceaseless intrigues', and numerous other character-studies — Pauline is one of them — drawn with an exquisitely sure touch and amazing self-confidence, by a novelist who is not after all a native of the country. Similarly, the evocation of the sun-parched waste of Botswana, with an occasional desert 'bloom' such as the village of Golema Mmidi; the slow almost imperceptible changes of the seasons and the unhurried accumulation of the physical details of everyday life, these are just some of the achievements of this South African novelist. This materiality of everyday existence happens to be the most difficult thing to achieve in a novel; and yet recreating in fiction the microcosm of the larger social world, and breathing a new life into the harshly familiar and the unrelentingly dull, is what writing novels used to be about; Bessie Head manages her task with immense skill and sympathy.

Her first novel, *When Rain Clouds Gather*, was soon followed by another, titled *Maru*, in which the same type of community was depicted; poor in resources, rich in malice, but not incapable of responding humanly to suffering when good leadership is given. This time the centrifugal forces of hate, love and ambition revolve around a young unmarried school teacher, Margaret Cadmore, offspring of a Masarwa ('Bushman') woman who had given birth to the child 'on the skirts of a remote village', and 'wore the same Masarwa ankle-length, loose shift dress which smelt strongly of urine and the smoke of outdoor fires. She had died during the night but the child was still alive and crying feebly when a passerby noticed the corpse.'[61] This child is brought up by an eccentric English school teacher, the wife of missionary who provides for her a wholesome environment of love and protection; all the same in a community where the Masarwa are still owned as slaves the little girl cannot be unaware of her status as a social outcast. 'There was no one in later life who did not hesitate to tell her that she was a Bushman, mixed breed, low breed or bastard.'[62] Having equipped her with a good education the Cadmores return to England, young Margaret becomes a school teacher, and is immediately plunged into a more abrasive atmosphere of unruly pupils who torment her by asking such questions as, 'Since when is a Bushy a teacher?'; and a school principal who bluntly proclaims: 'Either the Masarwa teacher goes or I go.' The parallel with South Africa becomes unavoidable: this is a society which practises racial discrimination against an ethnic minority defined by physical features. 'Who could absorb the Masarwa, who hardly looked African, but Chinese?'[63]

Again and again Bessie Head returns to this vision of a 'power-hungry' and 'exclusive' Africa; but her obsession with this theme, one suspects, is rooted in her insecurity as a mulatto, shared, too, in a less desperate measure, by other coloured South Africans. Ironically enough, this feeling is less pronounced in South Africa, where the coloured writer enjoys the psychological support of what has become a large national minority, with its own separate identity; but this sense of security diminishes when the coloured writer ventures outside the borders of the republic, and is thus forced to assume a larger African identity. Brutus expresses this same subtle sense of displacement in one of his poems: 'I'm an alien in Africa and everywhere only in myself, occasionally, am I familiar.'[64]

As novelist, however, Bessie Head is interested in the drama of inter-personal relations, not sermons. However twisted and grasping they appear to be, the characters of her novels encounter each other as living people with comprehensible human needs, frailties, and a proper measure of individual heroism: they hurt one another, they suffer, but in the end they learn that growth is possible even in the narrowly confined environment that Bessie Head has made her speciality. Thus, despite the evil passions released by Margaret Cadmore's presence at Leseding School, she also becomes a catalyst for change: Maru, the young chief, Moleka, the son of another, both fall in love with her, with consequences for everyone else that could hardly have been foreseen. So does Dikeledi, Maru's sister, in her own way, fall in love with the Masarwa school teacher, complicating even further her unmastered passions for Moleka. More important, these three do not only give Margaret Cadmore their friend-ship and protection, but in the end are themselves forced to revise their atti-tudes toward the Masarwa slaves they own, even to the point of abandoning the institution altogether. With its delicacy of feeling and subtle evocation of character; above all, its proper sense of place, this is as nearly perfect a piece of writing as one is ever likely to find in contemporary African literature. If one is right, such a conclusion makes even more surprising the disastrous failure of. Bessie Head's third novel, *A Question of Power*, with its unassimilated use of religious mysticism and classical symbols. Although we can grasp the *ne plus ultra* of that mental suffering, the unyielding subjectivity of the writing limits our sympathies.

But '*Maru*' is a different book altogether: within the limited scope of a mere 127 pages, we are presented with a rich interplay of character and social scene, and Bessie Head's broad sympathies for the outcast, for the lonely and the mentally broken, are given a convincing social framework. The simplicity of the narrative line, the careful economy of its language, and the poetic fragility of its texture, makes this one of the most exhilarating books to read. Its plea for recognition of the humanity of others is explicit but its fervour is dis-creetly suppressed and never fiercely insisted upon. In its quiet way what the novel finally suggests is the overwhelming need for love and protection in the world; for love, the invisible power of love as it shapes us and heals those we love, is the book's most controlling emotion.

Sex has very little space in Bessie Head's novels, it is merely acknowledged as an unpleasant necessity. For example, Elizabeth, the heroine of *A Question of Power*, sums up with a disconcerting forthrightness what must be the author's profoundest conviction about the insignificance of sex in contrast to the healing power of love: 'It was not maddening to her to be told she hadn't a vagina. She might have had but it was not such a pleasant area of the body to concentrate on, possibly only now and then if necessary.'[65]

All along I have insisted, perhaps insisted too often, on the pressure of the autobiographical on South African fiction, a feature common to the European writers who experienced at an uncomfortably close range the horrors of the Nazi holocaust; the passion to make the fact of personal experience a governing emotion in the works of these writers becomes a compulsive disposition. Nevertheless, where a writer is absolutely in control over the materials of his life the pressure acts as a necessary key which unlocks the imagination and provides us with the necessary means for reconciling the author's private world of subjectivity with objective world of universal significance.

The difference between Mphahlele and Bessie Head is the difference between a writer who throws in every flotsam and jetsam from his private life into a novel, in an untested supposition that we, as readers, will find significance in it, and a writer who constructs out of these fragments 'a separate place', full of meaning and instruction for us. Significantly, in *A Question of Power*, a novel in which the autobiographical element holds an intolerable sway over the novelist, the mental breakdown of the heroine is accompanied by a parallel breakdown in communication, with an increasing loss of this power to instruct or arouse sympathy, which is only intermittently relieved by periodic flashes of intense illumination.

Sooner or later we have to come back to the question of 'protest' and 'commitment' which looms so large whenever South African fiction is discussed. Bessie Head is not a political novelist in any sense we can recognise; indeed, there is ample evidence that she is generally hostile to politics. Far from being an axiomatic proposition, as some critics with an innate hostility to politics tend to believe, this lack of precise political commitment weakens rather than aids Bessie Head's grasp of character. Makhaya, the hero of her first novel, becomes blurred at precisely the moment that we fail to comprehend the nature of his political commitment. Having engaged in underground political work in South Africa, his abhorrence for political solutions is, to say the very least, inadequately explained. Contradictions in the ideas he holds remain unresolved and rather puzzling. 'Why not leave this country, even Africa, to trial and error?' Makhaya asks.[66] A little later, even more incomprehensibly, the author asserts about someone who has fled South Africa as a political refugee: 'Makhaya did not care because, more than anything, he hated politics.' Toward the end of the novel, in a way which must surely violate our comprehension of his character, Makhaya is made to confess: 'I'm tired of counting the change. I'm going to be a millionaire. All poor people stick on me and they have to become millionaires with me.'[67]

It is an absurd dialogue, rooted in the author's own confusion whenever she enters the realm of political ideas. Her natural sensitivity and individualist beliefs pull her toward religious solutions. In *A Question of Power* Elizabeth's greatest distress stems from the loss of internal equilibrium which she experiences as a greater threat to her well-being than any physical disability. As she puts it:

I am panic-stricken. My internal life is all awry, and when I'm assaulted there I'm broken. I've withstood a lot of external hardships, but I'm incapable of withstanding internal stress, not the abnormal kind that's afflicting me.[68]

7

Fact, raw experience, and the aching memory of what it 'felt like', become in D.M. Zwelonke's novel, *Robben Island*, the only recognisable conditions for the operation. This is as far away as we are likely to get from 'art for art's sake'. A former inmate of South Africa's notorious island prison, currently holding more than 250 political prisoners, including Nelson Mandela, Zwelonke has joined the ever-expanding community of South African exiles now living abroad; but the authority of this book comes from the suffocating intimacy with which he re-enacts for us the daily brutality and the physical squalor of political prison life. There is very little in the book which owes its existence to purely aesthetic considerations. If, as Macaulay once put it 'the sure sign of decline in art is the frequent occurrence, not of deformity, but of misplaced beauty', Zwelonke shows us how extreme anguish can be turned into viable art in which artistic effect has no autonomous claim on our response separate from the claims of truth.

Of the few intelligent reviews I have read of *Robben Island*, the one written by John Goldblatt comes closest to defining the book's most congenital characteristics: 'Just as kinetic art, *musique concrete*, and science fiction are new aesthetics of the twentieth century, so too is the literature of political imprisonment.'[69] Goldblatt remarks on the difficulty of 'criticising' this kind of writing; for this tale of beatings, torture, homosexual rape, the almost pointless violence, the mental and physical degradation, impose demands upon author and reader alike, which bring into fretful and uneasy question the very nature of a literary discipline like criticism. We are not here investigating a literary artefact whose existence is casual, whose formal qualities can bear an easy, relaxed, contemplation. Our relation with the book is tense, painful and contaminating, requiring us to discriminate between the tragedy of political internment and the 'corrupting eloquence' which so often feeds on it; the very rawness of the language, the book's dry and violent factuality, create conditions for our appreciation which are inseparable from its palpable intention to shock us out of our assumed literary poise and professional equanimity.

There is no point in presenting a detailed analysis of the plot of this novel. As Goldblatt points out, *Robben Island* is as factual as its name. The story of Bekimpi, almost programmed from childhood to pursue a life of criminality and confrontation with the law; his almost involuntary politicisation; his imprisonment, torture and murder in an isolation cell, constitute a simple narrative whose force lies mainly in the bleak, self-contained autarchy of its language. Telling in one and the same voice the story of his survival while detailing the process of liquidation of intransigent men like Bekimpi, Zwelonke succeeds in creating for us a world we can only enter with a profound sense of discomfort; we do not belong here, the light is too lurid for us to stare unblinkingly into its glare. All the same, we shall thoroughly misread this book if we see it merely as a piece of documentary writing from which literary strategy is absent: we are not confronted here with 'a chaos of facts'; behind the selection of every image is the presence of a 'reflecting, judging mind', organising for us an intelligible picture of extreme brutality, of a horrendous mental and physical torture; and yet, here is the heart of a paradox which is perhaps the very nub of the mystery of all artistic operations, this picture of evil is presented in a language which can be incongruously poetic at times, in spite of its uncompromising rejection of 'misplaced beauty'. Nowhere is the presence of this literary sensibility more evident than in Zwelonke's evocation of Robben Island — of 'its thick palpable mist, through which a bird cannot find its way, but knocks itself against the walls'.[70] This is more than a picture of an island; through its mist and drizzle we are made to experience the slow sapping of the prisoner's morale:

> When there are clouds, they are dark clouds, not bringing sudden storms but a patience-devouring drizzle that can wet a cat through to its skin, so that it cringes and groans from the biting, frozen air of the Antarctic.[71]

As an example of a new genre of twentieth-century literature, describing essentially the same phenomenon, *Robben Island* shares with other works of its kind a harrowing tone — 'howling' would be a more precise word — of a defiant universality, rootless, potent, disturbing. Do we not, after all, imagine we have read this same account by other political prisoners in Brazil, Spain, Portugal or Greece:

> The keys clanked and rattled as the iron bars swung open. The heavy paw on my shoulder jerked me into the cell. The privy-stink greeted my nostrils, the stink of fresh fart. The lights clicked on as a man rose from a little bucket, pulling his trousers up. A concentrated stink diffused from the bucket, filling the cell, now that the buttocks that had been its lid were removed.[72]

However, what finally distinguishes this book from, let us say, the South African sections of a novel like *The Wanderers*, is the fierce 'wit' which turns suffering into an object of grim, barely suppressed comedy. Beneath its surface of anguished recollection there is a vein of incredible gaiety and defiance. Again and again Zwelonke shows us how even in a South African dungeon it is possible to construct out of the ordinary, neglected objects of our daily lives the structures which make civilisation possible. Awaiting trial in solitary confinement, his morale at its lowest ebb, the author is given a copy of the Bible: 'I read it avidly', he tells us. 'I asked for one written in Shangani. I liked the language . . . Then once I also found in the prison library a historical novel set in the Roman Empire, which set the corpuscles of my blood circulating at cosmic speed.'[73]

Zwelonke, Carim, and South Africa's newest poets like Mtshali and Mattera, have managed to construct from the shattered fragments of life under oppression, a literature of value and defiant self-assertion which goes beyond simple 'protest'.

REFERENCES

1   Doris Lessing, *The Grass is Singing*, Heinemann, London 1973, p.30.
2   Nadine Gordimer, *The Black Interpreters*, Spro-Cas/Ravan, Johannesburg, 1973, p.51.
3   *Ibid.*
4   *Ibid.*
5   Lewis Nkosi, 'Fiction by Black South Africans', in G.D. Killam (ed.) *African Writers on African Writing*, Heinemann, 1973.
6   Enver Carim, *Golden City*, Seven Seas Books, Berlin, 1970, p.132.
7   Gerald Moore, *The Chosen Tongue*, Longman, London, 1969, p.203.
8   Carim, *Golden City*, p.132.
9   Joseph Conrad, 'Heart of Darkness' in *Three Short Novels*, Bantam Classic, New York, 1960, p.6.
10 *Ibid.*
11 Modikwe Dikobe, *The Marabi Dance*, Heinemann, 1973, p.67.
12 See Mazisi Kunene's *Zulu Poems*, André Deutsch, London, 1970.
13 Carim, *Golden City*, p.149–50.
14 *Ibid.*, p.12.
15 *Ibid.*, p.24.
16 *Ibid.*, p.99.
17 *Ibid.*, p.128–9
18 Enver Carim, *A Dream Deferred*, Allen Lane, London, 1973, p.102.
19 *Ibid.*, p.110.
20 *Ibid.*, p.99.
21 *Ibid.*, p.131.
22 *Ibid.*
23 *Ibid.*
24 *Ibid.*, p.155.
25 Alex La Guma, *In the Fog of the Seasons' End*, Heinemann, 1972, pp.52–3.
26 Carim, *A Dream Deferred*, p.137.
27 *Ibid.*
28 *Ibid.*
29 *Ibid.*, p.188.
30 *Ibid.*, pp.11–12.
31 Lessing, *The Grass is Singing*, p.178.
32 Carim, *A Dream Deferred*, p.12.
33 *Ibid.*, p.66.
34 *Ibid.*, p.67.
35 *Ibid.*, p.81.
36 Ezekiel Mphahlele, *Down Second Avenue*, Seven Seas Books, Berlin 1962, p.194.
37 *Down Second Avenue*, p.220.
38 *Down Second Avenue*, p.218.
39 Ezekiel Mphahlele, *The African Image*, Faber, London, 1962, p.223.
40 *Ibid.*
41 See Ezekiel Mphahlele, 'A Reply', included in Gerald Moore (ed.), *African Literature and the Universities*, Ibadan University Press, 1965.
42 Mphahlele, *Down Second Avenue*, p.164.
43 See interview in Dennis Duerden and Cosmo Pieterse (eds.), *African Writers Talking*, Heinemann, 1972, p.106.
44 *Ibid.*, p.217.
45 *Ibid.*, p.110.
46 *Ibid.*
47 Ezekiel Mphahlele, *The Wanderers*, Macmillan, London, 1971, p.212.
48 *Ibid.*
49 *Ibid.*, p.122.
50 *Ibid.*, p.163.
51 *Ibid.*, p.116.

52   *Ibid.*, p.127.
53   *Ibid.*, p.241.
54   *Ibid.*
55   *Ibid.*, p.203.
56   *Ibid.*, p.198.
57   *Ibid.*, p.222.
58   Nkosi, 'Fiction by Black South Africans', pp.113−4.
59   Mphahlele, *Down Second Avenue*, p.195
60   William Walsh, *V.S. Naipaul*, Oliver and Boyd, Edinburgh, 1973, p.30.
61   Bessie Head, *Maru*, Gollancz, London, 1971, p.12.
62   *Ibid.*, pp.15−16.
63   *Ibid.*, p.108.
64   Dennis Brutus, *A Simple Lust*, Heinemann, 1973, p.121.
65   Bessie Head, *A Question of Power*, David Poynter, London 1973, p.44.
66   Bessie Head, *When Rain Clouds Gather*, Gollancz, 1968, p.84.
67   *Ibid.*, p.144.
68   Head, *A Question of Power*, p.69.
69   See John Goldblatt's review of *Robben Island* in *Index on Censorship*, 3/1974, pp.99−101.
70   D.M. Zwelonke, *Robben Island*, Heinemann, 1973, p.41.
71   *Ibid.*
72   *Ibid.*, p.5.
73   *Ibid.*

CHAPTER SIX

MODERN AFRICAN POETRY:

ITS THEMES AND STYLES
A   THE PIONEERS

1

In the following two chapters I propose to make a broad survey of modern African verse of English, French and Portuguese expression. In a very summary fashion I mean to indicate the main themes and styles and to point out in broad general terms what the achievements of African verse have amounted to, and also, no less important, what have been its failures and shortcomings. For purposes of convenience alone I have divided my treatment of this subject into two main sections: the Pioneers and the Moderns.

To those already familiar with African poetry, and for the growing number of specialists in the field, a treatment of the kind I have chosen may seem somewhat superficial, at the very least, insufficient; after the recent spate of numerous introductory textbooks on African literature, a much closer analysis of the works of individual poets rather than a broad synopsis of the field may now seem a more useful enterprise for the contemporary critic to undertake.

My immediate answer is that, desirable as such closer analyses of the texts are, African literature is still a relatively young discipline. To capture even partially the flavour of what has become a rapidly growing volume of work by modern African poets some effort is required.

Scattered as they are over a vast continent, increasingly subject to a perplexing variety of social, cultural and political pressures, these poets may reveal through the themes they choose and the manner in which they execute them, the full extent of the diversity and, equally, the underlying unity of the African cultural situation. It is to be hoped that a survey of this kind will provide the reader with an excellent opportunity for observing within a single context the contrasts as well as the similarities in style and content of much of the poetry that has been produced by Africans in just a little more than half a century.

It can never be too strongly emphasised or emphasised often enough that African poetry does not commence with the advent of colonial education in Africa; nor does African poetry, properly speaking, begin with the training of native speakers in the use of the European tongues. As in other parts of the world, poetry in Africa, its use and enjoyment by ordinary members of the community, is as old as organised society itself: the African languages, through the 'oral literatures', are repositories of some of the finest verse in epic form as well as in the shorter lyric which has survived to our own day under very testing conditions. A great deal of this oral poetry, whether it is the praise-poems of

South Africa, the sacred songs of the Masai, the *Odu* corpus of the Yoruba, or the religious chants of the Igbos, or the funeral dirges of the Akan, has fertilised much of contemporary African verse in the European languages: even when it has not palpably done so it has sometimes created a healthy tension between traditional African modes and the acquired Western techniques.

Regrettably, for our present purposes, we can only confine ourselves to what is called, for lack of a better term, "African verse in the European languages", most of which, to the eternal discomfiture of the the Africans themselves continues to be written in the languages of former colonial masters; the relevance to poetry of the adopted means of expression is of the most immediate kind. Between a poem like *Song of Lawino*, first written in Acoli, and then translated into English, and any poem written directly into a European language, is a difference not merely in linguistic procedure but in the social attitudes implied in the choice of one language rather than another. A European language can simultaneously liberate from certain rigidities of traditional forms while imposing newer and unexpected restrictions on the spontaneous African feeling. As the chapter on negritude tried to demonstrate, the African poet is thus perpetually engaged in a struggle to maintain his essential identity against the constricting measures of another tongue.

2

Historically, it is possible to trace the beginnings of African poetry in the European languages, not in African itself but among African exiles in Europe and among slaves and the ex-slaves of the New World. Thus from the very start African writing in European languages betrays its deepest characteristic: first, alienation from African soil, both physical and psychological; secondly, an awareness, even though sometimes painfully suppressed, of politics as the conditions of its operation, while simultaneously serving to inaugurate that first serious split between those writers and poets who would carry out the 'task' of defending African interests, and those who for whatever reason − of convenience or necessity − were content to hide behind a 'mask' of a newly assumed culture.

Slavery was a great initiator of a new consciousness among African exiles. The various forms and degrees of this bondage had some unforeseen consequences. After being taken into captivity, some slaves were taught to read and write, and, occasionally, were even encouraged to dabble in the so-called 'civilised arts' of their masters such as music, painting and literature. A great deal of research awaits to be done in this area, but already work of some impressive scholarship has been undertaken in collecting and annotating writings in prose by African exiles and ex-slaves such as Olaudah Equiano, Ignatius Sancho, Ottalah Cuguano and others; there is also sufficient evidence, as the historians of African literature have been pointing out, that individual Africans wrote verse in both classical and modern European languages which was of more than passing interest.

As far back as the 16th century we encounter in Spanish Granada a figure like Juan Latino, a slave in the household of the Duke of Sesa, brought to Spain from Africa with his enslaved mother at the age of twelve. Educated with the

Duke's young grandson at the cathedral school, Latino later went on to the University of Granada where he studied poetry, music and some medicine.[1] He married the daughter of a Spanish nobleman, and wrote the standard eulogies in Latin of the high dignitaries, including an elegy to Pope Pius V in four parts, the two-part *Austriad* which celebrates the victory of Don Juan of Austria at the Battle of Lepanto, and the *Epigrammatum Liber* composed in honour of the birth of Prince Ferdinand in 1571. Though we can safely assume that Latino became as fully integrated into Spanish society as it was possible for a man of colour to be in a slavocratic society of sixteenth-century Europe, he never entirely lost his sense of identity as an African. Nor, as made obvious by Encisco's drama about the poet, would the Spanish let him forget his colour. In a play that often reminds us of Desdemona in *Othello*, Doña Ana, Latino's wife, is made to protest her husband's nobility though she never questions, except by implication, her belief in the superiority of a white colour:

> You make of color sole criterion,
> Discounting that fine equilibrium
> That comes from mind well poised, and noble works
> Born of that rational tranquility.
> Are yearnings of the heart as naught to you?
> If heaven decreed this object for my love,
> The height of his perfection can be read
> In those same terms that measure my descent.
> The world holds his embrace dishonored me —
> His loving arms left stain of ugly black.[2]

And she goes on:

> Love forces me to give my hand to one
> Who, although black, deserves the name of man.
> In giving I win back all that I lost
> In those embraces of his dusky arms.[3]

Obviously a bold, self-confident man, Latino seems to have seen himself as a unique poetic voice, as he makes obvious in the prologue to *Epigrammatum· Liber* when he announces: 'Unique is the victor and seeks a unique poet/A great deed requires an author; a poet ought to have been born for your brother, greatest Philip.'[4] As Professor Dathorne puts it 'his was the first individual African poetic voice to address the pope and royalty'[5] and Latino's awareness of his racial identity emerges clearly in the lines:

> For if the Blackness of our king offends your official ministers
> Your whiteness does not delight the men of Ethiopia
> There, whoever in his whiteness visits the East is scorned,
> And there are Black leaders; the King too is dark
> Queen Candace and her race of black ministers
> Had sent her son in a chariot to Christ.[6]

All the same, proud as Juan Latino was of his colour, such was his upbringing and training, that he seemed not only to have accepted Christianity unconditionally but seems also to have become more of a Spanish patriot than an African nationalist. Forgetful, or not caring to mention the reasons why he and his mother had been brought to Spain in the first place, Latino now chooses to praise Philip for bringing Christianity to the Africans. 'Famous Philip, you are my protector against the Turks/Reigning as a Catholic, you have been accustomed to defend our countries, and in a more holy way to cherish the Faith.'[7] As Spratlin rightly sums up: 'Juan Latino, though proud of his colour, was hardly an advocate of racial culture. Turning his back on the tribal gods, he accepts Christianity as the universal religion and commends Philip for his missionary efforts among the Africans.'[8]

In his recent work Professor Dathorne finds an element in Latino's work, which he describes as his 'preoccupation with panegyrics'. Dathorne seems to detect here an emotional link with African 'praise-poetry' and explains Latino's 'preoccupation' as having been 'the result of his African origin'.[9] Before we get carried away by this sort of speculation it might be well to reflect that Latino arrived in Spain at the age of twelve, and received almost all his education in Spanish and Latin; writing laudatory verses to the great and powerful was a fairly widespread practice in Europe and required no particular African predisposition.

The list of Africans who found themselves in Europe during and immediately after the Renaissance and wrote some verse which may seem to us now only interesting as curiosities can be extended to include James Eliza John Capitein, carried off from West Africa to Holland as a boy, who thereafter received his education at the University of Leyden, and later not only translated the Bible into Fanti, one of the Ghanaian languages, but improved on the Ten Commandments – so thorough was his 'education' in the hands of the rich Dutch merchants – by substituting in the place of God the following: 'I am Jan Company who brought you out of Egypt.'[10]

The other was Anton Wilhelm Amo, born in 1703, also from what is now Ghana, who was brought to Amsterdam as a slave when he was only four years old. Presented to the Duke Anton Ulrich von Braunschweig Wolfenbuttel, he attended the University of Halle, after gaining a degree in law, went to Wittenberg University where he obtained a degree in philosophy.

However, of those Africans who had recourse to the art of versification during slavery and after, no example is more celebrated or more potent for what it can tell us of the stifled creative potential of many blacks taken into captivity than the plight, in many ways a less desperate one, of Phillis Wheatley, a Senegalese girl disgorged by a slaveship in Boston in 1761. Aged only seven when she was brought to the American colonies the African slave girl was sold to one wealthy Bostonian, John Wheatley, in whose family she was later brought up. Noticing the girl's unusual intellectual flair, John Wheatley's wife taught the young Senegalese to read and write and encouraged her other intellectual pursuits. Phillis Wheatley became not only a cultivated slave woman, familiar with the currently admired English writers of her day, including Alexander Pope, whom she largely imitated; her poems were also full of classical allusions deriving from her wide reading of Latin authors, chiefly

Ovid. Not a great poet by any means, she nevertheless wrote verse sometimes superior to that of her white contemporaries, and if she is not as widely known as they the fault lies with historians of American literature who have been slow to accord Phillis Wheatley her rightful place in American letters.

As the first skilful poet of her race in America a curious ambiguity attaches to Phillis Wheatley. She was, to say the least, something of a social climber, determined like her Renaissance African counterparts in Europe, to please her captors, and the bulk of her work 'consists of poems addressed to people of prominence',[11] including the Earl of Dartmouth, the Countess of Huntingdon, and King George III. She was obviously a far more complex individual than might at first appear from the effusive platitudes of much of her verse. During the struggle for American independence she evinced an ardent patriotism which was presumably shared by many other slaves, some of whom actually fought side by side with American rebels in the exaggerated hope that once the war was over they might extract some concessions for their own race. About Africa and about slavery Phillis Wheatley was, however, curiously reticent; where she had occasion to remember Africa, her native land, she was invariably patronising or apologetic:

> 'Twas mercy brought me from my pagan land,
> Taught my benighted soul to understand
> That there's a God and there's a Saviour too;
> Once I redemption neither sought nor knew.[12]

If the name of Phillis Wheatley is evoked here it is not out of any desperate wish to stake a claim upon her poetry as *African*. I cite her name mainly for two reasons. The first concerns matters of historical fact: Phillis Wheatley was an African, although it is possible to argue that her upbringing and education made her first a royalist, and, paradoxically for an African slave, an American poet. The second reason has something to do with the social and political conditions in which African poetry in European languages has its origins: Phillis Wheatley's barely suppressed hostility to her native land, her unctuous, unquestioning Christianity, her anxious servility and her precipitate desire to flatter her superiors, are not as we have already seen, isolated qualities for which we should single her out among the poets of her time. By the time we reach the modern period at the beginning of the century, the conflicting but pressing claims of Christianisation and Western education on the one hand, and the need to defend the validity of an African civilisation as well as to assert the birthright of a dispossessed people on the other, had created sufficient tension within the main body of African writing to enable us to talk meaningfully of a 'split personality'. For the first time in African literature we are confronted with the phenomenon of the so-called 'man of two worlds'.

3

The advent of missionaries in Africa brought to the African communities the printing presses and the written scripts, and with these the first translations of the Bible and the church hymns; from this fare, supplemented by simplistic moral tales designed for the new converts, were laid the foundations for a literary activity that would soon include the rendering into vernacular languages of the more adaptable narratives of European literature such as Bunyan's *Pilgrim's Progress*, Defoe's *Robinson Crusoe*, Swift's *Gulliver's Travels*, and the timeless plays of William Shakespeare. Almost everywhere in Africa the pattern was the same. By the 1820s in South Africa the Scottish missionaries had firmly laid the groundwork for the literary activity which would culminate in that first flowering of African literature the most notable representatives of which were Mqhayi, Jolobe, Bereng, Vilakazi and H.I.E. Dhlomo.

The last two are among the founding members of the very strong protest movement which has been the marked feature of South African verse in more than a quarter of a century. In his two poems, 'Because' and 'On the Gold Mines', first written in Zulu and later translated into English, B.W. Vilakazi, the late Zulu scholar and poet, took up the cause of the newly urbanised African worker, especially the severely exploited mine labourer, in verse which showed in its content if not in its style a major break with previous African poetry in which the element of 'protest' had been carefully muted. Noting the immense disadvantages under which the African labourer produced wealth for the privileged white minority, noting also the supposed acquiescence of the African worker because of a not clearly articulated sense of grievance, Vilakazi self-consciously assumed in his poem, 'Because', the artless voice of the common man in order to protest his condition:

> Because, when night approaches,
> You see me loosening the chains
> Of daily drudgery,
> And, meeting people black like me,
> Dance with new-born energy
> While chanting tribal songs
> That rouse our stifled zest
> And banish weariness:
> You think me but an animal
> Who, should it die, is soon replaced.[13]

Nevertheless, for all its worthy sentiment, the poem's disguised persona, a highly educated university professor assuming the offended *naiveté* of a mine worker, unintentionally gave to Vilakazi's protest message, especially in the last stanza, a stilted, even patronising, tone. In contrast, his other poem 'On the Gold Mines' had a straightforward approach, a distinctness of voice, that only sharpened the 'protest' and helped to improve the diction — at any rate, in the English translation. This description of the white foreman is typical of the poem's chilled accuracy which somehow managed to slough off the naive sentimentality of the first:

> Bellow you frenzied bulls of steel!
> Far is that place where first you came to life
> And — roasted by fiery furnaces
> Until you were ready and only ash remained —

Were quickly dispatched, and having crossed the sea
Were loaded on trucks, for puffing fuming engines
To bring you to Goli,[1] place of gold, and us.
Loudly you bellowed, till we, like frightened dassies
Swarming towards you, answered your strident summons.[14]

All the same, Vilakazi's poems, especially in their English translation, present the critic with a special problem: do these poems belong to African verse of English expression or do they remain essentially Zulu works whose rendering into English merely distorts the poet's intention? The problem is compounded by Vilakazi's largely wasted attempts to apply the laws of English prosody to the Zulu originals, so that in so far as we can speak of Vilakazi's verse at all in English translation, we are forced in the end to fall back on the content. Only of the Zulu originals are we entitled to speak confidently in regard to their diction, metre and rhyme; and where these are concerned, while Vilakazi clearly realised the potentially fruitful use to which traditional 'praise poetry' could be put, the more pervasive influence in many of his compositions is that of English romantic verse. To put it as bluntly as possible, Vilakazi's revolutionary themes are not matched by a similar revolutionary approach to poetic technique. Consequently, repeatedly aware of these echoes from another tradition, we are obliged in discussing Vilakazi's work to confine ourselves only to those of his achievements about which there can be no dispute: these pertain mostly to the strong 'social content' for which Vilakazi was rightly admired, the open political 'protest' for which he is judged to have elevated vernacular literature from its habitual attachment to folklorish material into a medium capable of dealing with serious social issues.

As a 'mission school' product Vilakazi was less fettered by his background than many of his contemporaries. This becomes immediately apparent when we examine the work of a poet like J.J.R. Jolobe. A respected Xhosa poet and minister of the Presbyterian church, he too, translated some of his verse into English; but whereas the 'mission school' influence is evident throughout Jolobe's work, especially in his deep commitment to Christian values in opposition to the 'pagan' religion of his people, or his adherence to the notion of some more enlightened European culture compared to whose dazzling light he regrettably saw around him only 'the gloomy shadows of our land/Of darkness and of ignorance', Vilakazi, by contrast, is obsessed by thoughts of a departed glory, by the grandeur of vanished African kingdoms.

When first I heard our tribal songs
They seemed to me of little worth;
But now their message echoes in my heart.
Secrets and timeless passions haunt a lilt
Inspired by Zululand's sons and their traditions.
These songs recall a past so swiftly fading
That now I fear its meaning may elude me
Although I weep with longing to preserve it.[15]

113

Thus Vilakazi was not only the first vernacular poet in South Africa to bring to African verse a very acute sense of social conflict, deliberately spelled out in class terms, a fact which may account for his popularity with the left,[16] but he also injected into his poetry an increasingly rueful note of nationalistic protest, lamenting what he saw as the colonial spoliation of traditional African cultures. Himself a linguist, dedicated to the study and renewal of the Zulu language, Vilakazi wrote largely in his mother-tongue; nevertheless in his own translations and those of his admirers his was a voice that would somehow manage subtly to penetrate the barrier between Zulu originals and the English translations of his work.

Herbert I.E. Dhlomo, another Zulu poet, also a playwright and vigorous commentator on culture and politics, did not have to face problems of translations. He wrote directly into English. With his sharply polemical essays and with the publication in 1941 of his long poem, *Valley of a Thousand Hills* he gave to South African 'protest poetry' its single most extended work. The poem's ambitious scope, its combination of a 'nature' theme familiar to lovers of traditional English verse, with a vigorous protest at the defeat and humiliation of Zulu power, were crucial in ensuring for the author a wider attention at its publication than had hitherto been accorded a work by an African writer. Norman Head's effusive introduction to the 1941 Knox edition was typical of the wide, sometimes astonished, welcome by white liberals for a work which, if it did nothing else, proved, at least, an African could fashion words into a recognisable poetical pattern worthy of serious critical attention. Head wrote that the poem:

> . . . carries an exciting narrative quality that gives it a special interest apart from its metrical form and the beauty of its language. Starting out from a deep underground spring of agony it flows forth as a swift river, a strong current of feeling pouring through a conducting body of pure lyricism. It is the cry of a once-proud nation stricken to the dust, mortified of body, its spirit humbled, its conscience burning and alive.[17]

Head's delineation of the major themes of the poem was generally correct but his enthusiastic praise of its method strikes the modern reader as somewhat exaggerated. Judged by modern standards, and placed alongside such modern practitioners of the art of verse in South Africa as Dennis Brutus, the late Arthur Nortje or even a more tradition-conscious poet such as Mazisi Kunene, Dhlomo's *Valley* seems 'poetical' in a strained, old-fashioned way, too much beholden to an outmoded English diction and metre: words like 'yore', 'writ', 'ambrosial' and 'beauteous' — words which had become the 'stock-in-trade' of traditional English verse — occur throughout the poem; add to this the frequent references to classical European mythology and a certain clumsy inversion of syntax, mannerisms which were, incidentally, equally typical of the West African poets of the pioneering school, the result was the engendering of certain atmosphere in the poem which smacked of a synthetic literary style, depriving the poem of an authentic African voice. Here, for instance, in Dhlomo's description of Shaka, king of the Zulus, sometimes compared to 'Jove', we see exemplified a great deal of what went wrong with the poem:

> Born sealed with immortality
> Hymned Shaka, god of war-writ fame,
> Homeric feats attained, and we
> Plumed Trojan Black Bulls, claim a name![18]

Though there is an unmistakable similarity between Dhlomo and
Vilakazi's failure to adapt lessons learned from English verse to their own native
tradition, Vilakazi at least enjoyed the advantage of having written mostly in
his mother tongue, with the result that however derivative his poetics it could
not include the use of an exact European imagery and terminology as Dhlomo
was sometimes compelled to do. Regrettably, in spite of Head's assertions to the
contrary, except very intermittently, lyrical 'purity' is precisely what Dhlomo's
poem fails to achieve. Too many hackneyed phrases from English verse adhere
to what is paradoxically a poem about a very tradition-conscious people; even
where the poet exploits the heritage of 'praise-poetry', as Maria K. Mootry so
rightly observed,[19] the metrical movement of the lines remains that of English
formal verse.

Since Mphahlele's initial comment on Dhlomo's poem[20] critics have tended
to over-emphasise the author's debt to Shelley, Byron and Keats to the exclusion of any other influences; but in his handling of syntax Dhlomo often draws
on even earlier sources, chiefly in his attempts to emulate Milton's weightier
moral tone. A line like 'Hold still/You gasping craggy heights, you valleys
deep!'[21] even tries to convey the music of Miltonic verse.

Romantic in tone the poem generally is, but Mootry rightly defends
Dhlomo against Mphahlele's more wanton strictures;[22] whatever its failures
may be, *Valley of a Thousand Hills* remains an important contribution to
Anglo-African poetry of the pioneering school; in its subject-matter if not in its
technique, in its tone of protest and its unrestrained nationalist feeling, it
charts a new course for African verse of English expression which was increasingly to reject white missionary tutelage in favour of a new African identity, a
cultural development whose political consequences were soon to become
obvious. At the time, a missionary commentator who clearly discerned the
directions in which African poetry in South Africa was moving, wrote with
enthusiasm of what he thought had already been achieved:

It is one of the heartening features of the present time that although Bantu
poetry is in a transition stage between the old and new — between the poetic
outbursts of the praises of the Chief and new forms for which European
poetry has supplied the patterns — there are signs of promise of a new age of
Bantu poetic expression. Men like Mqhayi, Jolobe, Bereng, Vilakazi, H.I.E.
Dhlomo and others are making no little offering to the literature of the
race.[23]

If Dhlomo's efforts toward this end were continually frustrated by a sub-
servience to an alien poetic tradition which was incapable of supporting too
strict a revolutionary break with a Western manner of making poetry, we must
remember that short of a conscious attack on language itself a great many poets
both in Europe and the colonies were equally incapable of initiating a poetry of

115

true originality, properly attuned to the spirit of the times. Not until the innovations of Pound and Eliot were fully assimilated was a new poetic idiom fashioned out capable of expressing the true genius of contemporary life. The modern African poets no less than their European counterparts were to benefit from this sudden release from the constricting measures of traditional English verse.

Having said that, we should still be in a position to appreciate the achievements of men like Dhlomo, even allowing for the kind of limitations they were unable to transcend. Occasionally, through an intensity of feeling and the sincerity of the emotion, Dhlomo does manage to attain impressive heights of lyrical power. A sense of loss, a feeling of genuine distress at the impoverishment and decline of a once-powerful nation, counter-balanced only by an admiration for the natural beauty of the land, constitute the nodal points of tension in the poem:

> A bird
> Sung song was never heard before by men
> Around the Valley of a Thousand Hills!
> In mingled joy and pain heard I and cried:
> 'From whence you come, pain, beauty, love and joy
> Have mingled out into a bloom of song!
> But here on earth Man's Soul remains the toy
> Of inharmonious processes which long
> Have raged; here where our youth and joys are mocked
> By want and tears; where, like the dead, foul dust
> Shuts tight our door; where age, deemed wise, is rocked
> By scourge and fear and hate! here where we must
> Deceive and fawn, serve shams, and crawl like worms a place
> To find, and die to live! Where crafty eyes
> Of gain and power, devour devoid of grace!
> Not like thy song do men here fall . . . then rise!'[24]

But what status can we assign to that other poet, Jolobe, already mentioned in the same context as Dhlomo and Vilakazi? That after Mqhayi, who wrote only in Xhosa, Jolobe was one of the best Xhosa poets of the pioneering school there can be no doubt; but against his best virtues must be set those negative qualities which characterise the work of most of the 'mission school' poets who, to use Mazisi Kunene's thesis, were persuaded that 'their ways are evil, that they have a repulsive system of values'.

Although this could not have been wholly the view of a poet like Jolobe, in South Africa as well as in West Africa, in the works of a man like Jolobe, as in poems of Osadebay, Casely-Hayford and Armattoe, we encounter in terms that can allow no doubt at all the initial crisis of those African poets who were too obviously indebted to missionary influence for their original impulse to write. Clearly, they found it difficult to harmonise the conflicting claims of the two ways of life, the African and the European ones, which had so decisively shaped their consciousness in the way that Ezekiel Mphahlele, a man of a later generation, was to claim he could.[25]

This conflict of loyalties between the Western and African traditions, the tendency encouraged largely by the missionaries to regard African culture as 'pagan' and, therefore, as somehow 'degenerate', is best exemplified by a passage in Jolobe's long narrative poem, *Thuthula*, which dramatises the struggles between Ngqika, the young prince, and Ndlambe, his uncle and regent.

Initially the cause of the conflict seems to have been political, the consequence of a struggle for succession between uncle and nephew, but later the dispute degenerates into a contest between Christians and anti-Christians of which a plan to abduct Thuthula from Ndlambe, her royal husband, is only one cunning part. There is very little attempt in the poem to integrate the two themes, the private and the public, the marital and the political; but somehow attached to the main strands of the narrative is the episode relating to Ntsikana's conversion to Christianity. In Jolobe's poem, Ntsikana, a revered poet-prince of the Xhosa people, and the first royal convert to Christianity, first appears at Ndlambe's wedding on the eve of his conversion to the new faith, Ntsikana is invited to take part in the Xhosa wedding dance but declines. No doubt, fully accepting the teachings of the Christian missionaries, who frequently regarded African dancing as sexually gross and immoral, Jolobe carries this attitude right to the centre of the poem. Ntsikana's rather Pauline conversion is staged against the background of the festive Xhosa dance; and soon enough it becomes obvious that so far as Jolobe is concerned this dance symbolises everything in African culture that is 'pagan' and 'benighted' from which Ntsikana must eventually be saved. Indeed, from the moment that Van der Kemp succeeds in imparting the evangelical message to Ntsikana the latter becomes, to use Jolobe's own delightfully apt simile, as 'game' pursued by the 'Hound of Heaven': and though Ntsikana is present at the dance, and though his mates call encouragingly to him, 'inviting him to come/And join them in the dancing step', Ntsikana continues to sit passively, wrapped up in his blanket, meditating:

> At last he rose in readiness to dance.
> The Grace of God, however, intervened,
> As if an angel waved its wings with might
> A whirlwind strong did rush across the court
> And down he sat. He had not raised a foot.
> In course of time again he stood to dance:
> The mighty wind once more did rush and blow.
> Ntsikana grave responded to his call.
> His goods he now collects and gives command
> To his dear wives with him home to return.
> Forwith he cleansed himself of ochre red,
> And uttered some strange things by word of mouth.
> He said, 'This thing I hear says we must pray.'
> He raised his voice, appealing to his tribe
> To shun all evil and embrace the good.[26]

Just as in the case of Dhlomo and Vilakazi, Jolobe's technique, if one can call it that, owes almost everything to European prosody: in this respect, his sonnet, 'To Light', is particularly enlightening.

In spite of Jolobe's not very secret aversion to African religious custom and practice, which is constantly reinforced by the use of such imagery as 'darkness deep/Of mind and soul' or 'gloomy shadows of our land'; in spite of his abiding faith in British democracy and the much vaunted British sense of fair play; in a poem like 'To the Fallen', which registers the full natural shock about the Second World War casualties, one begins to sense in Jolobe a troubling ambiguity which is only made sharper, not blunter, by his almost desperate willingness to find a brighter side to every national calamity. The comforting rhetoric of lines like 'They looked beyond and saw the fruit, vast gains/To their own race, to mankind and the world,' was now increasingly undercut by the worried recognition that black volunteers may have been sacrificed to defend an Empire that had always ill-used its black subjects and, more culpably, had no intention of modifying its attitude.

4

Various commentators have emphasised the 'public' nature of the first output by African poets, the constantly 'moralising' tone into which they so casually slipped, but I think we ought equally to recognise the sense of responsibility which encouraged these pioneering poets to assume such public postures. Chief Dennis Osadebay, the Nigerian jurist and politician and author of a collection of verse, Michael Dei-Anang, a Ghanaian civil servant, and producer of two collections of verse, Raphael Ernest Grail Armattoe, the late Gold Coast physician, anthropologist, historian and poet, and Gladys Casely-Hayford; they are just some of the poets who were not simply interested in the technicalities of the art of versification, though in his introduction to one of his collections Armattoe made a brave attempt to represent himself as such; as can be seen from the varied professional interests they represented, they were also public figures in their own right who saw themselves as 'pioneers' in the great movement for the modernisation of the continent. As far as these men and women were concerned, verse had a decided function to serve in society: and this function was to 'educate' and to 'uplift'. What, therefore is so often dismissingly described as 'public posturing' in their verse derives in part from this sense of 'mission', so that we can apply to them the term 'missionary poets' in a double sense: firstly, in the sense of their having been influenced by missionary education, and secondly, for having been committed to the notion that those Africans who had acquired an education had to 'uplift' and 'improve' the condition of their fellow Africans. The pride, the intention, the sense of urgency in their task can be gathered from Osadebay's poem, 'Young Africa's Explanation' in which he plainly asserts:

> I am a critic
> And never take a thing for granted;
> Assumptions of my fathers' days
> Are stumbling blocks across my ways;
> To clear them in my duty call,
> To walk erect and never crawl.[28]

This sounds very much like a blanket rejection of African value-systems in a scramble for Western novelty; but in fact Osadebay was very much a committed nationalist who clearly saw part of this 'task' as assisting in the regeneration of Africa.

Out of this school of West African poets a more racially combative poet than the Ghanaian, M.F. Dei-Anang, would be difficult to find: full of allusions to the decayed grandeur of the African past, inspired with new hopes for the future, the themes of Dei-Anang's poetry consist of the usual paraphernalia of black nationalism: there is the constant reiteration of past African achievement, so precisely stated in his lines, 'I love to dwell in the past/Among the ruins of long ago'; there is the usual modulation from a vision of pre-colonial Africa in its pristine purity and nobility to an angry record of its debasement and humiliations during the colonial era, from the Africa 'who nursed the doubtful child/Of civilization' to an Africa 'Partitioned and pawned/In centuries of greed'; in all this, pride of race is the engine of Dei Anang's poetry. His inclination toward negritude themes before he was obliged to reject these tendencies on ideological grounds, can be seen in his humorous version of the creation in which the white race is seen to be the result of God's failure to repeat his initial success when creating the blacks; in the view of the poet the whites are a pathetic result of the 'water-colour' growing 'faint and limpid:/Too pale to make another Darkie'. However, as with most 'pioneer' African poets who wrote on the eve of the post-war independence movement, after recapitulating the history of Africa's trials and sorrows, there is a great surge of optimism that deliverance must be at hand. After the lamentation, there comes a testament of faith contained in the ringing declaration: 'Dark Africa!/My dawn is here'.

The effort to stimulate interest among Africans in the past achievements of their race, and the certainty that it is familiarity with this history which will inspire the new generation to strive harder in their own chosen tasks, is the subject of Dei-Anang's long and ambitious poem, 'Awake, Ye Gold Coast Sons!' in which the author attempts nothing less than a summary of the history of the black race. It is an account of the movement of the African people from the region of the Nile across the Sudan, the raising of once-powerful empires, their final decline and fall. Throughout the poem racial pride is mitigated only by a melancholy sense of loss about the immense squander of the material and spiritual heritage of the African people. Describing the journey of the African peoples from Upper Egypt across the Sudan the poet mourns:

> Those tunes
> They sang
> That took away
> The treach'rous pang
> Of desert thirst,
> Or kept the lion
> In bloody lair
> Are lost today.[29]

Until the distressingly inept attitudinising of the later verse of *Ghana Glory*, which is not only jingoistic in tone but seems in its discussion of public issues to be governed entirely by the poet's relations with the Nkrumah regime as its court-poet, Dei-Anang's previous work had always exhibited moments of sharp clarity, despite the usual limitations in technique, which were reflected in the acid simplicity of the language. Of course, one need not exaggerate the achievements of poets like Dei-Anang; indeed, there has often been greater temptation to belittle everything these poets wrote; but occasionally, it seems to me, one comes across some lines which can stand with the finest in the English language. The first stanza of Dei-Anang's 'Blest are the Ears' even succeeds in echoing the breathless majesty of Henry Vaughan's 'I saw eternity the other night'. Here it is:

> Blest are the ears
> Attuned to hear
> The distant music
> Of the spheres[30]

And in the third stanza there is a line which contains the harsh proposition that 'living is strife', that the joy of living belongs to 'the happy few'; but the last four lines present us with something of a metaphysical conceit which brings out with excellent economy the sense of uninterrupted enjoyment of leisure; the conceit is in the form of a paradox, a sort of progression without movement from one state to a similar one, when life is pictured as

> a ceaseless conference
> With joy, a smooth sequence
> From mirth to mirth.[31]

In *Ghana Glory*, a collection of verse launched in 1965 with the prestige of a Foreword by the late Kwame Nkrumah, Dei-Anang's patriotic fervour, previously always tempered with a proper degree of realism ('I bring thee now/No vain recollection/Of former power') has degenerated into the sycophantic banality of 'Inside and Outside', a poem extolling the virtues of Kwame Nkrumah's book, *Consciencism*. In its meretriciousness, this kind of feeble versification is exceeded only by the embarrassingly vapid rhetoric of another poem, 'Come to Ghana', which suggests the fabricated stridency of the writers of travel brochures:

> Come to Ghana
> When it's April
> There's beauty everywhere;
> Come to Ghana
> When you are lonely
> There's gladness everywhere,
> There's beauty all the way.[32]

How a mind as complex as that of the late Raphael Grail Armattoe, another poet of the 'pioneering school', would have responded to this kind of super-patriotic mush it is difficult to imagine. After all, he, too, had once written a 'nice' poem about his native Denu, which he described as a 'land of the cane and palm/Where men are strong and calm/And girls are straight and true',[33] lines which may strike us as better poetry than Dei-Anang's 'Come to Ghana', but not as constituting a very great advance, either in critical vigour or the choice of imagery. And yet, and here is the paradox, any critic who has read Armattoe with, at least, a certain measure of sympathy and care, must harbour the suspicion that he would have dismissed 'Come to Ghana' as the kind of 'charming' nonsense that he so repeatedly and cruelly satirised.

If this is so, justified or not, that suspicion must tell us something about the kind of man Armattoe was. A man of complicated sensibility, except in minor details, his social background was not so different from that of many West and South African intellectuals of his generation. Born in what was then the Gold Coast, he had left for Europe aged only thirteen in order to pursue further studies. Qualifying as a medical doctor, he practised in Northern Ireland for ten years before returning to the Gold Coast in 1950, partly to enter politics. Donatus I. Nwoga properly observes that when Armattoe returned to the Gold Coast he found it 'impossible to fit into the political scene in the country'. An impression left on the reader, as much by Armattoe's writing as by the manner of his falling out with Ghanaian politicians, is of a vigorous intellect marked by a morose irascibility, a sharp tongue which was always coated with a melli-fluous but damning phrase; for what makes Armattoe's voice unique among his generation is not so much his preoccupation with the twin concerns of all the African nationalists of the time — colonial freedom and material progress — but a temperament in which anger and impatience were barely controlled by a well-developed talent for sharp satire.

The querulous tone characteristic of so much of Armattoe's poetry is typi-fied by, among other things, his choice of words for dedication of his *Deep Down The Blackman's Mind* to the 'loving memory to Kwame Nkrumah and his friends who wanted to bury the author alive in 1902',[35] or that other caustic dedication of 'The White Man's Grave' to Sir Francis Galton, F.R.S., founder of the Galton Laboratory, University College, London, who, according to Armattoe, 'hoped the yellow races of China might "extrude hereafter the coarse and lazy Negroes from at least the metaliferous regions of tropical Africa".'[36]

Indeed, the tone of the two dedications has the further function of illu-minating for us the dangerously exposed, and rather ambiguous position of men like Armattoe, eminent in their own right as scholars or public figures, often born in privileged positions of social ease, and therefore naturally inclined to see themselves as part of some vaguely defined aristocratic class: all the same, the social climate of the time, which has not changed that remark-ably since, ensured that even if these men had wanted to there was no easy way in which they could have escaped the common injury daily inflicted on their more lowly fellows for the imaginary sin of being born black; for they were often tarred, to use an apt popular phrase of the time, with the same brush. In his self-chosen role as a defender of the status of black people, Armattoe's position was a particularly ambiguous one: while railing endlessly against their shiftless-ness, he was, obviously, as much concerned for the well-being of black people as he was sometimes inclined to be impatient with what he regarded as their lack of push and initiative. As he once wrote in another poem: 'Is there aught to keep him (the Negro) down/But his whining lowdown moan?' And in the preface to *Between the Forest and the Sea* Armattoe was explicit on this point: 'The African people are a gay, improvident people full of charm amidst misery and desolation. To an outsider they seem to be in a perpetual turmoil of hilarity.'[37]

The words 'gay' and 'charm' suggest at once a talent for making the provocative statement while hinting, perhaps, at Armattoe's tendency to adopt toward black people the lofty air of a paternalistic observer of their follies; similarly, his poetry is an amalgam of nationalist sentiment, declarations of racial pride, epistles to imaginary poets and living acquaintances, some polemical stuff, and, above all, satirical sallies against the offending shortcomings of his contemporaries.

It is in his sardonic wit, his willingness to use ridicule impartially to lash out against the frailties of his own kind as well as against those he came to recognise as the true enemies of the black race, that Armattoe's uniqueness among pioneering poets can be said to lie. The 'pioneers' were generally a humourless lot, heavy with moral purpose. Armattoe's fierce pride, on the other hand, was tempered by a mordant wit which seemed uncommonly suited for castigating the peccant and the corrupt. The racial pride is real enough and publicly stated. As he himself was to express it in one of his poems: 'I like being prouder than all men.' This assertion is supplemented by a whole range of minor poems which can be said to belong roughly to the negritude theme. 'Our God is Black' is perhaps his most famous:

> Our God is black!
> Black of eternal Blackness
> With large voluptuous lips,
> Matted hair and brown liquid eyes.[38]

But as always with Armattoe, his statements of the race theme were always governed by an underlying irony, sometimes barely hinted at, which always seemed to provide an escape hatch from the intolerable hyperbole. For instance, it is difficult to know in what spirit we are expected to read some of the lines in 'Negro Heaven':

> But somewhere, not here, liveth He,
> Blackest of the Blackest of men
> Coal, coal-black of form, dark of mind,
> Omnipotent, immense, profound,
> He protecteth the little tadpoles
> The blind mole and other black things[39]

At first this seems a straightforward statement of the negritude theme until we get to the lines about 'Angels black as Indian ink' and 'dark saints' singing 'In that blissful heaven of blackness' and suddenly it seems possible that the poem could be read in two ways in which the distancing critical faculty of one part of the poet's personality is perpetually and secretly mocking the other, racially assertive one. Indeed, for all Armattoe's pride of race, the dominant note of his poetry is one of a subtle contempt for his weaker, less intellectually equipped, brothers. Such fund of charity as he possessed, in any case never in large supply, was quickly exhausted, and what remained behind was the humour, often bitter, malicious, tormenting and tormented. Indeed, Armattoe's impatience with the frailties of others must have struck some readers as bordering on a kind of arrogant self-righteousness. Nothing save Armattoe's excessive pessimism could justify the view of humanity put across in a poem, 'The Human Race' in which we mortals are seen as somehow lower than the wild beasts:

> Give me always the willing beasts
> Which are never on bended knees
> To mortals worse and less than beasts.
> Beasts never fawn, cringe, whine nor curse
> Nor owe, own, steal nor lend their purse
> To fiends pretending to be friends.[40]

The final conundrum about a man of Armattoe's literary ambition is his failure to address himself adequately to the problem of poetical technique. The result of this failure was to reduce the content of his verse to doggerel trivia, some of which is seen to great disadvantage in an occasional poem like 'Why I sing'. The following lines, 'I sing because I'm sad/Or because I'm glad', is an occasion neither for great poetry nor awe-inspiring philosophy. Nor was Armattoe always noticeably hampered by any tendency toward immense originality; frequently he took an easy way out: the lines of the poem, 'The Month of May' ('Now is the month of May/For the hawthorn is in bloom'),[41] must have been snipped off from the poetical hedge of an English garden; and, 'Mother, you said/We shall not always wail/While others smile' had Countee Cullen's famous lines in *From the Dark Tower* as their true pedigree.

These failures seem strangely paradoxical given Armattoe's elevated opinion of his own poetic ability, or rather his high sense of mission. As Armattoe stated the matter: 'How then is it that the Negro in West Africa has done so little creative writing with his incomparable gift of song?'[42] And in this connection the poet spoke of 'the poverty of literary effort' among fellow West Africans which he said had 'induced' him to write his own verse.

Even more paradoxically, Armattoe's brief comment on poetic form is not only penetrating and unquestionably just but contains the only devastating indictment of the kind of verse his generation had produced, including his own output. Armattoe wrote: 'If the African is to command genuine respect and esteem among the great races of the world, he must know his past and express that past in authentic and unmistakable accents.'

Such a combination of tasks and responsibilities was to prove to be extra-ordinarily difficult for men like Dhlomo or Armattoe. About the African past they knew a great deal but an 'authentic and unmistakable accent' they certainly failed to achieve. Armattoe comes closest to expressing the true quality of his mind, which was scientific and objective, not in poetry of deep emotional profundity, but in light satirical verse in which he pointed off much that is idiotic in human conduct. Subtly ironic, but genial in tone, was the epistolary form he sometimes adopted. In 'A Letter to an African Poet in 5,000 A.D.', Armattoe could afford to poke fun at what he obviously put down as the 'gaiety' and 'charm' of the Africans while preserving a genuine affection for the human qualities of his people. Presumably written from beyond the grave, in this letter Armattoe requests information from an African poet living in 5000 A.D.:

> Are Nuba girls still tall and gay sentient
> and free, and are the virgins, tantalent
> and true, in our land? Do coy vestal
> maidens clad in beads, with ankle bells and
> parrot plumes, still dance in trance, with
> bobbing heads and lilting lips, round the
> iron trident of the Thunder God?

Armattoe could never let go of a good joke once be had found one.

> Confide to me . . . What new prophet is
> worshipped here below . . . But more amusing
> to my cold mind it would be if Negroes
> still believed in their immortal souls and
> white men came to take them seriously . . .
> And do good Americans, when they die, go
> to Paris still, and Negroes to heaven?[44]

5

I suppose what I have been at pains to make obvious here is the inconclusiveness of Kunene's model of the African 'elites' as mere collaborators with the colonial system, invariably sycophantic in their attitude towards their masters, when this model is applied too rigorously in explaining the particular predicament of the 'pioneering poets'; often products of the missionary insitutions, and frequently 'bourgeois nationalists', the 'pioneering poets' were by no means wholly lacking in a political consciousness of a kind: it is not as if their intention was always to deliver their people, kicking and screaming, to their new foreign masters; the issue was more complicated than that. Even in the verse of an avowedly Christian poet like Gladys Casely-Hayford, there is an easy acknowledgement of what she calls 'a glorious heritage/If you are black, or brown.'[45] When they occasionally promoted Western values, including Christianity, in opposition to African ones as the basis for that modernisation which they so honestly and fervently wished for their people, this advocacy was not without a troubled ambiguity. It is true that this ambiguity would acquire its most authentic articulation in the successful fusion of African and European images contained in the poetry which came to be written by the writers of the next generation. To define the nature of this technical advance, to state the variety of themes and styles which came to occupy the succeeding generation of poets, will now be our task.

REFERENCES

1   An account of Latino's life is contained in V.B. Spratlin's *Juan Latino, Slave and Humanist*, Spinner Press, Inc., New York 1938.

2   See *The Famous Drama of Juan Latino* by Diego Jimene de Encisco which is included in Spratlin's biography, p.186.

3   *Ibid.*

4   All my translations are based on extracts from Spratlin's *Latino* with corrections to the text made by comparison with the 1583 edition of Latino's poetry in the British Museum.

5   O.R. Dathorne, *The Black Mind: A History of African Literature*, University of Minnesota Press, Minneapolis, 1974, p.69.

6   Cf. Spratlin's version on p.41 with Latino's original.

7   Spratlin, p.46

8   Spratlin, p.42

9   Dathorne, p.69

10 See Janheinz Jahn, *A History of Neo-African Literature*, Faber, London, 1968 p.35.

11 James Weldon Johnson (ed.) *The Book of American Negro Poetry*, Harcourt Brace & World, New York, p.29.

12 *Ibid.*

13 B.W. Vilakazi, *Zulu Horizons*, rendered into English verse by F.L. Friedman from the literal translations of D. Mck. Malcolm J.M. Sikakana, Witwatersrand University Press, Johannesburg, 1973, p.93.

14 *Ibid.*, p.124

15 *Ibid.*, p.33

16 A collection of Vilakazi's verse was translated into Russian.

17 See Norman Head's Introduction to the first edition of Herbet I.E. Dhlomo, *Valley of a Thousand Hills*, Knox Publishing Company, Durban 1941.

18 Dhlomo, *Valley of a Thousand Hills*, p.1.

19 See Maria K. Mootry: 'Literature and Resistance in South Africa: Two Zulu Poets' in E.D. Jones (ed.) *African Literature Today*, 6, Heinemann, London, 1973, p.114.

20 Ezekiel Mphahlele, *The African Image*, Faber, 1962, p.183–6.

21 Dhlomo, *Valley of a Thousand Hills*, p.20.

22 Mootry, 'Literature and Resistance in South Africa: Two Zulu Poets', pp. 123 – 4.

23 See R.H.W. Shepherd, *Bantu Literature and Life*, Lovedale Press, Cape Province, January 1955, p.183.

24 Dhlomo, *Valley of a Thousand Hills*, p.14.

25 Mphahlele, *African Image*, p.53

26 James J.R. Jolobe, *Thuthula* (A Poem), Arthur H. Stockwell, London 1937, pp.15–16.

27 See, for example, Donatus I. Nwoga's Introduction to 'The Pioneer Poets' in *West African Verse*, Longmans, 1967, pp.121–4, and Gerald Moore and Ulli Beier, Introduction to *Modern Poetry From Africa*, Penguin, London 1963, pp.20–1.

28 Dennis Chukude Osadebay, *Africa Sings*, Arthur H. Stockwell, 1952; contained in Kraus Reprint, Nendeln, 1970, p.12

29 M.F. Dei-Anang, *Cocoa Comes to Mampong and Some Occasional Verses*, Methodist Book Depot, Cape Cost. Reprinted by Kraus, Nendeln, 1970 p.14.

30 Dei-Anang, *Cocoa* p.39.

31 *Ibid.*

32 Dei-Anang, *Ghana Glory*, Thomas Nelson, London, 1965, p.21.

33 From 'To Denu' in R.G. Armattoe, *Deep Down the Black Man's Mind*, Arthur H. Stockwell, 1950, p.5.

34 Nwoga, *West African Verse*, p.131.

35 Armattoe, *Deep Down*, p.8.

36 *Ibid.*, p.26.

37 R.G. Armattoe, *Between the Forest and the Sea: Collected Poems*, Lomeshie Research Centre, Northland Road, Londonderry, N. Ireland, p.2.

38 Armattoe, 'Deep Down', p.14.

39 *Ibid.*, p.13.

40 *Ibid.*, p.31–2.

41 *Ibid.*, p.31.

42 See Armattoe's Introduction to *Between the Forest and the Sea*, p.1.

43 *Between the Forest*, p.1a

44 *Ibid.*

45 Gladys Casely-Hayford, 'Rejoice' in Nwoga *West Africa Verse*, p.5

CHAPTER SEVEN

MODERN AFRICAN POETRY: ITS THEMES AND STYLES
B THE MODERNS

1

African literature is full of ambushes and minor booby-traps for anyone who relies too uncritically on the terminology of Western criticism. What, for example, makes one type of African poetry 'modern' and another not modern is the kind of problem which bedevils current discussion of African literature for the simple reason that our usual notion of the opposition between 'modern' and 'traditional' is insufficient to account for certain African poets the most sophisticated of whom have been trained in the handling of European verse forms but for reasons of choice and temperament continue to borrow a great deal of their technical equipment from the oral tradition.

Kofi Awoonor, Mazisi Kunene and Okot p'Bitek, to name only three African poets, have fashioned out a style and idiom that is very largely indebted to the oral traditions of their people; but it would be more than obtuse to consider someone like Awoonor anything but an exceptionally 'modern' poet and a very gifted one at that. In the case of Mazisi Kunene and Okot p'Bitek a separate argument can be made out, I think, of their being 'traditionalists' of some sort, but even with these two, the moment we start comparing their work with the general output of what we have come to call the 'pioneering poets', it becomes immediately apparent that their very deliberate and intelligent use of traditional forms, in some curiously paradoxical way, makes for a different kind of poetry from that of the 'pioneering school', a poetry that might even be said to be more 'modernist' in its tendencies.

The next problem in the discussion of modern African verse relates to the African poetry of French expression. The difficulty arises out of the confusion as to how to place French-speaking African poets who belong in time to the same period as the 'pioneers' of Anglophone Africa but are poets who, while handling similar themes, wrote verse strikingly different in tone and technical competence from that of their English-speaking contemporaries: Senghor, Dadié and the two Diops are some of the poets that readily come to mind.

It has become fashionable, I think, to regard the negritude poets who produced their best work just before and immediately after the Second World War as representing a stage in poetic development roughly parallel to that of the 'pioneering poets' of Anglophone Africa; in actual fact, even at their most conventional, French-speaking African poets seem in comparison to their English-speaking contemporaries to have produced a verse much fresher and more striking for its vigour and originality.[1]

What perhaps emerges most clearly from any comparative study of French and Anglo–African poets of this period is how totally men like Dhlomo,

Vilakazi, Dei-Anang, Osadebay and Armattoe were victims of a cranky form of conservatism in African education which, until very late in the day, remained particularly resistant to the kind of innovation which Pound and Eliot had already brought about in English verse: in most African schools the only kind of verse which continued to be considered legitimate was of the extremely conventional type, rigidly bound to regular metre and standard rhyme. Not until the succeeding generation of Anglo-African poets, a generation sufficiently aware of the latest experiments in English verse, does a new poetic sensibility begin to emerge. In many ways we can view the early work of such poets as Lenrie Peters, Abioseh Nicol and Gabriel Okara as providing a kind of bridge to the works of younger poets in which a new accent and a new diction became the most striking features. This experimentation, the attempts to integrate African and European linguistic elements, still goes on and shows no signs of declining, as can be attested to by the works of such poets as Awoonor, Soyinka, Wanodi, Lo Liyong and numerous others.

It is true that among the Nigerian poets the initial enthusiasm for Hopkins, Yeats, Eliot and Pound seems at times to have been vastly excessive: to take one case in point, in spite of some lines of remarkable beauty and purity Okigbo's earliest verse, apart from the African elements in it, can sometimes strike the reader as consisting largely of a pastiche of all the modernist poets he admired, chiefly Pound and Eliot but also the French symbolists; what is not in doubt, however, is that such 'imitations' − if imitations they were − were compelling the younger poets toward new explorations of language, enlarging the range of their expression, and enabling them, finally, to discover a proper register where the adopted language and the African sensibility could most be properly united.

Under the heading of 'the moderns' we shall, therefore, be discussing a variety of African poets, with a heterogeneity of styles and techniques; in the end what seems to unite them, and equally what seems to separate them from 'the pioneer poets', is a fundamental preoccupation with technique as important both in itself as well as providing the essential means for expressing a radically transformed cultural and political situation.

In contrast, what seems to have absorbed all the energies of 'the pioneer poets' were certain themes they regarded as urgent, method was left to look after itself: these themes, the fate of the Africans, the vicissitudes of colonial politics, pride in race and in African culture, were the overriding concerns. All the same, lack of a fresh and original approach made the verse seem dull and uninspired.

With the succeeding generation of poets the development of a proper style and idiom came to mean almost as much to them as content, if not more: the most traditional and the most experimental of the poets discussed under this heading are united only by their attitude to poetry, first and foremost as a way of using *language* in a certain way, and finally, as a way of communicating whatever ideas they wished to express more effectively.

2

In 1937, at the age of 36, Jean-Joseph Rabearivelo, one of the most celebrated

Malagasy poets this century, committed suicide in his native city of Antananarivo. 'I am alone and depressed,'[2] he wrote. 'The truth is I suffer and suffer all the more because there is no one in whom I can confide completely.'[3] Complaining of solitude, of feeling 'abandoned', and 'forgotten', Rabearivelo finally took his own life by swallowing cyanide on 22 June 1937. In the diary which he left behind he invoked the names of French poets who had similarly taken their lives in relatively early age. 'I sign myself J-J Rabearivelo. At the age of Gherin, at the age of Deubel, a little older than you, Rimbaud *ante-néant*.'[4] Thus ended one of the most remarkable lives in French Malagasy letters. Also, it is fair to say, from that very moment an enigma was born: that enigma, briefly stated, is how was it possible for a personality so sensitive to the predicament of the colonial subject, a talent so specifically endowed with an explosively rich creative vitality, to expend so much of that energy in producing poetry which even at its best seems to feed on pure air, seems, in fact, to feed on the liquid fragility of its own skies!

In their brief but excellent introduction to Rabearivelo's recently published volume of poetry, John Reed and Clive Wake allude to a 'disjunction experienced in [Rabearivelo] himself, between race and culture'.[5] In another brief notice of the poet's work, Ulli Beier observed that

> . . . nothing could be further removed from the themes and images of current French African poetry than the writing of Rabearivelo. Colonialism and the African personality do not figure in it, There are no tom-toms, palm trees, and black nude women.[6]

Although Beier obviously intends this as a compliment, the bare outline of the poet's life suggests that far from enriching his poetry, this deliberate exclusion of 'oppression and revolution' impoverished it; above all, the sense of isolation from his own people and the intense longing after metropolitan Parisian culture helped literally to kill Rabearivelo.

A largely self-educated man, the off-spring of an unmarried Hova woman, Rabearivelo not only taught himself enough to become one of the best of the minor poets of the French language, but increasingly he felt himself alienated from his own people and the life of the island around him. More and more he yearned after the culture of metropolitian France with which he strongly identified and from which he felt himself unfairly 'exiled'. In this regard he stands in sharp contrast to two other well-known Malagasy poets who succeeded him: Flavian Ranaivo, whose subject-matter and technique derive from the life and traditional songs of his people, and Jacques Rabemananjara, then a revolutionary poet whose identification with the island was of the most direct and political kind, some of his poetry having been composed in prison while awaiting execution.

Jean-Joseph Rabearivelo was, however strikingly different. He had succeeded not only in turning himself into a 'highly cultured Malagasy Frenchman', but in the words of Edouard Eliet, became 'a being apart, neither Malagasy nor French, something like a spiritual mulatto'.[7] 'Existentialist before its time, as Boudry says, his reading was wide, especially in the poetry of the French symbolists (what Boudry described as 'the nebulous symbolism') and the 'decaying Romanticism', with which 'he was saturated as the body of a drunkard is saturated with alcohol'. These 'rotted and distracted his mind'.[8] Predictably, this did not endear him to the rather provincial French colonial society of Malagasy; until he acquired a position as a proof-reader at the Imprimerie de L'Imerina, he was often unemployed, and, not surprisingly, apart from the literature which nourished his intense isolation he sought the means of escape in all forms of sensual excess, including gambling, drink, sex and drugs. In his desire to break away from this sense of isolation he kept up a ceaseless correspondence with numerous French writers, but like the bull of his poem, 'Zebu', who 'leaps' and 'lows' but who 'will die without glory' he was 'trapped' on the small island 'which he experienced as a prison'.[9] His feelings of 'loneliness', of being 'abandoned,' confirm this first impression of a poet whose absorption into an alien culture was so complete, or nearly so complete, that by comparison the life of his own island people seemed intolerably drab and profitless. It is not surprising that Rabearivelo's suicide came shortly after plans for him to join a Malagasy contingent to the Paris Exposition Universelle of 1937 had been brutally cancelled by the French administration and a group of basket-weavers sent there instead.

At this stage, a reader may well wonder just to what extent these minutiae of Rabearivelo's life may be said to bear upon the quality of his poetry. After all, we have the poems, he may argue, and like Russell in Joyce's *Ulysses*, he may well insist, 'When we read the poetry of *King Lear*, what is it to us how the poet lived?' In this case, I would suggest, everything. Rabearivelo's form of aliena- tion deserves special attention. His 'consumption' of large doses of French literature of a particular character was as much a form of dependence as his reliance on drugs and sex in a vain attempt to escape his condition.

We have throughout stressed the close connection between politics and the development of African poetry in the European languages; in Rabearivelo's case, a touchy personality, his frustrations and resentment of his colonial status on the one hand, and his attempts to escape his spiritual prison by the means provided by a European literature of such soul-weary decadence, impelled him in the end toward a poetic style, often brilliant in the evocation of 'death' or 'decay' but completely lacking in the force and energy that a close identi- fication with the life and political fortunes of his people might have produced.

Rabearivelo published more than half dozen volumes of poetry, most of them no more than pamphlets: they include *La Coupe de Cendres* (The Bowl of Ash) 1926, *Sylves* (1927) *Volumes* (1928) *Prèsque Songes* (1934) and *Chants pour Abeone* (1935). A marked feature of Rabearivelo's work is its repeated striving toward a language of musical abstraction, of reverie, a kind of 'Innerlichkeit', which would enable the poet to break loose from the intolerable burden of his colonial status and become attached, by some kind of strenuous intellectual effort, to the metropolitan culture of France. That the symbolist tradition which this Malagasy poet was attempting to imitate with such zealous effort had long reached its point of exhaustion merely added to the tragic irony of his situation.

As early as his *Sylves* period Rabearivelo's flirtation with death is already apparent in a poem like 'Postlude'* with its uneasy acknowledgement that decay has already set in in early age:

> But in vain am I saddened and alarmed by your fate,
> ineluctable flight, ineluctable death
> Of my first youth at the turning of the alleyway.[10]

As so many other critics have remarked, these early poems are highly derivative both in diction and in sentiment. For instance, it might seem strange to readers of Rabearivelo's work that a writer who have never left his country should find it necessary to lament, as he does in 'Zahana', a poem about a Malagasy tree, what he calls 'the long exile from places of which we are the natives' or in another poem, 'Filao', that he should somehow grouchily surrender to this sense of 'displacement' in lines such as the following:

> But now that exile has cracked your skin,
> the waning vitality of your
> drooping leaves gives to birds shelter without a shade. . . [11]

Our surprise at these sentiments lasts only long enough for us to start reminding ourselves that the 'exile' Rabearivelo is so frequently bemoaning is 'self-willed'; some might even say it is a borrowed emotion. This evocation of an incomprehensible sense of estrangement, at once studiedly languid and fretfully elegiac, is followed in 'Zahana' by images of 'sterility' and 'decay' in which the 'succulence' of a fruit dries away in 'the harsh and sterile soil'. The last stanza effectively fuses the image of a withering tree and that of a poet who has reached a point of exhaustion:

> Comme le mien ton front n'offre plus au matin que les dernières fleurs d'un arbre qui s'éteint et la defaite est soeur de celle de ma race!

> (Like me your face at the break of day offers only the last flowers of a tree which withers away and your decay is sister to that of my own kind.)[12]

It is a mysterious world that Rabearivelo reveals to us, a world of violent stillness, of living death, solitude, estrangement. It is, above all, a world of dreamlike unreality, with one nightmarish image following after another. Even the mildest images have a ring of oddity about them: 'a forest astir with stillness', 'a tree without a trunk', 'a crow that feeds on stars'. Or take this image of dawn in the poem, 'Daybreak,' pictured as resembling someone who 'holds a torch in hands/stained black and blue like the lips of a girl/munching mulberries'. The effect aimed at seems always to be to provide a metaphor for

---

* Although in these texts I have relied a great deal on Reed and Wake's selections, where they have seemed to depart too much from the originals I have substituted my own translations from the French versions.

deformity and emasculation in which natural objects are either incomplete or have been deprived of their expected attributes such as the image of 'naked sailors/with their tongues cut out'.

Rabearivelo's maturest poetry is a sequence published under the title *Traduit de la Nuit* (1935), but even in these poems 'meaning' is secreted in a language of dreamy and shadowy fantasy in which the troubled figure of the author can be viewed as though through an opaque window, distantly emerging from 'the vasting and shining sea'. Some of the these lines especially in the later poems, show Rabearivelo in the best command of his idiom, at times producing the most delicate music to fit the image to the sense. For instance, I can think of no possible equivalent rendition in English which can convey the dreamy music of wistful reverie contained in the lines of Section 1X of *Traduit de la Nuit*:

> Butinez-y, abeilles de mes pensées,
> petites abeilles ailées de son
> dans la nue enceinte de silence;
> chargez-vous de propolis
> parfumée d'astres et de vent:
> nous en calfeutrerons toute fente
> communiquant au tumulte de la vie.[13]

Alienated Rabearivelo may have been, but there is no question that he was devoted to his native land, to the blue horizons of the 'vast Iarivo sky'. Nevertheless, whether by temperament or by choice he seems to have relied too much on the second-hand ideas of metropolitan French poets for guidance to address himself adequately to the problems of his own people – or as Reed and Wake put it, 'to interpret the Malagasy soul to the French-speaking world outside'.[14] Reed and Wake also make out a convincing case for what they call 'the inauthenticity of so much of his life, and death'.[15] One recalls pretty much the same charge made against Ezra Pound: 'The impression persists', argued Charles Olson, 'that the only life he had lived is, in fact, the literary . . .' Reed and Wake also refer to a 'mass of literary allusion' which they claim to have been typical of Rabearivelo.[16] The editors of *Poètes d'expression française* similarly speak of the 'instability the perpetual restlessness of a being who is no longer a pure native without being truly a European'.[17] All this would seem to confirm Kunene's thesis about the underlying pathology of the indigenous elites during what he calls the 'second phase' of colonial occupation:

In this phase the occupied country already boasts of a large number of those not only 'educated' in the colonising power's sense but also who are so totally sterilised of their own culture that they are foreign in their own country. Thus is born the phenomenon of the *assimilado*, a group of people who are so alienated from the realities of their own country that they consider their own colonisation as part of a grand divine plan.[18]

Undoubtedly, Rabearivelo provides classic example of a 'deracinated' intellectual; but once again the web of tensions and strands of conflict in the life of such an alienated poet are not without an element of ambiquity. 'The most outstanding feature of this indigenous elite', Kunene argues, 'is its total loss of cultural roots'.[19] Yet Rabearivelo was not completely unware of the value of his own cultural heritage. He used or translated traditional Malagasy poetry popularly known as the *hain-teny*, a word which means in Malagasy, according to Jean Paulhan 'the science of words';[20] and which the Rev. James Sibree, quoting from Dahle's book, refers to as 'somewhat lengthy clever speeches'.[21] According to Sibree 'many of the shorter of these "flowers of oratory" have the sententious forms of proverbs; and others take the shape of a conversation between imaginary persons, whose names often afford a key to the sentiments they express'.[22] A typical example of the *hain-teny lavalava* is this song of mutual love:

> Let us two, O friend, never separate upon the
> high mountain, nor part upon the lofty rock, nor
> leave each other on the wide-spreading plain.
> For, alas! that this narrow valley should part
> such loving ones as we are; for thou wilt advance
> and go home, and I shall return to remain, for if thou,
> the traveller, shouldst not be sad, much less
> should I, the one left. I am a child left by its companions,
> and playing with dust all alone;
> but still should I not be utterly weak and given up
> to folly, if I blamed my friend for going home?[23]

This form of folk poetry has shaped the work of other Malagasy poets, especially Flavien Ranaivo, who makes the *hain-teny* an integral part of his verse-making, much more so than Rabearivelo, whose *Vieilles chansons des pays d'Imerina* read more like translations than original compositions.

3

Flavien Ranaivo provides an interesting contrast to Rabearivelo. In his preface to Ranaivo's collection, *Mes chansons de toujours*, Senghor argued that he proceeds by an 'opposite movement'[24] to Rabearivelo's literary development. Born in 1914, the son of the Governor of Arovonimamo, Ranaivo's first compositions were initially influenced by the romantic school of French poetry, but later he was to rediscover the resources of his own folk tradition, thus bringing to his verse what one critic calls 'the expression in the French language of thought which rests on Imerinian foundations'.[25] Whereas Rabearivelo wished to be 'a Latin among the Melanians', Ranaivo wished his work to be firmly anchored in the folk tradition of the *hain-teny* and Malagasy songs. For such an enterprise, he was, of course, exceedingly well qualified, having learned to sing his people's songs before learning to write and having travelled widely around the island in his youth. As can readily be seen in his poem, 'Chant pour deux Valiha', dedicated to Senghor, the influence of the vernacular song is most dominant in Ranaivo's verse:

Voici venir la nuit,
la nuit de la forêt:
comment t'abriteras-tu
de ses tracasseries?
E eniah o,
e eniah e:
ainsi dansent les ingénus. . .

(Here comes the night
the night of the forest
how are you to shelter
her vexations
E eniah o
e eniah e:
Thus dance the initiates . . .)[26]

Of Ranaivo's style Senghor has stated that it is 'dense, studded with antitheses, parallelisms and asymmetries, with inversions, ellipses, syllepses: a style of the 'strong beat', made for economy and surprise'.[27] To this catalogue we may add wit and humour, and a tendency toward the enigmatic statement, all of which are recognisable elements of the *hain-teny* or the 'poetry of disputation'. The arch cleverness of the *hain-teny*, which is like the proverb forms, is not unlike the 'conceit' of the 'metaphysicals': 'Tears of the cicada, friend/they fall drop by drop/but they drown the entire earth.' The *hain-teny* is also, essentially, a poetry of love, and in Ranaivo's handling of the form tender sentiments are expressed in subtle verse full of mordant wit and humour; and every stanza is carefully planted with 'land mines' and 'booby-traps' of amusing but perplexing conundrums.

Quelle est celle-qui-fait-claquer-ses-pas-sur-la-terre-ferme?
— C'est la fille du nouveau chef-de-mille.
— Si c'est la fille du chef-de-mille.
dites-lui que tombera bientôt la nuit
et que je troquerai des amours corallines
contre un soupçon d'amitié.

— Quelle est celle-qui-vient-du-nord?
— C'est la soeur de la veuve-au-parfum-de-jamerose.
— Dites-lui d'entrer sans retard,
Je lui préparerai une franche lippée.
— Elle n'en goûtera point, que je sache:
elle ne prend qu'eau de riz,
non parce qu'elle a soif
mais caprice a votre égard . . .

(Who is that-who-makes-his-footsteps-clatter-on-the-firm-land?
— It is the daughter of the new chief-of-thousand.
— If it is the new daughter of the chief-of-thousand.

133

say to her that night will soon fall
and that I'll exchange loves of the coral reefs
against a mere hint of friendship . . .

— Who is that-who-comes-from-the-north?
— It is the sister of the window-with-the-jamerose-perfume
— Say to her to come in at once
I will prepare her a delicious mouthful.
— She will hardly taste it, that I know
That one takes only rice-water
not because of thirst
but for sheer caprice where you are concerned . . .)[28]

4

If Ranaivo represents 'an opposite movement' to Rabearivelo's poetry, Jacques Rabemananjara, lawyer, poet and playwright, and, before independence, a leading figure in the anti-colonial struggle against the French, has written a body of work which provides the most complete antithesis to the kind of verse which Rabearivelo was determined to write. The two personalities are not only different but their social intentions or lack of them, the manner in which the two men perceived their roles as poets, bring out in the most dramatic way the natural opposition between a poet who was obliged to fabricate a 'mask' for himself and one who was equally resolved to carry out certain political 'tasks'. Indeed, leaving aside for the moment Ranaivo's own special contribution, the more one reflects on the situation of these two poets, the more one is struck by the terrible irony of Rabearivelo's fate.

Having left school at 13 years of age, Rabearivelo, the passionate auto-didact of French culture, was from the start engaged in a slow, wasting struggle to support himself and his poetry; but Rabemananjara, born in 1910 of the Belsimisaraka stock, once described by a popular writer as 'a favourite of the French', seems to have encountered no such difficulties. After receiving his education from the Jesuits of the Antananarivo College, he went on to work for the local administration as a somewhat privileged civil servant. Later, in 1946, at the age of 36, he was to become the youngest of the five elected deputies to the French national Assembly in Paris, representing the rich plantations of the Second District. Again, in contrast to Rabearivelo who lived precariously on the margins of Malagasy society in the boundless hope of one day reaching the French capital, Jacques Rabemananjara was earlier on enabled to sample the heady life of literary cafés[29] when in 1938 his teachers obtained for him a post in the Ministry of Colonial Affairs in Paris. Like so many others before and after him, it was while living in the relative comfort of Paris that Rabemananjara 'found himself' and became an ardent nationalist and patriot.

He saw France fall; he saw the Germans march in to occupy Paris, and all France. He saw the whole long humiliation, the collaboration, the Resistance, and the Liberation. He saw French friends vanish in the night.

His education was not sentimental. So France formed this Malagasy poet and patriot — and martyr.[30]

Back in Malagasy after the war, Rabemananjara joined the radical Democratic Movement for the Revivification of Madagascar (MDRM): 'his speeches . . . became indeed inflammatory, full of phrases such as "Have you the souls of slaves?" "How can you respect the French?" ',[31] and when the abortive uprising of 1947 took place, followed by widespread bloodshed and severe repression by the French, Rabemananjara was tried along with two top MDRM leaders and found guilty of 'treasonable crimes' against the state: he was sentenced to life imprisonment with hard labour. *Antsa*, Rabemananjara's long, patriotic poem about Malagasy, bears the dateline: May 1947, Antanimora prison, Tananarive. All the same, even during these harsh times, the poet's luck seemed to have held. He was not to stay in prison for more than three months: in August 1947, following a demand by the French National Assembly, Rabemananjara was once more in Paris, this time to present to the French Assembly a special report on the events that had just taken place on the island: in France he was obliged to remain until 1963.

Thus if we contrast the lives of these two poets, Rabearivelo and Rabemananjara, at every juncture we find ourselves compelled to take into account a singular chain of ironies. Rabemananjara, who started his career with everything, whom we should consequently suppose to have most to lose in any change in *status quo*, not only became a committed poet, bent on action where Rabearivelo tended to brood eternally in isolation, but Rabemananjara's political activities also led to imprisonment and exile in Paris: surely, the greatest irony of all, that despite Rabearivelo's eager court-ship of French culture and society, it is Rabemananjara, the revolutionary poet rather than Rabearivelo, the romantic idealist, who is finally obliged to spend more than a decade in the superheated atmosphere of post-war literary Paris, universally listened to and widely feted as a victim of colonial society.

To a degree rarely encountered before in Malagasy poetry Rabemanan-jara's compositions are abundantly charged with a patriotic fervour which is almost wanton in its undiminishing intensity: poetry and action seemed to have found in his life their most perfect conjunction. At his most passionate, his verse, as François Mauriac once called it, becomes a cry elicited by 'l'amour et la douleur'. Even when handling a tight sonnet form Rabemananjara's lyricism explodes like hot lava: it is the laudanum of exultation which laces his most casual declarations of his love and devotion with a bitter tinge of intemperate *jouissance* and relentless energy. He can turn the humblest shelter into a sacred shrine so that the hut becomes 'a fireplace/ where we come to burn our hearts and our trump cards'.[32] and in the passageway of the temple 'the smallest far away sound' resounds in the poet's heart.

The love for the island of Madagascar and the love for a woman become in Rabemananjara's verse twin emotions, often interchangeable, the woman and the island becoming royal recipients of his boundless adoration and limitless passion. 'J'exalte ta beauté hautaine et la noblesse/ de l'encolure ou vient folâtre mon Désir.' (I exalt your proud beauty and the nobility/ of your neck where my Desire comes to frolic.)[33]; and more than either Rabearivelo or Ranaivo,

Rabemananjara is the one Malagasy poet most easily identifiable with the Negritude Movement, identifiable with a programme, if you wish, whose objective is to summon 'the ancestors and the Race' so that they may together plot the future of the island. 'Il nous faut conjurer les Aieux et la Race.'[34]

If Rabemananjara's writing is invariably distinguished by its rhetorical fervour and plangent tone, it is in *Antsa*, his long patriotic poem about Madagascar, 'the island of flaming syllables', that Rabemananjara pours forth his most impassioned lyricism. Alternately exalted as proud mistress and supreme sovereign, the island of Madagascar features in this poem as both Goddess and violated Virgin whose lovers must raise her from the ashes of her humiliation and restore her to her former dignity; and it is 'love' in its grandest conception and 'will' in its most obdurate form, which determine the weight and limit of that legend, for the poet refashions legend even as he recreates it:

> L'immensité de ta légende,
> le renouveau de ton renom
> ont pris l'espace pour mésure.
>
> Mon amour fixe l'infini
> et ma foi fixe la durée
> Madagascar!
>
> (The immensity of your legend,
> the renewal of your renown
> have assumed their measure
>
> My love fixes the infinitude
> and my will fixes the duration,
> Madagascar!)[35]

Half the poem is concerned with the glorification of the island ('I bite your red and virgin flesh/with the sharp fervour/of the dying flashing teeth/Madagascar!') and the other half, which becomes the antistrophe to the first, is a ringing hymn to Liberty ('the savana is in delirium: Liberty!') At once priest, philosopher, and magician, the poet performs his sacred rites through the pronouncement of the one word: Liberty.

> . . . . Of all the dancing virgins
> it is you alone, O Dzirah,
> it is you the Preferred One:
>
> From the charm of your breasts
> rises like a star
> in an unexpected rhythm
> the dance of the Race:
> Liberty.[36]

Finally, like many contemporaries who absorbed the ideas of the negritude movement the poet proposes an organic unity between man and nature, between man and woman, between the living and the dead, all of them themes very central to the negritude philosophy, with its insistence on the sustaining power of sexuality and fecundity, and the rhythmic flow of the universe:

> Dans le ventre de la mère
> l'embryon sautillera
> Dans les entrailles des pierres
> danseront les trepasses.
>
> Et l'Homme et la Femme,
> et les morts et les vivants,
> et la bête et la plante,
> tous se retrouvent. haletants,
> dans le bosquet de la magie.
>
> (From the belly of the mother
> the embryo will explode
> In the entrails of the rocks
> will dance the departed.
>
> And the Man and the Woman
> and the dead and the living,
> and the beast and the plant,
> all rediscover themselves, painting,
> in the magic grove.)[37]

And rhythm, of course, in its cosmic yet palpable sense, is what gives physical drama to these ideas, what welds them together, and, indeed, endows them with their unique energy. Unlike Rabearivelo, the tragic poet whose personality and humanity in the end seems to melt into vanishing abstractions, Rabemananjara is a communal poet, never lonely: he is passionate, zealous, public, very confident of his audience. The dramatic monologue suited perfectly the dramatist in him, his patriotism became his mantle: in *Antsa*, especially, the red earth of Malagasy mingles symbolically with the blood of the martyred insurrectionists of 1967.*

5

In Africa itself, as distinct from Madagascar, three African poets can be said to be the founding fathers of African poetry of French expression. They are Léopold Senghor, President of the Senegalese Republic, the late David Diop, born in Bordeaux of a Senegalese father and Camerounian mother, and Birago Diop, a Senegalese veterinary surgeon and diplomat, as well as a trusted

---

* We can only view with astonishment Rabemananjara's tortuous career which included his participation as Foreign Minister in his country's policy of détente with South Africa until once again he was obliged to leave for Paris where he is currently living in exile.

member of Senghor's present cabinet. This trio was the only one from black Africa to be included in Senghor's 1948 collection, *Anthologie de la Nouvelle Poésie Nègre et Malgache de Langue Française*, which is now universally acknowledged as an important landmark in black literature of French expression.

To these three we can perhaps add the name of Bernard Dadié of the Ivory Coast who since 1950, has published three volumes of poetry, some folk tales, two novels and has had plays produced in Africa and France; Lamine Diakhathe, a Senegalese who since 1954 has published three volumes of poetry, Antoine-Roger Bolamba, a Zairean who published his first book of verse in 1955, and Malick Fall, the Senegalese poet and playwright. This first generation of poets and novelists of French expression has now been joined by younger poets, the most distinguished of whom is the Congolese poet, Tchicaya U Tamsi: they include such poets as Paulin Joachim, Joseph Miezan Bognini, J.-B. Tati-Loutard and others even younger still.

Since Senghor, the two Diops and other pioneers of African verse of French expression began publishing their works in the 1940s the themes of this poetry have changed but little. Broadly speaking, they can be said to represent the two poles of negritude: firstly, that side of it which is concerned with racial identity and the excavation of the African cultural heritage, and, secondly, that part of it which has continued the specific tradition of militant anti-colonial protest first pioneered by David Diop. For both these wings of negritude, post-independence African politics has created a new climate and with it new problems.

After all, if our insistence is correct as to the close connection between politics and the development of African poetry, and if that connection continues to hold to this day, then it must be clear that without taking into account the changed circumstances of cultural life in post-independence Africa, French-African poetry cannot hope to develop any further; it can only atrophy and die; for both in its search for a specific identity and in its character of militant social protest, negritude poetry was rooted in certain specific political conditions and a definite psychological climate created by the anti-colonial struggle. That struggle is now over or nearly over but new exigencies have come to light. And it is in their willingness or unwillingness to face up to their new social responsibilities that the poets who were once conveniently grouped together under the umbrella of negritude are once again dividing themselves into two inimical camps.

The deep fission between the negritude represented by Senghor and the negritude, if one can call it that, represented by Diop, was already apparent at the time of the first Congress of Negro Writers and Artists held in Paris in 1956 but remained temporarily concealed by certain overriding common interests. It is by no means an accident that of the three poets already mentioned — Senghor, Birago Diop and David Diop — it was the latter, from the beginning the most radical, the most aggressively direct and frankly internationalist in his concerns, who also thought it necessary to caution against a poetry which was merely committed to the 'revival of the great African myths'. For David Diop liberation from economic exploitation as well as liberation from racial oppression became two major, closely connected concerns; the assertion of an African cultural heritage was only an aspect of and never a negation of a belief in the common fraternity of the world's labouring masses.

As early as 1956, in a poem like 'Vagues', Diop was already championing the universal struggle of the oppressed, willing to applaud 'the Suez docker, the Hanoi coolie' for flinging 'their huge song into breakers' and for 'lashing, lashing the maddened Beast'[38] of colonialism and Western economic domination of the world. In yet another poem, 'Certitude', he warned those whom he described as growing 'fat on murder':

> I tell them that the heart and the head
> Join each other in a straight line of combat.[39]

The original collection of David Diop's verse, *Coups de Pilon*, contains only seventeen poems, and a later, posthumous edition published in 1973 included another thirteen; hardly what one might call a substantial amount of published work; yet the impact of his aggressive style far outweighed the slenderness of his output: among the younger generation of African poets his influence remains considerable, and his untimely death in an air crash in 1960 aged only 33, removed one of the most powerful voices in the anti-colonial literature of French expression. The surrealism of Breton, Eluard, and Césaire, the themes of political revolt inspired by Marxist economics, the black consciousness movement of the Harlem Renaissance in the 1930s and the 1940s; these are the evident influences in Diop's work, as indeed they were to leave their indelible mark on the work of nearly all the other black poets who began publishing in the first half of the 20th century.

If Surrealist imagery and an austere blank verse mark Diop's style, the condition of the colonised people everywhere became his subject matter: it was the actual condition of black people rather than the mythologies of blackness which drew from him the warmest response. He wrote in 'La route veritable':

> Brothers from whom they would wrest your youthful innocence
> Do not seek for truth in the grimace of their phrases
> In their patronising pats and bedroom betrayals.
> Do not seek for beauty in this mask which trembles
> And soaks with perfume the hideous sight of their wounds
> Nor love in those exposed thighs
> Coining adventure in the pick-up bars
> Truth Beauty Love
> Is the worker breaking the murderous calm of their salons . . .[40]

The energies of Diop's poetry is politics. In a paper written for the 1956 Congress of Black Writers and Artists in Paris, Diop stated unequivocally, 'form is only there to serve the idea',[41] adding that for Africans 'poetry must reflect the world and maintain the memory of the African heritage'.[42] Clearly, such a formulation owes a great deal to the Marxist theory of 'reflection'. About negritude as a fashionable mystique of the times, Diop had some cautionary words to utter. An African poet, he argued, might 'cram' his compositions with words borrowed from his native language. He might explore what he thinks

139

'typifies' his particular culture, joining in the enterprise of reviving 'the great African myths' to the accompanying sound of loud African tom-toms, but he would find in the end that 'he had only given back to the bourgeois colonialist the reassuring image which the bourgeois wishes to see'. This, Diop argued, is the surest means of fabricating a 'folklorish poetry' for the European salons.

Against such tendencies Diop's conception of the mission of the African poet was more ruthlessly austere: it was not through 'assimilation' or 'facile Africanity' that an African poet could best contribute to the growth of an African civilisation. It was by 'fighting with all of his writings for the end of the colonial regime that the Black creator of French expression contributes to the rebirth of our national cultures'.[43] Toward this end, Diop called for a poetry, whether written in the formal style of the Alexandrine or composed in free verse, which would 'burst the eardrums of those who would not listen'. In this brief but combative statement Diop effectively set forth his position as lying far to the left of the other African adherents of negritude.

To evaluate properly the nature of Diop's veiled attack on the official position of negritude we shall have to recognise that the 'folklorish' quality that he was warning against was becoming only too evident in some of the more ludicrous simplifications of negritude poetry: it is present in a great deal of Birago Diop's 'Leurres at lueurs', in some of Bernard Dadié's 'Afrique debout' and 'La ronde des jours' and in some of Senghor's own work. Anchored firmly in African religious belief, a poem like Birago Diop's 'Souffles' could success-fully convey the actuality of traditional African thought; but obliged simply to exploit the unexacting contrarieties of the black-versus-white schema imposed by negritude, the poet could achieve nothing deeper than the surface exoticism of 'Diptyque'.

Dadié's work had a more complex appeal. In common with works produced during the colonial period his earliest verse contains much vigorous social protest. Sometimes it is defiantly anti-French, that is to say anti-colonialist; sometimes it is saturated with a sense of injured pride. In 'La vie n'est pas un rêve', Dadié writes of a French governor wishing to 'make of Africa one prison/an immense charnel house'; and more bitingly in another poem about 'the warmongers' he calls upon ancestral spirits:

> And you, gods, spirits, phantoms
> What keeps you from speaking the word
> In the face of monsters
> Who feed their cannons
> With the children of the people?[44]

Dadié wears his *négritude* like a garland; the gentle irony of 'Je vous remercie mon Dieu' conceals an immense tidewash of bitterness. Nevertheless, a great deal of his verse is devoted to a nostalgia for an uncorrupted Africa, desecrated but unbowed, abandoned but faithful to her children. It is to this Africa that the poet, guilty and chastened, returns to address himself in 'Sèche tes pleurs':

Dry your tears, Africa
Your children return to you
Their hands full of toys
The heart full of love.[45]

This reference to 'hands full of toys' has a special significance in any attempt to understand Dadié's kind of nostalgia, for this is undoubtedly a poetry of childhood; its impulse is one of retreat to a sheltered innocence before Africa fell victim to the twin evils of colonialism and modernism. It is this same yearning for a retreat to a more stable past which is expressed by Lamine Diakhathe in the lines: 'Let us take out our wings of light and go/soaring off to a gentler time.'[46]

When Dadié needs a respite from denouncing the colonialists and their 'humid prisons', he wishes to take refuge in an Africa of 'dreams'; of night 'beautiful as the smile of a child'; a charmed continent of 'limpid skies' and the 'savana drenched with sunlight', a land of plenitude and social harmony, an Africa of perfumed forests and the tom-tom, of the lute and the dance and the laughter of children without a hint of pain; an Africa we are finally tempted to say, which never was! And the weakening grasp on social reality in a poem like 'Confession' is reflected in a language steeped in dream and reverie.

But if Dadié and Diakhathe merely express a hankering after an Africa of 'childhood' in which fear, hunger, and violence are conveniently absent, in a poem like 'Bonguemba', with its uncomplicated language and rhythm, Antoine-Roger Bolamba attempts to reconstruct for us a world of utter simplicity and joyful innocence in which can be glimpsed 'singing women/wrists and heels tinkling' and 'crocodiles in the water' which 'weep with joy'. The simplicity is admirable, the clarity achieved has a certain subtle power, not to mention charm, but it is a dangerous charm that the poem works on us: with its enchanted images of tribal innocence the poem leans heavily on the spurious appeal of the travel poster which is so cruelly mocked in Malick Fall's short poem in which tourists 'want to get a close-up view/of the crocodiles asleep/Along the Avenue de la Liberte'.[47]

As for Senghor he was different only in his ability to evolve a strategy which tended to conceal similar weaknesses through a skilful combination of lofty theme and lofty style of expression. By a recourse to the verbal music of an incantatory style, and thereby evoking in the reader a hypnotic trance which lulled his critical powers into temporary idleness, Senghor was able to command assent to ideas which on second thought seemed, to say the least, extremely dubious; indeed, the element of myth-making seemed a necessary part of Senghor's verse-making. With others less talented the gap between symbol and reality became too great to be papered over by such an inflated rhetoric.

Nevertheless, we must not exaggerate differences between Senghor's romantic negritude and what one might define as the 'social realism' of David Diop, differences which are in actual fact counterbalanced by what was in this period a large measure of agreement and similar concentration on certain fundamental themes. For all his internationalist outlook, for David Diop as much as for Léopold Senghor Africa was to remain the area of primary interest.

In poems such as 'Africa' and 'Black Dancer', Diop, too, was ready to gratify what had become a growing passion for negritude themes. These themes were exemplified by the now all too familiar tendency to romanticise about the 'Africa of proud warriors in ancestral savannahs'; by a readiness to contrast some mythical 'African innocence', the purity of which was asserted rather than shown, with the corrupt artificiality of European society. Frequently, by the manipulation of symbol and by bald assertion, blackness was made to carry the weight of symbolical meaning which was too great to do the poem any good. The opposition of 'black' to the 'white' colour, the implied authenticity of one against the falsity and fecklessness of the other, was a comforting reversal of values long imposed by Europe, but required on the part of even the African reader too great a suspension of belief to shore up his sense of doubt. According to this schema, beauty, truth, emotional warmth, and sensuality were the attributes of African civilisation: greed, exploitation, severe repression, a sterile eroticism and desperate alienation, were the attributes of European civilisation. As Senghor was to put it: 'sensualité, oui, pas l'erotisme'. In his poem, 'New York', Senghor writes:

> New York! I say to New York, let the black blood flow
> into your blood
> That it may rub the rust from your joints of
> steel, like an oil of life.[48]

Diop, too, went in for this kind of thing. In 'Black Dancer', for instance, the figure of the dancing black woman was converted into a symbol of fresh innocence and spiritual regeneration: she was the 'warm rumour of Africa' possessing 'secret powers', capable of 'restarting the world' by the magic of her loins. The theme survives among some of the younger poets of the succeeding generation like Siriman Cissoko of Mali who writes about a girl whose loins are 'more fertile than the banks of the Nile' and A.Y. Diallo who regrets having abandoned mother Africa for 'the langourous embrace of the unknown' instead of remaining within 'the vigorous embrace/of your muscular thighs'.[49] These poems constitute a variation upon a theme made popular by Senghor in his poem 'Femme Noire'. However, even in poems of African 'innocence' and 'ancestral glory' Diop's apparent 'romanticism' was invariably tempered by a harsh and sharpened sense of political realism! David Diop never neglected to pose uncomfortable questions. 'Africa,' he wrote 'tell me Africa/Is this you this back that is bent/This back that breaks under the weight of humiliation?'[50]

By comparison Léopold Senghor and Birago Diop appeared to be distinctly conservative. The son of a Serer landowner, a Roman Catholic and the product of the French Lycée and the Sorbonne, and a former deputy of the French National Assembly, Senghor seemed particularly attached to the 'rich soft soil' of France. In the chapter on 'Negritude' we have already explored at some length Senghor's ideas touching on African metaphysics, what Senghor calls an 'African ontology'; we could, had space and time allowed, have extended our enquiry to the examination of the extraordinary lengths to which Senghor was prepared to go in an attempt to express this African *uniqueness*, while, simultaneously, accommodating himself just as easily to French culture.

Indeed, some have even questioned the claim that Senghor writes verse which is in any way uniquely African.[51]

Reed and Wake, the most devoted annotators of Senghor's poetry, make nearly the same point: 'The French gave to Senghor and those like him everything French culture could offer, not to enable them to carry their countries to independence but to make them Frenchmen. . .'[52] For if Senghor was a Serer from the Senegalese coast, forever dreaming of 'the Kingdom of Childhood . . . among the sea-flats of Dyilor', he also remained the child of the French nation whom he extolled for having 'opened my heart to the understanding of the world'; the French, he wrote elsewhere, 'brought me The Good News, Lord, and opened my heavy eyelids to the light of faith.'[53] In the same poem, which comes at the end of *Hosties Noires*, Senghor offered this passionate prayer to God, that 'among the white nations, set France at the right hand of the Father'. Although he admitted 'she too is Europe' Senghor was prepared to forget her 'mask of smallness and hatred', for, as he honestly confessed, 'I have a great weakness for France'.[54]

It is an extraordinary poem, one which it is impossible to imagine David Diop ever writing; its dedication to the late President Pompidou and his wife, Claude, is equally intriguing though finally understandable, for Senghor went to school with Georges Pompidou and remained to the end a very close friend. Double loyalty to Senegal and to France seemed to be the poem's main motif and it is written with commendable, if troubling, honesty. The poem also introduces us to the key phenomenon of French colonisation, which was the policy of assimilation, the attempt to create out of the colonial subjects a ruling class that was no less French than the metropolitan Frenchmen. Against such a background there is now, understandably, a growing tendency in African thought to see negritude as a reactionary movement of assimilated elites, whose passionate expression of loyalty to the indigenous cultures was inspired by guilt and nostalgia for what they had already betrayed.

There is a grain of truth in such a general formulation; but from the point of view of literary criticism nothing can be more mistaken or indeed more sinister than to minimise Senghor's contribution to African literature on the basis of an antipathy to his conservative stance in African politics. His flirtation with the racist government of South Africa is shocking, his continued identification of Senegalese interests with those of France is suspect, his domestic policies have come increasingly under attack in recent years; yet I believe Senghor to be a great African poet who, despite questionable metaphysics and aesthetic principles founded on shaky psychological doctrine[55], has managed to create a body of work which commands our attention for its consistently high quality and because in it Senghor has provided a valid poetical structure for his ideas and obsessions.

From his first collections, *Chants d'Ombre* (1945) and *Hosties Noires* (1948), through *Chants Pour Naett* (1949) and *Ethiopiques* (1956) to *Nocturnes* (1961), in their grave meditative rhythm these poems create a devotional atmosphere quite appropriate to the immediate purposes of a poet who is determined to re-enact the ceremonial procedures of the traditional *griot* and the incantations of the Roman Catholic mass: throughout Senghor's work this duality of inspiration and the duality of means is kept up. Simultaneously, he is keen to create a body of imagery in which philosophically, aesthetically and socially, Africa and Europe are seen as two antithetical systems of life: this simple opposition provides the underlying tension in *Hosties Noires* (1948), the poems set among the destruction and debris of World War II during which the poet fought on the side of France and was captured by the Germans. The turbulence of the European conflict — 'the panic of black soldiers in the thunderstorm of tanks' — is contrasted with the peaceful 'evenings of Dyilor/That deep-blue light of the night sky on the land sweet at evening',[56] just as the 'blue metallic eyes' of downtown New York were to be sharply contrasted with Harlem pavements 'ploughed by the bare feet of dancers'. In *Chants d'Ombre*, these poems of nostalgia and ancestral worship provide an opportunity for organising an impressive imagery drawn from memories of childhood:

> And you, Fountain of Kam-Dyame, when at noon among my naked sleek companions decked in bush flowers
> I drank your mystical waters out of my cupped hands.[57]

He is the master of the long Whitmanesque line which carries the reader inexorably forward in a surge of emotion or reflective thought: lines which seemed to be created especially to be read aloud to the accompaniment of musical instruments, as indeed many of them are. Imitating the procedures of the traditional poet-singers, the *griots* of West Africa, Senghor has written verse to be chanted to such African musical instruments as the *kora* and the *tama*, the *khalam* and the *balafong*. However, in his major work the African and the European poetic traditions converge: apart from the traces of sur-realism sometimes apparent in the juxtaposition of incongruous images — 'streams of black milk' — Senghor admits to the influence, among others, of the verse forms of Paul Claudel, the Roman Catholic poet and diplomat, but rightly argues: 'one only imitates those whom one resembles, like the son his father, more exactly perhaps, the brother his elder brother'. It is in that spirit that he has described Claudelian verse as 'the most Negro'. He says it was while translating some Negro-African poems into French (which 'broke the narrow framework of the Alexandrine') that he recognised the parallel.

But apart from his success with language, a fact of which we are bound to take increasing note in any assessment of poetic ability, Senghor's specific greatness lies in the general feeling we receive from reading his work that he *typifies* and unites within his poetic sensibility all the aspirations, the contra-dictions, the strengths as well as the weaknesses, of a whole generation of French-speaking West Africans who now occupy positions of influence in business, politics, and cultural institutions, a generation which was profoundly affected by Western education, African yet proud of their Frenchness, rooted in the cultures of Africa but yearning for the 'rich soft soil' of France; they were bitter in the hour of their rejection, nostalgic in the hour of assimilation, at once militant and accommodating by turns. Though many of them shared these ambivalent emotions none can be said to have created a body of work in which this internal drama of conflicting emotions is given such eloquent expression.

6

In English-speaking Africa, as we have already noted, an equivalent generation of poets arose which came under the powerful sway of the Christian missionary education; their idea of progress was the missionary idea of progress; and even when they came to reject Christianity it was not so easy to shake off the central ideology or the underlying assumptions of the Christian mission in Africa; but no single English-speaking African can be said to have emerged during this period who was able to articulate the aspirations and frustrations of this generation (the pioneers of Anglophone Africa provide only a patchwork of poetic sensibilities and incompletely realised struggles with language); only in French-speaking West Africa, especially in Senghor, and later, Tchicaya U'Tamsi, do we have a major and a minor but significant poet who, toiling with the inexhaustible energy of powerful intellects, were able to weld together disparate ideas, emotions, guilts and frustrations, into a coherent body of work.

To characterise U'Tamsi as a minor poet may seem to many admirers singularly parsimonious given his already notable achievements both in terms of his prodigious output and the quality of his verse; but I consider such an estimation a just one and in due course I shall try to give reasons for making it.

Since 1955 U'Tamsi has published six volumes of verse, each exploring in varying degress of intensity, the poet's state of consciousness on the one hand, and the vicissitudes of the black race on the other. The two themes, one concerned with self-exploration and self-knowledge and the other with the tragic history of the African people, are indissolubly linked in U'Tamsi's verse, the latter merely helping to feed the former and the former being ceaselessly clarified by the latter. Like the modern Jew, emotionally fraught, worn and frangible, U'Tamsi is burdened with the disabling memory of racial persecution: he is, as he aptly epitomises himself 'the Jew-negro wanderer/in the desert of my country's heart. . .'[59]; and recalling the brutality of slavery, he writes in *Brush Fire*: 'my race/remembers/the taste of bronze drunk hot'. The violence which accompanied colonisation and decolonisation, the Atlantic slave trade, Western racism, and, in the face of these crimes, the continual failures and hypocrisy of the Church, form the larger backdrop against which the poet, born in the Congo but educated in France, attempts to reconstruct a personality already too fragmented to achieve a proper self-definition.

The reflective voice in U'Tamsi's verse, ribald, confessional, self-dramatising, accusing yet tormented, is that of a man with an excruciatingly heightened form of consciousness, full of strictures for the failures of the West but unflinchingly honest about his own moral shortcomings; above all, he is aware of many self-betrayals as well as the betrayals of those others, his own people for example, who might have legitimately expected a better intellectual leadership from its elite. U'Tamsi's self-mocking irony is a well-conceived strategy for alerting us to his acute perception of his own imperfections while serving as a form of self-protection against any moral charges we might be tempted to press against his kind. He writes in 'The Promenade': 'behold me here in Europe/No cane in my hand/mouth bunched into a trumpet/expansive/more French than Joan of Arc'.[60] Or he will confess: 'I don't know how to save myself/then I dreamt of returning to my village/with eyes behind dark glasses.'[61] The frequent slyness and archness of manner is a kind of armour against which our fiercest accusations bounce off without inflicting too much injury.

U'Tamsi's wit has been much remarked upon by critics and rightly so. In all six books examples of it abound. He is a poet of extreme equivocation, given to quick denunciations but given also to self-doubt, to circumspection and even to some inconvenient retraction. Tempted to deliver a dazzling aphorism or offer a profundity about the mystery of the Congo he will step back at the last moment:

> I know nothing of it nothing
> and I have used the excuse of my rotten teeth
> to keep my mouth shut
> decently[62]

and like the French poet he most resembles he can turn this wit into a lethal weapon against all the hated, repressive institutions he has chosen for his targets; against the Church, for example, which remains a powerful presence in most of his verse; against its minister, 'the popes and priests without shame', who remain the irredeemable butt of his humour: 'yes on top of Vesuvius, of Kilimanjaro one sees the pope like Churchhill smoking cigars. . .'[63] The eccentric nature of U'Tamsi's imagery, what Claire Clea calls 'les tableaux hétéroclites'[64] an aspect surely of the surrealist and symbolist tradition in French verse, can administer a salutory shock in the readers's response such as is produced by the sexual imagery in 'Low Watermark':

> above a herd of rutting buffaloes shines
> a moon narrow as a virgin's cunt
> the ship of my loves sank deeper
> between two grins of a caressing dawn
> the winds seated themselves on the knees of my sister
> laughing at the knife drawn between them[65]

Professor Dathorne, among others, makes an assertion which is never substantiated, that U'Thamsi's verse is 'linked to oral poetry'.[66] Whether such a claim can ever be proved is extremely hard to determine by reading U'Tamsi's verse. On the other hand, the poet's 'links' to the arid psychic wastes of contemporary European life and thought is apparent not only in the hopelessly mutilated language and extreme imagery which is the heritage of Baudelaire, Rimbaud and Verlaine, a tradition which reaches to him via Césaire and the surrealist poets, but this link is obvious also in the exploration of certain themes concerned with alienation, moral uncertainty and even sexual self-doubt. Sometimes U'Tamsi's verse seems a witty paraphrase of Rimbaud's frenetic expressions of disgust with Christian bourgeois culture, and what he called its 'just passion for death'. Rimbaud's rebellious cry in 'Mauvais Sang', 'I'm leaving Europe . . . remote climes will darken me', has its most ironic counterpart and final reversal in U'Tamsi's inversion, 'I'm more French than Joan of Arc.' Both poets are in revolt against Christ, for Rimbaud because he is the 'perpetual thief of energy'[67] and for U'Tamsi because you soil yourself by mixing with the bourgeois,'[68] and both wish to recover their 'pagan past' as a source of vitality: as U'Tamsi puts it: 'To be a pagan at the pagan renewal of the world. . .'[69]

But finally, we must return to the ticklish question of why despite his obvious poetic gifts — his wit, his critical intelligence and social awareness — the total impression left on the reader by U'Tamsi's verse is of a minor poet rather than a major one. This impression is not dispelled by the fact that U'Tamsi is a congenial companion. He may be more progressive than Léopold Senghor, but he still seems a much lesser figure than the elder, more conservative poet of 'African civilisation'. Notwithstanding the amazing energy and intensity of feeling, and, perhaps, partly because of this energy and intensity, U'Tamsi's verse often gives the impression of a restless poetic sensibility which registers a series of fragmented states of consciousness, the succeeding one sometimes cancelling the one before, without eventually being integrated into any unified vision of society.

To give one example: U'Tamsi's tragic view of African history is often modified, sometimes totally cancelled out, by his prankish, highly playful wit, a mode of writing which has led Moore to describe him as 'totally undidactic. . .a poet who would not dream of bullying words into the service of any external purpose whatever'[70] an alarming commendation. To prove this point Moore constantly refers to Césaire whom the Congolese poet superficially resembles; but despite the strangeness of much of Césaire's imagery the Martiniquaise is a model of clarity compared to U'Tamsi's manner. Those who wish to satisfy themselves on this point can take another look at *Cahier*. It is not simply that U'Tamsi's surrealist technique, the mutilated imagery, the extreme condensation and displacement, contributes to our lack of secure anchorage in much that he writes; it is simply that when all this impressive technical machinery is set to work his procedure of repeated verbal *non-sequiturs*, the thought-formulations abandoned in the middle of a line, add up to no final statement about society: we are never sure what attitude he wishes us to assume to the larger questions he constantly picks up and quickly lets drop.

For all U'Tamsi's rage about the murder of Emmett Till, the persecution of blacks in Durban and Harlem, the lightness of tone, contributed, I would say, by a literary technique which sometimes declines into playful gesture, often makes him sound, to borrow a phrase, like a poet of lamentation without genuine sorrow. On the other hand, U'Tamsi is able to satisfy, at least partially, our craving for a message by a reiteration of certain themes, symbols and motifs which extends from one book to the next, a network of themes and recurrent motifs which help to knit his work together into some recognisable whole. He is the most impressive modern poet of the Congo:

> I longed to make love
> to this river
> having done so I rejoiced with all my soul
> my voice striking the bush in ecstasy[71]

7

To turn away from French-speaking African poets of U'Tamsi's stature to their

English-speaking counterparts is to enter a different domaine of cultural activity in which certain themes may indeed remind us of Senghor, Diop and U'Tamsi, but in which the technical achievements of the verse seem less impressive and the scope less sweeping. In fact African poetry of English expression only achieves a measure of technical mastery over language, over form as opposed to content, relatively late in the day; to be more precise this development occurs toward the end of the 1950s and for reasons too numerous to discuss here this development coincides with the advance of Anglophone African states toward political independence. The creative freedom and the widening scope of literary activity were perhaps among the first consequences of the new political order; this in turn meant wider contacts among African artists themselves and new experimentations with the art of poetry.

Immediately, we can distinguish two lines of development along which Anglo–African poetry was to proceed. The first stems from a group of poets who seemed eager to respond, and some would say too anxious to attach themselves, at whatever cost, to the modernist movement in Europe and America. This movement led by the Nigerian troika, Christopher Okigbo, Wole Soyinka and John Pepper Clark, was to pay particular attention to the technical achievements of Hopkins, Pound and Eliot, while bringing into the verse the vast panoply of African myth and subject-matter. The second group, which at times developed as a direct reaction to the increasing dominance of the first, fought to recover the idiom of oral African poetry and to make it the basis of a new manipulation of the English language. The Ghanaian, Kofi Awoonor, the Ugandan, Okot p'Bitek, and the Zulu poet, Mazisi Kunene, are three prominent representatives of this second group. It is important to note, however, that the two tendencies were never mutually exclusive. As I have already pointed out before, someone like Kofi Awoonor, while determined to maintained a close link with the Ewe oral tradition, was also a sophisticated modernist who could be said to enjoy an ambiguous status between two tendencies, using an idiom that is clearly open to both influences:

> They say, they say,
> The day they release the prisoners
> There will be blessings
> And joy will be found again
>
> But who will release the prisoners?
> And break the poor-man's hunger?
> I was there when they released the prisoners.
> I heard tears of anguish
> And the agony of the hungry.
> Let the earth keep silent
> And let us hear![72]

Also there is a sense in which the traditionalists' attempt to exploit the resources of oral speech could itself be seen as part of the modernist tendency which, in English poetry at any rate, tried to do away with the kind of 'poetic diction' which was so beloved of the pioneering school. The jettisoning of this excess poetic baggage was long overdue even if, as sometimes happened, this meant substituting African mannerisms for the discarded English ones.

There is no doubt that for many modern African writers the oral tradition can be a source of strength. All the same, some poems first composed in the African languages, then translated into English, raise problems of diction which are hard to resolve. Kunene can be a very powerful poet, for instance, when the images assume a concrete shape, but the image is hard to grasp where Zulu rhetoric is allowed to play too crucial a part:

> Those whose minds are centred on a sacred stone
> Offering their limbs of existence,
> Are destined for the rebuffs of life.
> They will die in the thickets of reeds.[73]

Against lines like these we can set the simple lucid dignity of his single-stanza poems like his 'The Day of Treachery' and their most effective use of the proverb and riddle forms:

> Do not be like the people of Ngoneni
> Who rushed with warm arms
> To embrace a man at the gates
> And did likewise on the day of treachery
> Embracing the sharp end of the short spears.[74]

The Zulu praise-poetry on which a large proportion of these poems is modelled is a type of poetry which is singularly unsuited for the withdrawn meditative voice, working in isolation from an immediate audience; even when the poet is soliloquising, the requirements of a public audience, however 'invisible', are too great for us not to sense a deep internal disorder in the poetry. This feeling of tension, even embarrassment, such as we feel when we overhear an individual talking aloud to himself can only be ameliorated, never completely dispelled in a poetry that cries out to be chanted or performed while it is simultaneously written for the silent page. On the other hand, reading a poet like the late Christopher Okigbo creates no such emotional disturbance; whatever can be said about certain African elements in Okigbo's poetry the verse is not indissolubly tied to this 'invisible' audience as in Kunene's poetry. Okigbo is closer to the individualistic ethos of European poetic self-expression in a way that Kunene could never be as long as he continues with his chosen enterprise of writing traditional Zulu poetry for English translation. I hope I need not point out that this is a description of a state of affairs, not an approval of any one type of poetry. Perhaps to be truly appreciated *Song of Lawino* and Kunene's *Zulu Poems* have to be read in their original languages. Yet when the transference of Zulu lines into English works reasonably well the gain in richness and power is immense, as can be seen in another of Kunene's poems called 'The Night':

> The heart of the earth is covered with weeds,
> Darkness descends from the path of the skies.

The black tails of cows shake against the wind,
Beating the sea with the fence of dusk.
It is as if people crawl in the islands of the light:
He who was as tall as the forest
Creeps on his belly dancing in the embrace of a dream;
The wilderness of the earth holds its head in its hands.
The little children have fled to their holes:
The hole is a great home of the ancestral spirits
Where grief hangs above like ribs,
Where the great day sends its forerunners
The white hair, the white hair of the sun.
You will also carry the cripples across the streamers.[75]

The linguistic phenomenon of which poems like these are a product is determined by a different set of values and calls for a different kind of literary evaluation. The problem of how to deal with them is raised in an acute from in Okot p'Bitek's otherwise admirable *Song of Lawino*. The poem is a long monologue uttered in public by an 'uneducated' woman whose values are still rooted in a rural native culture; in contrast her husband, Ocol, prides himself on being 'a modern man/A progressive and civilized man'. As someone has said the 'internal structure' of the poem is that of 'a dialogue, or a debate: a debate between two sets of values, Western and African, symbolised in the person of Lawino, on the one hand, and Ocol her husband, on the other'.[76]

The poem requires us, first of all, to distinguish between two types of speech: that of an uneducated 'bush' woman and that of a Westernised husband. Almost immediately the question which confronts us is whether the terms in which the debate has been conceived and executed are not already those of the author himself, highly sophisticated and learned, whose mode of disguise in the humble habits of Lawino finally proves unconvincing. Lawino's penetrating observations on the politics of Uhuru, her lively satirical disquisitions on church institutions, Protestant and Catholic, while protesting her lack of comprehension, become in the end an unworkable device.

The debate about what language is appropriate when translating African speech into a European language has been going on for some time now[77] and remains inconclusive; but we must wonder whether there is not involved here something more than an attempt to find a proper equivalent in English for African speech when Lawino says of Ocol 'he has read extensively and widely'. That very tautology 'extensively and widely' belongs to a different set of linguistic possibilities and choices and seems unlikely to be the product of rural speech.

Elsewhere p'Bitek succeeds admirably in bringing to the surface the wealth of African language. The strength and dignity of oral poetry, the organic nature of language in a community in which the *use-value* of objects is still paramount, can be seen in Lawino's biting description of Ocol :

My husband's tongue
Is bitter like the roots of the *lyonno* lily,
It is hot like the penis of the bee,

Like the sting of the *kalang*!
Ocol's tongue is fierce like the arrow of the scorpion,
Deadly like the spear of the buffalo-hornet.
It is ferocious
Like the poison of a barren woman
And corrosive like the juice of the gourd.[78]

A more serious question is whether the oral tradition and the poetic forms within that tradition can be made to yield models which can be mechanically repeated under new conditions of literary production. For this reason we must treat with severe caution the new craze for the oral tradition in modern African literature. Nothing is so distracting as the whimsical, undigested use of the oral tradition in current African writing, even if we must commend the utterly serious approach of the three leading exponents of this movement, namely Mazisi Kunene, Kofi Awoonor and Okot p'Bitek. In fact, I am not at all sure that tradition can ever be preserved; perhaps it can only be changed or challenged.

8

For nearly two decades now, since roughly the middle of the 1950s, African poetry in English has been engaged in a compulsive search for a language and idiom which would bring about a synthesis of what is best and viable in the Western and African traditions. The Western and the African traditions have been acknowledged, sometimes reluctantly, as the basis for constructing a new literature, able to fulfill new social needs. So far as literature was concerned the first requirement for this to happen was precisely to articulate the socio-cultural conditions in which the modern African writer had to function, the heterogeneity of cultural experiences among which the poet had to pick his or her way. The dilemma and the way out is pointed to with exceptional subtlety in Abioseh Nicol's most successful poem, 'African Easter' in which the assemblage of images drawn from Christian, Islam and indigenous African religions provide us with the true 'objective correlative' for that complexity of cultural facts which make up the world of an African intellectual in a West African city. The first part of the poem is well worth quoting in full :

> *Ding dong bell*
> *Pussy's in the well.*
>
> Another day . . .
>
> Sleep leaves my opening eyes slowly
> Unwillingly like a true lover.
>
> But this day is different.
> The lonely matin bells
> Cut across the thin morning mist,
> The glinting dew on the green grass,

> The cool pink light before the heat of day,
> The sudden punctual dawn of tropic skies,
> Before the muezzin begins to cry,
> Before the pagan drums begin to beat.[79]

Immediately, we can isolate certain lexical items in the text which are so organised as to create the impression of a jumbled confusion of religions and cultures : *matin bells* (Christian), *muezzin* (Muslim), *pagan drums* (Negro African). The choice of these special, highly associative code words and phrases, intended to yield special significance in the organisation of the total structure of meaning, is maintained throughout the poem. In their symbolical representation certain items stand in natural opposition, the figures of Shango and Christ for example, as are the words *chalice* and *libation*. However, it is the Christian symbols which dominate the poem: *rock, chalice, dove, sepulchre, Aramic agony*, etc. The English nursery rhyme which opens the first stanza 'Ding dong bell/Pussy's in the well' suggests that enclosed, pampered world of European childhood, so anomalously transferred to 'the sudden dawn of tropic skies'; and the jingle quickly establishes the intellectual training of the modern African intellectual as artificial and lacking in coherence; and it is through this constant opposition and juxtaposition of imagery that the actual meaning of the poem is constructed, the alienation of the African intellectual from his true heritage, his embrace of bourgeois Christian values, which is fully brought out in the communicant's cautious acceptance of the chalice from the priest: 'I only mind/That he wipes the wet rim/not to spread dental germs' and the pharisaical boast, 'A tenth of my goods/I give to the poor/through income tax.'

It might well be argued, and with some justice, that the poem does not finally achieve a proper synthesis of the diverse religions and cultures which African writers often profess to be their goal; that just as the Christian imagery dominates the poem, in its conclusion the poem also presents us with triumph of that uncorrupted Christian ideal which, we are told, is 'concealed in mumbled European tongues', in the 'thick dusty verbiage/of centuries of committees'. That in this situation African tradition is losing out is made clear enough, and it is a state of affairs which Nicol apparently accepts with equanimity :

> Easter morning.
> Where are my ancestral spirits now?
> I have forgotten for many harvests
> To moisten the warm earth
> With poured libations.[80]

This theme of culture-conflict and the need to reconcile the various strands of it, especially the Western and the African tradition, is a major pre-occupation of another fine West African poet, Gabriel Okara of Nigeria. In his poem concerning a winter visit to North America, Okara's approach to this theme is even more discreet and oblique than Nicol's handling of it; but on the whole he follows the same pattern of constructing meaning by a careful grouping of images through which culture-conflict, social dislocation, and alienation can be glimpsed as through refracting glass. Meaning in an Okara poem is rarely expressed through a process of 'ratiocination'; instead it is conveyed to us through a systematic arrangement of a constellation of images, each of which is associated with certain cultural attributes; only this way is the theme of culture-conflict and possible conciliation worked out.

We can note, for instance, that in this particular poem, 'The Snow Flakes Sail Gently Down', the major opposition is between those images which, like 'snow', 'winter-weary elms', 'funeral cloth', 'vigil', and 'grief-stricken mourners', are not only associated with death but are by extension made to stand for the whole of the Western way of life and its inhuman materialism : against these symbols of death ('the weight of weightless snow') are opposed the imagery of the restless black birds : 'birds . . . nesting/and hatching on oil palms bearing suns'. We can also see that unlike Nicol, the Nigerian poet leans toward his own tradition, finding in it the 'roots' which are so strong that they dent 'the uprooters' spades'. The same schema is repeated in 'Piano and drums', with 'drums' representing traditional African values and the 'piano' symbolising European culture. The opposition in the 'drum' and piano' passages is extended to rhythmical organisation of the poem. Compare the bouncy, leaping rhythm of the 'drum' passage with the liquid-flowing movement of the 'piano' concerto :

> (drum) When at break of day at a riverside
> I hear jungle drums telegraphing
> the mystic rhythm, urgent, raw
> like bleeding flesh, speaking of
> primal youth and the beginning,
> I see the panther ready to pounce,
> the leopard snarling about to leap
> and the hunters crouch with spears poised.

> (piano) Then I hear a wailing piano
> solo speaking of complex ways
> in tear-furrowed concerto
> of far away lands
> and new horizons with
> coaxing diminuendo, counterpoint,
> crescendo. But lost in the labyrinth
> of its complexities, it ends in the middle
> of a phrase at a daggerpoint.[81]

The resolution in both Nicol and Okara's poems, the former by embracing Christ/('You can come out now/You see we want to share you/With our masters, because/You really are unique') and the latter ('lost in the morning mist/of an age at a riverside keep/wandering in the mystic rhythm/of jungle drums and the concerto . . .'), are no resolutions at all : at least, Okara does not pretend they are : he is poised, so to speak, on the dagger-point' between the two ways of life, between the two systems of value. However, what both poets have succeeded in doing is to provide us with an index of the widespread social dislocation and the resultant loss of cultural equilibrium; for that purpose these poems are excellently rendered; they are perhaps more 'truthful' in what they tell us of this particular state of affairs than the hasty denials by some critics of African literature that such a state of affairs exist at all.

In a sense, I suppose, we can look upon these two as representatives of the 'transitional school' of poets who fall somewhere between the 'pioneers' and the ultra-moderns of whom Okigbo was the most impressive practitioner. Among these poets we can include the works of most of the older generation of Ghanaian poets, notably Kwesi Brew, A. Kayper-Mensah, G. Adali-Mortty. The Gambian poet, Lenrie Peters, would have fitted naturally in this group were it not for the cosmopolitan nature of his themes. These poets keep pretty close to the modern idiom of versification; but though conventional in comparison to ultra moderns like Okigbo there is not nearly so much of the English Romantic or Georgian rhythms in their poems as so disastrously crippled the works of the Pioneering School. Nevertheless, their poetry still seems a battlefield of two main poetic sensibilities, of the European and African poetic idioms, which may very well be an objectification in literary form of the actual contradictions in the society at large. Change brings with it the threat of vast social dislocations or vast social progress, and in either case the role of tradition is called into question. The whole drama of social change, so painstakingly plotted in these poems, seems to be played under the surveillance of ancestral eyes. As G. Adali-Mortty has said: 'Old suns set/ new suns rise.'[82] Kwesi Brew elaborates this mood in one of his poems, 'Ancestral Faces':

> They could not hide the moss on the bald pate
> Of their reverent heads,
> And the gnarled barks of the wawa tree:
> Nor the rust on the ancient state-swords,
> Nor the skulls studded with grinning coweries
> They could not silence the drums,
> The fibre of their souls and ours — [83]

9

With younger West African poets like Soyinka, Clark, the late Christopher Okigbo, and then the others even younger than this generation, the range of subject-matter which poetry is allowed to deal with is considerably enlarged; technique equally becomes a subject of absorbing interest. Nevertheless the theme of social dislocation, the focus on the problem of achieving continuity between traditional cultures, and the new modern social structures, never totally disappears from the foreground of poetic reflection. What does happen with the modern school of poets is that the conflict is now enacted through language itself and through those symbols which are the very embodiment of the drama of external conflict now internalised and transfigured into a private vision. In consequence, the language of these poets becomes more recondite and difficult to decode. However, at all times we must remind ourselves that however private the language of some of this poetry, it could never entirely succeed in separating itself from the external world and some of its basic social considerations. As the Russian linguist, V.N. Volosinov, emphasised : 'The word is the most sensitive index of social changes, and, what is more, of changes still in the process of growth . . .'[84]

Of the three well-known Nigerian poets — Wole Soyinka, John Pepper Clark, and the late Christopher Okigbo — only the latter seems to have maintained a consistently high standard of craftsmanship while showing a deepening emotional response to experience. Thus, up to his tragically premature death during the Nigerian Civil War, Okigbo's career is appropriately one of expanding human interest as well as a refinement of poetic technique; or rather — since from the very beginning Okigbo had revealed a high level of technical competence — we must observe only that his later development showed a gradual unloosening of emotion from too tight a bind in the purely formal aspects of composition.

Among Okigbo's generation, a generation weaned on Eliot, Pound and the Classics, a certain notion rapidly gained ground that to be taken seriously at all poetry not only had to be made 'new' in the Poundian sense but that it had to be made difficult as well; but few were to achieve the exacting purity of language which Okigbo brought to the art of versification.

His careful attention to craft, his deep love for music, his wide reading outside the usual staple of English literature, especially his obvious familiarity with the French symbolist tradition, enabled Okigbo to widen the scope of his technical achievements so that throughout the 1960s he seemed the very embodiment of the new avant-garde in Africa.

It is true that many of Okigbo's earlier poems sound like a pastiche of the American and European masters he admired, chiefly Pound and Eliot: 'Rays, violent and short, piercing the gloom/foreshadow the fire that is dreamed of' has a typical Eliot music just as this stanza from *Labyrinths* is bound to strike the reader as having the same provenance:

> so comes John the Baptist
> with a bowl of salt water
> preaching the gambit
> life without sin. . .[85]

And yet not all Okigbo's borrowings are as obtrusive as these: indeed, the point which needs emphasising is that Okigbo's choice of models was the right one for his kind of interests and temperament and it was one that actually advanced his technique. Between Pound's unusual enthusiasm for Provençal and early Italian poetry and Okigbo's strong attachment to the Classics lies a conjunction of interests which enables the younger poet to put to good use whatever he has assimilated from the great innovator of twentieth-century English verse. The end of 'The passage', despite its obvious debt to Pound, shows a marvellous delicacy of feeling and a simple felicity of line which does no discredit to Latin pastoral verse:

> For we are listening in cornfields
> among the windplayers,
> listening to the wind leaning over
> its loveliest fragment[86]

By the time of his death and the composition of the last poems 'prophesying war', Okigbo's development as a poet had attained impressive heights of maturity and confident command over his materials. The social tensions which led to the 1966 army coup in Nigeria and the prospects of a war of secession darkened the mood of these last poems, but the vision of the apocalypse which increasingly dominates Okigbo's consciousness at this time seemed to impart a new emotional vigour to the writing, though nowhere does the verse show any inability to cope with the accumulating pressures and the new sensation of a rapidly approaching catastrophe. The lines simply feel more compact now because there is more inside them:

> The chief priest of the sanctuary has uttered
> the enchanted words;
> The bleeding phallus,
> Dripping fresh from the carnage cries out for
> the medicinal leaf. . .[87]

Okigbo's earlier poems are mostly about a young man's quest for experience and the attainment of true self-knowledge; and since the pagan setting of the classical texts he had studied in Latin and Greek provided such a close approximation to the religious context of African art and performance, Okigbo tries to combine these two elements within his own work; his more ambitious undertaking, however, lies in the attempt to fuse Christian and African forms of religious ritual, with their accessories of myth and symbol, into a unified sensibility able to resolve the personal dilemma arising out of the conflict between the Western-Christian culture on the one hand, and the indigenous African tradition on the other.[88] A Roman Catholic in his youth and a product of a Western university education, Okigbo was acutely aware of the spiritual distance he had already travelled from his native culture which in specific terms meant a severance from that segment of the population who remained the custodians of the indigenous culture; part of his poetic effort, therefore, is directed toward regaining this lost equilibrium by reintegrating himself into his indigenous culture and religion.

Time and again the poet sees himself as a 'prodigal son', an 'exile', who has journeyed far from ancestral shrines only to find uncertain refuge in the temples of Western culture and the Roman Catholic Church. Of 'Limits' Okigbo says: '(It) was written at the end of a journey of several centuries from Nsukka to Yola in pursuit of what turned out to be an illusion.'[89] It is this search for equilibrium, conducted through the medium of poetry, which provides the unifying theme for Okigbo's work: similarly, the partial adoption of the mythological frame for the unfolding of the poet's consciousness furnishes us with the primary symbol for the poems, which is a double adventure of human growth from childhood to manhood paralleled by artistic growth from apprenticeship to poetic maturity. A cluster of ritual images encapsulating the process of self-surrender, initiation, and ultimate self-realisation, mark out the main stages of this spiritual journey and poetic development.

> For he was a shrub among the poplars
> Needing more roots

> More sap to grow to sunlight,
> Thirsting for sunlight,
>
> A low growth among the forest.
>
> Into the soul
> The selves extended their branches,
> Into the moments of each living hour,
> Feeling for audience.[90]

In both 'Heavensgate' and 'Limits' Okigbo reinvents himself into the poem, mingling the autobiographical details with peripheral social observations, sometimes making witty comments on the figures who have taught, influenced, aided or abetted his progress. What frequently characterises the works of great poets, and what is evident in the poetry of Christopher Okigbo, is a dual approach to creative function: that is to say, the poet first wishes to give expression to his poetically charged imagination; but simultaneously with this function he also assumes a task whose object is a prolonged meditation on the process of creation itself. This meditation on method can be explicit, sometimes it can only be construed from any number of clues which are conveniently scattered through the text.

At all events, what emerges in the end is a general philosophical view of life which can never be fully grasped from random poetical inspiration, the kind which gives rise to the occasional poem. In the total work of a major poet there are usually recurring images, themes and motifs, which taken together, present us with a total vision of the world, of society, of men and things, and the act of creation which knits them together; and in my view, these are the qualities which characterised Okigbo's approach to poetry, and seemed to confer upon him the hopes for the emergence of a major poet in English-speaking Africa.

To a certain extent the same kind of internal unity links together the works of Wole Soyinka, the Nigerian playwright, novelist and poet. One of the best known of modern Nigerian writers, Soyinka has established a reputation in the theatre with plays like *A Dance of the Forests* (1963), *The Road* (1965) and his superb comedy, *The Lion and the Jewel* (1963); despite its obvious structural defeats and the usual verbal excesses, his first novel, *The Interpreters* (1965), has scenes of savage power alternating with passages of mordant satire not easily matched by any other African novelist in English-speaking Africa.

With the publication of his two collections of verse, *Idanre and Other Poems* (1967) and *A Shuttle in the Crypt* (1972), Soyinka has now created enough work in three major genres to enable us to form a judgement about the general philosophical position he has assumed and the manner in which this position affects the value and character of his work. Unfortunately, while useful to many readers understandably confounded by Soyinka's clotted language and deliberately obscure imagery, the kind of close textual exegeses which up to now have been characteristic of most commentaries on Soyinka's work, tell us nothing about the ultimate meaning and value of that work as a social product. This reticence on the part of the critics is even more astonishing given Soyinka's declared position against the notion of 'art for art's sake' and his having gone on record for insisting that writers have a social function.[91]

Literature is a branch of human knowledge, a tool of 'perception' as well as a process of 'transforming the world'. If that proposition is true we have a duty to examine Soyinka's work not only for the recurring motifs and symbols which run through it, but for what these motifs and symbols add up to when they are reconstructed. What do they tell us, for instance, of Soyinka's view of society and his position in that society?

The answer to that question must be sought in the writer's work as a totality; for what connects works so diverse in nature and purpose — the novel, the plays and the poems — is Soyinka's central preoccupation with the question which, as we have already seen, other African writers have posed but none with the ferocious intensity which Soyinka brings to it. Briefly summarised the question amounts to this: what possible meaning can tradition be made to yield toward a reordering of African society, toward the creation of a new African sensibility? The second question, very much linked to the first, can be construed from a close reading of his play, *A Dance of the Forests*, from his prose-work and from several poems; and the question is whether African society is capable of benefiting from the folk experience which tradition actualises in the form of myth, legend, as well as other types of artistic projection.

I believe that Soyinka's work, both in its reworking of myth and its general observations on contemporary African society, constitutes a series of answers to the first question. As to the second it would seem, by the very nature of the enterprise he has set himself, namely the investigation of many aspects of tradition, presumably for what they can tell us about the range of possibilities open to us when dealing with certain ethical problems, that Soyinka believes contemporary African society can and should salvage something from its past. Otherwise, there would seem to be very little value in his present exercise. Yet a reading of *A Dance of the Forests* and some of the poems raises serious doubts; the sentiments contained in some of the passages imply an almost pessimistic view of the future of African society.

As a poet, novelist and dramatist, Soyinka is rightly appalled at the 'inauthenticity' of many aspects of African society, at the internecine struggles and seemingly endless cruelties and bloodshed which are the outcome of the furious contest for control among the different segments of the new civilian/military bureaucracies. In their bitter reproachfulness some of the lines in 'Conversation at night with a Cockroach' could stand as a monument to the once limitless optimism among many Nigerian intellectuals which characterised the years immediately after independence, especially among the young writers recently emerged from the universities, which was later to be so lamentably eroded by the grimly exhausting strife of the Civil War:

> . . . We sought to speak
> Each to each in accents of trust
> Dispersing ancient mists in clean breezes
> To clear the path of lowland barriers
> Forge new realities, free our earth
> Of distorting shadows cast by old
> And modern necromancers. No more

Rose cry and purpose, no more the fences
Of deceit, no more perpetuity
Of ancient wrongs.[92]

Soyinka himself who, it must be acknowledged, had from the start shown an almost clairvoyant premonition about the nation's possible failure to make the historical leap without a rupture in the system, became one of the most notable victims of that crisis. Nevertheless, the scale of the disaster, the brutal statistics of the war casualties and his own imprisonment, must have come as a shock to a writer who had occasionally seemed to celebrate 'death' as a necessary key capable of unlocking the mysteries of human existence. This, at any rate, is one of the most curious aspects of Soyinka's work: his fascination with Death.

Sometime ago Soyinka was quoted as saying he believed in capital punishment because society periodically needs blood sacrifice. As late as the composition of *Idanre* it was pretty obvious that destruction and creativity, the two contrary inpulses deified in Soyinka's personal god, Ogun, formed the two poles of tension in his work. As Soyinka himself wrote: 'growth is greener where/Rich blood has split'. And Egbo in *The Interpreters*, staring at a point in the river where his parents drowned,

. . . acknowledged it finally, this was a place of death. And admitted too that he was drawn to it, drawn to it as a dream of isolation, smelling its archaic menace and the violent undertows, unable to deny its dark vitality.[93]

In *The Road* the enigmatic Professor declares: 'The Word may be found companion not to life, but Death.'[94] Nevertheless, looked at not as some metaphysical necessity in a game of philosophical inquiry; seen in its purely physical reality and actual impact Death was more horrible, more meaningless and obscene, than even Soyinka could have supposed. Thus the horror darkens many of his later poems:

Not human faces, hands, were these
That fell upon us, nor was death withheld
Even from children, from the unborn.
And wombs were torn from living women
And eyes of children taken out
On the points of knives and bayonets.[95]

Unlike many African writers Soyinka has never subscribed too much to the negritude myth of a once innocent Africa, a black Garden of Eden, which had to await the advent of white colonialism before happily succumbing to Evil; on the contrary he sees human society, including the African one, as caught up in an 'eternal cycle of Karmas that has become the evil history of man': escape is possible, certainly, but only through some evolutionary 'kink' in what would otherwise be a 'doom of repetition'.[96] The underlying motivation in Soyinka's work seems to be 'a search for authentic values in a degraded world', but it is interesting that far from seeing the attainment of 'authentic values' as being dependent upon the triumph of a certain class in which repose all our hopes and aspirations, Soyinka advocates a peculiar sort of heroic values based upon the 'creative dare' of the isolated individual. This aristocracy of the few who are endowed with the creative spark, ready to follow their insights where they lead them, willing if necessary to break the bonds of conventional restraints like 'the stray electron, defiant/of patterns' will teach the rest of us how to recover our 'authenticity.' Such is the Promethean ideal which Soyinka holds out toward the end of his long poem, *Idanre*:

> . . . he who guards the Creative Flint
> Walks, purged spirit, contemptuous of womb-yearnings
> He shall teach us to ignite our several kilns
> And glory in each bronzed emergence.[97]

If as we have already suggested, current African literature answers to a feeling of dislocation and a sense of incoherence which continue to grip African society in its post-colonial phase, Soyinka's major writings can be seen as one writer's response to this state of affairs. To this mood he responds in a number of ways but his most efficacious weapon has been satire which is never totally absent even from his tragedies. From the very beginning, in poems like 'Telephone Conversation' or 'The Other Immigrant', Soyinka showed just how sharply he could press the knife. 'Civilian and Soldier' is a more sombre poem but Soyinka has never been able to resist the ridicule of the dull-witted and insensitive:

> You stood still
> For both eternities, and oh I heard the lesson
> Of your training sessions, cautioning
> Scorch earth behind you, do not leave
> A dubious neutral to the rear.[98]

The best part of Soyinka's writing contains this trenchant criticism of the unexamined brutalities of modern African society, of the emptiness of its ideals and the shallowness of its perceptions, but Soyinka is unable to suggest any movement forward because a mixture of mythic 'occultism' and artistic 'messianism' cannot be made to replace a proper analysis of the choices available. Indeed, much of the obscurantism and mystification which have increasingly troubled critics of Soyinka's work[99] in recent years can partly be attributed to this deeper ideological confusion. Clearly Soyinka has not worked out for himself how and within what economic system or political framework the problems he so persistently holds up to scrutiny can be solved; and I fail to see this deficiency can be alleviated by the kind of appeals to the redemptive 'power of myth' so eloquently explicated by Stanley Macebuh in a recent article published in Soyinka's own journal.[100] As for certain strains in the language Macebuh thinks that it is our failure to recognise that Soyinka is attempting to translate into English the cultic, masonic language of Yoruba ritual which makes us unable to appreciate it:

Language in Soyinka is difficult, harsh, sometimes tortured; his syntax is often archaic, his verbal structures sometimes impenetrable . . . There is, nevertheless, the possibility that a good many of Soyinka's critics have, in identifying this difficulty, yet failed to pay sufficient attention to the internal, that is, ethnocentric compulsions in his poetic dramas that render this condition nearly inevitable.[101]

Not to put too fine a point on it, 'nearly inevitable' is a very prudent way of expressing the argument since 'ethnocentric compulsions' can be made to serve as an explanation for every kind of stylistic failure. Soyinka has always been less fortunate in idolators than in his critics: it is high time that a great number of Soyinka's solecisms are recognised for what they are: failure to communicate clearly. Poems like 'Telephone Conversation', 'Death at Dawn', 'Season' or 'Massacre October '66' may treat different events, they may deal with a variety of emotions, but what make them successful as poems is their combination of a critical realism with an uncluttered simplicity of line which releases the experience from the usually dense coagulation of his syntax, what Moore calls 'a tendency to overload his lines, creating an effect of strain and turgidity'.[102] The self-defeating obscurantism of a stanza like this one from 'Après la guerre' shows what happens when Soyinka overworks the lines and mixes his metaphors:

> Do not cover up with scabs
> And turn the pain a masquerader's
> Broken-tongued lament
> Its face a painted mask of veils
> Its breath unmoistened by the run of bile
> A patchwork heart and death-head grin
> To cheat the rigors of
> Exorcism.[103]

John Pepper Clark, the third poet in this triumvirate, is less ambitious in his programme than either Soyinka or the late Okigbo; his line is usually the standard line of modern English verse, usually indebted to Eliot, Yeats or Hopkins. He has no particular theme unless one accepts the recent civil war as the main source of his inspiration for many of the poems featured in 'Casualties'. Like Soyinka, Clark has written some fine individual poems, but both are erratic performers who frequently fall below their true measure.

In Clark's first collection of verse, *A Reed in the Tide* (1965) there are about half a dozen poems which deserve our attention. These include 'For Granny', 'Night Rain', 'Agbor Dancer', 'Girl Bathing', 'Fulani Cattle' and 'Imprisonment of Obatala'. Nearly all of these are poems which rely on a strong sense of locale. To these we can add 'Cry of Birth' and 'Child Asleep' which form part of the Moore and Beier selection of modern African verse. In these poems Clark employs to good effect imagery strongly evocative of the Delta region of the Niger, imagery depicting the tropical swamps, heavy rainfall, special vegetation and many vignettes of village life. His rhythms can be monotonous, keeping to an unvaried pattern, as in 'Olokun'; but in his best poems he displays a faultless visual sense, an admirable fluency of line and an almost desperate clarity in the underlying thought or sentiment. Two stanzas from 'Agbor Dancer' will be sufficient to indicate this facility:

> See her caught in the throb of a drum
> Tippling from hide-brimed stem
> Down lineal veins to ancestral core
> Opening out in her supple tan
> Limbs like fresh foliage in the sun.
>
> See how entangled in the magic
> Maze of music
> In trance she treads the intricate
> Pattern rippling crest after crest
> To meet the green clouds of the forest.[104]

The last five lines of 'For Granny' have the same fluent yet concentrated power:

> Or was it wonder at those footless stars
> Who in their long translucent fall
> Make shallow silten floors
> Beyond the pale of muddy waters
> Appear more plumbless than the skies?[105]

Clark's second collection, *Casualties* (1970), brings together a number of compositions in which the poet comments on the 'casualties' of the Nigerian Civil War, but what strikes one about most of these poems is the casual nature of their execution, the slackness of the emotion perhaps because of the uninspired delivery. Unlike Okigbo or Soyinka, Clark is a poet with very little capacity for sustained intellectual thought; he is therefore at his best when writing a descriptive verse in which his excellent ability to 'think in images' is given full play.

There are one or two pieces in *Casualties*, especially the title poem, in which Clark allows himself more than the anodyne sentiment and shows even a willingness to introduce an occasionally, bitterly polemical note; his denouncing, for example, of 'the emissaries of rift/So smug in smoke rooms they haunt abroad . . .';[106] at such moments there is a sudden quickening in the writing and a much-needed tension in the line; but the rest, I fear, lack the emotional pressure you would expect from poems dealing with the loss of friends or with the description of personal relationships brought about by the turbulence of the Civil War. At any rate, that vivid sensual fullness of his mostly descriptive, earlier verse, the emotional immediacy of poems like 'Night Rain', 'For Granny' or the even more derivative 'The Imprisonment of Obatala', is now sadly missing.

It is difficult to find any evidence among these scattered, tired reflections that would justify Mr Udoeyo's assertion that 'the poetry of Clark's *Casualties* . . . is as violent and terrible in style as the events which inspired the work'.[107]

Neither the imagery nor the rhythm has much to suggest of that terrible blood-letting and the social dislocation which accompanied the Civil War. The first poem, 'Song', sets the general tone; it is an example of the relaxed, unengaged manner in which Clark deals with what can only have been momentous events in the life of his generation:

> I can look the sun in the face
> But the friends that I have lost
> I dare not look at any. Yet I have held
> Them all in my arms, shared with them
> The same bath and bed . . .[108]

10

In both the Portuguese and English-speaking parts of Southern African the struggle for emancipation from colonial rule has had the most direct impact on literature in general and on poetry in particular. This struggle has been more prolonged, more bitter and wasting than anything known in West Africa with the exception of Guinea-Bissau. At the time of writing this the political conflict has opened its more determined phase inside South Africa itself where still exists the strongest and most inflexible white minority regime in South Africa. Not unexpectedly, though the official languages may differ considerably the black writers of Southern Africa, both English and Portuguese-speaking, share certain common features. The majority of these writers have a profound commitment to the social and political revolution now taking place in the region; in Mozambique and Angola, it would be fair to say, almost to a man or woman these writers have been shaped by the struggle for political rights; first it gave them the motive to begin, then provided them with the goal, and continues to shape the ideals enshrined in the literature.

For reasons which are probably the same as those which have been responsible for the recent shift from prose to poetry in South Africa, writers in Angola and Mozambique have concentrated most of their energies in the writing of verse; for reasons of language very little of their work, either in prose or poetry, is known in the rest of Africa; but among the connoisseurs of African writing there has always been a general acknowledgement of the high standards achieved by poets like José Craveirinha, Angostinho Neto, Noemia de Sousa and others, but it needed the appearance of Margaret Dickinson's slim anthology with the prophetic title of *When Bullets Begin to Flower* to reveal the full range and diversity of talents that make up modern Africa poetry of the Portuguese language.

As the editor points out, the theme of that poetry is 'the struggle'; but it would be wrong to assume that it is all in order of 'agitprop' or verse written for the occasion. While remaining firmly committed to the struggle against Portuguese colonialism, the best of these poets were to stay in touch with those deepest emotions that can open up the warmest affections of lyricism in the Latin languages. Such, for instance, is 'Letter from a Contract Worker', by the Angolan poet, Antonio Jacinto:

> I wanted to write you a letter my love
> to bring back our days together in our
> secret haunts
> nights lost in the long grass
> to bring back the shadow of your legs
> and the moonlight filtering through the
> endless palms
> to bring back the madness of our
> passion
> and the bitterness of separation.[109]

The poignancy of the situation is fully brought out when we learn that the 'contract worker' cannot write and his love cannot read. These poems also show that just as it was easier for French-speaking African poets, with nearly the whole of the French rhetorical tradition behind them, to use verse as a vehicle for public themes, the same was also true of the African poets of Portuguese expression; they too being inheritors of the same Latin tradition. Such a tradition only had to be combined with indigenous forms of African poetry to provide a powerful example of the kind of verse which does not flinch from its public function. Right from the beginning, in its calculated gesture, its plangency of tone, the poetry of the Portuguese African colonies, like its French counterpart, was wedded to the public platform in a way that African poetry of English expression could hardly attempt. Since the seventeenth century and until Walt Whitman and his American heirs like Allen Ginsberg, English poetry had been growing more inward and reflective, fighting shy of rhetorical grandiloquence and large public gestures.

In his poem, 'I want to be a Drum', the Mozambican poet José Craveirinha brings these influences together in order to emphasise both the internal rhythms of oral literature and the aesthetic philosophy which underlies all such creations, while exploring the plastic Latinity of the Portuguese language:

> The drum is worn with its cry
> oh ancient God of men
> let me be a drum
> body and soul just a drum
> just a drum in the hot night of the tropics
>
> And not a flower born in the forest of despair
> Nor a river running to the ocean of despair
> Nor an assegai tempered in the living fire of despair
> Nor even poetry forged in the red pain of despair
> Nor anything
>
> Just a drum worn with its cry in the full moon of my land
> Just a drum of hide tanned in the sun of my land
> Just a drum hollowed in the hard-wood of my land
> *Eu!*[110]

Not unexpectedly politics, the passionate desire for change, has been the dominant theme of this poetry; and it was a group of poets — Agostinho Neto, Marcelino dos Santos, Jorge Rebelo, Costa Andrade and others like them — who gave to Portugese African verse its specifically political character. Neto's poetry is a good example of this kind of writing. A former frequenter of PIDE prisons in both Angola and Portugal under Salazar, later to become president of the Angola Republic, Neto was witness and recorder of his people's anguish under Portuguese rule who survived the twin companions of imprisonment and exile to compose a poetry bolder and more defiant, singing of hope, the desire for transformation through struggle, and the certainty of a new beginning. In his poem 'Bamako', written after a Pan-African conference held there, he cries:

> Bamako!
> there are our arms
> there sound our voices . . .
> dry the tears shed over centuries
> in the slave Africa of other days
> vivified the nourishing juice of fruit
> the aroma of the earth
> on which the sun discovers gigantic kilimanjaros
> under the blue sky of peace.[111]

Neto's poetry is nothing if not an attempt to give voice to the voiceless and the poor, to the brave and unarticulated hopes of the downtrodden and the forgotten: when he is not writing of the contract workers, the porters and the washerwomen of the *muceques* of Luanda (of 'the mulatto girl with gentle eyes/retouching her face with rouge and rice powder'), he is writing of poor peasants trying to scratch a living from the land, the impoverished and exploited. His most moving poem, for instance, is dedicated to his friend Mussunda, a simple African without any schooling:

> To you friend Mussunda
> to you I owe my life
>
> And I write poems you cannot follow
> do you understand my anguish?[112]

This is the deep anguish of every writer who wishes to communicate across barriers of language and Western education with the people to whom he belongs and without whose corroboration his vision is nothing but a blind prison. The rage at this feeling of distance from his own people and the sense of alienation from the land of his own birth is the truest echo in Neto's poetry and the nearest articulation of the revolutionary protest of the Senegalese poet, David Diop:

> I fled
> smiling and sad

smiling and empty
without land, without language, without country . . .

As we have already hinted, in the current literary activity in Africa, the most astonishing development has been the shift in South African black writing from prose and verse. In 1973 for instance, two hundred Black South African poets entered their works for the Roy Campbell Award competition for which they were turned down by the all-white committee;[113] but a number of them continued to write and publish in between political detention and imprisonment. As in prose the themes of this poetry are the violent oppression and the reaction of the majority to this oppression.

Dennis Brutus was the first South African poet to acquire a reputation abroad both for his writing and for his opposition to South Africa's race laws, having once been imprisoned and then been shot while attempting to escape. In their cramped violence and crushed tenderness Brutus's first collection, *Siren, Knuckles, Boots,* re-enacted the blistering, harshly enclosed quality of life under apartheid, with considerable effect. For those who know the poet well his 'Off The Campus: Wits' is startling for its subtly controlled bitterness and violence of emotion. The poem shows us the black students shunted off to the sidelines while their white classmates, uncharacteristically referred to as 'these obscene albinos', take advantage of the exclusively white sporting and social amenities; and the poet writes:

We cower in our green-black primitive retreat
their shouts pursuing us like intermittent surf
peacock-raucous, or wracking as a tom-tom's beat . . .
So here I crouch and knock my venomed arrows
to pierce deaf eardrums waxed by fear
or spy, a Strandloper, these obscene albinos
and from the corner of my eye
catch glimpses of a glinting spear.[114]

Within this arid landscape of violence and hatred Brutus was also capable of creating oases — more like mirages or 'illusions' — of peace, of human warmth and affection, as in his love poems for Bernice, though even in these love poems the sound of 'boots and sirens' was never too far away. When the poet is sent to jail, what will stay with him is 'the grave attention of your eyes/surveying me amid my world of knives.'[115] Sexuality itself, otherwise a balm to the bleeding wounds, seemed to detonate with hidden feelings of enmity and suppressed violence, as when he writes:

I pulse with phallic thrust
devouring your contoured loveliness.[116]

After *Letters to Martha*, which was mostly about his jail experiences, Brutus continued to produce verse at an alarming rate — *Poems from Algiers, Thoughts Abroad, China Poems,* etc. — and the quality declined in direct proportion to the growing, but what increasingly looked like a hasty, output. In exile, far away from South Africa, the rough energy which had animated his verse, seemed to flag: the poems about exile are repetitive in theme and too mechanical in their execution; so that on the whole they only serve to inform us about the places Brutus has visited and people he has encountered without conveying any enduring emotional power.

Once again we may have to look to the internal writers for the emotional vigour which all too often gets blunted by long sojourn abroad. This power the best of the new poets try to supply, though their grasp of technique is still uncertain; many of their poems remind us of LeRoi Jones' witty remark about poems which 'tell us the Black man has been oppressed' but 'very few . . . tell us what that is like, at least, very few do with even the intensity of Kipling telling us what it is like to do the oppressing . . .'[117]

As far as technique goes this may be true of some of the South Africans; James Matthews, for example, usually has some admirable things to say, but all too often his lines appear to be prose cut up to look like poetry. Some of this verse may lack the range and technical finish achieved by front-rank poets such as Mazisi Kunene, Arthur Nortje, Dennis Brutus or Willie Kgotsisile; poets like Oswald Mtshali, Wally Mongane Serote, Njabulo Ndebele, Pascal Gwala and James Matthews sometimes manage to achieve a bitter concentration in their imagery which derives from the immediacy of the experience with which they are dealing. Their verse benefits from the fact that they are writing from inside the contry, and their rage and bitterness fuel their verse rather than dampen it. At times the directness and plainness of the line may distress those brought up to expect much ornamentation in verse; but the poets seem to form a part of an honourable lineage in English verse which has always tried to strip language of all false and superfluous rhetoric in order to bring it closer to the rhythms of common speech. There is no better way of conveying the bare directness of some of this poetry than by quoting in full a short poem by Don Mattera, detained after the Soweto uprising:

> Each morning
>   corner of Pritchard and Joubert
>   leaning on a dusty crutch
>   near a pavement dust-bin
>   an old man begs
>   not expecting much
>
> His spectacles are cracked and dirty
> and does not see my black hand
> drop a cent into his scurvy palm
> but instinctively he mutters:
>   Thank you my Baas!
> Strange, that for a cent
> a man can call his brother, Baas.[118]

Some of these poets have literally come off the street and, while lack of formal training can be a handicap, they are learning as they go along, and they learn simply by practising their art. In some, like Oswald Mtshali, a kind of jailbird like Mattera, it is the irrepressible gaiety and a dauntless sense of the improbable, which feeds their satire; but there is also a new accuracy of *seeing* in the verse which goes hand in hand with a fresh sense of realism. This pronounced visual sense, when sufficiently disciplined, can acquire a tremendous sinewy power with a minimum of inflation of language! Here is Mtshali's brief portrait of Shaka, King of the Zulus:

> Ancestors forged
> his muscles into
> thongs as tough
> as wattle bark
> and nerves
> as sharp as
> syringa thorns.[119]

Like all good verse, lines such as these get very close to the spare quality of good prose, just as good prose, when it is done well, and without any undue recourse to flashy rhetorical devices, can sound like poetry. In their themes these writers show themselves to be closely attuned to the needs of the black community; that is to say, the deepest yearnings for change and renewal are reflected in their works, and must, in the end, transform the very forms within which they work. What we find in South Africa, therefore, is that nearly forty years after the fierce manifestos of the negritude poets in Paris, a Black Consciousness Movement is once again spawning a whole generation of artists and poets whose outlook has been shaped by the most intense kind of repression. Its most accomplished lyrical expression is to be found in the work of Mongane Wally Serote.

To date he has published two collections of verse, *Yakhal'inkomo* (1972), *Tsetlo* (1974) and a long poem, *No Baby Must Weep* (1975). His first collection showed a poet still uncertain in his handling of technique but already displaying an unusually fertile imagination for producing the freshest image; but it was in *Tsetlo*, in the tart richness of language which seems to be coined out of the untidy leavings of human existence itself, that we were able to get a hint of the lyrical powers which Serote has yet to exploit to the full. He has failed with his long poem, *No Baby Must Weep*, but the best of his verse reminds us of the lyrical purity of an Alexander Blok; under the lurid light of his poetic imagination the most insignificant details of the human landscape are greatly illumined and can gleam like a new pigment of paint. An 'imagist' before he had ever heard of such a movement, his lines can achieve the irresistible authority of someone who knows what language can do for him, like the Ancient Mariner who can detain the wedding guest with a hint of sordid power in his gleaming eye, something veiled and untoward:

> look into my eyes
> there, the story of my day is told.[120]

Or this sensuous detail from his poem 'Night-Time':

> trees seem to sweat in the dark
> and the street lights look like wet eyes . . .[121]

The visual intensity of his imagery can achieve the odd whimsicality of a surrealist painting:

> honey-child
> with eyes laid in their cushions like eggs in their nests,
>
> their whiteness clean like the whiteness of an egg,
> their dark dots glow
> shifting swiftly and slowing with the mood of an uneasy snake . . .[122]

If the tradition of English verse seemed too inward and too reticent to allow
for the same explosive use of imagery as the African poets of French and
Portuguese expression seemed to allow themselves, the example of black
American poetry had a liberating influence on black South Africans; but it was
the late Arthur Nortje, with his unusual ability to harness history and ideas to
the purposes of the highest poetry, who showed just how the exigencies of a
political situation can compel even the English language toward extreme
rhetorical fervour. A poem like 'Questions and Answers' acts as a touchstone for
a new kind of sensibility, capable of uniting the most personal elements in the
poet's vision with a deep concern for public issues. What constitutes a major
difference between Nortje's poetry and other types of earlier 'protest' writing is
its tone of rebellious self-assurance, its malevolent compulsion toward
aggression, the lack of plea in it: its tone is harsh and unforgiving:

> I will not slip across the border
> patrolled by men with leashed Alsatians
> snarling along the barbed wire fences
> looking for a disturber of something or other:
> I am no guerrilla
> I will fall out of the sky as the Ministers gape from their front porch
> and in broad daylight perpetrate atrocities
> on the daughters of the boss: ravish like Attila
> and so acquire more scars myself
> laughing as I infest the vulnerable liberals
> with the lice inherited from their gold-mine fathers . . .[123]

This survey, gives, I hope, some idea of the social, cultural and political
forces at work in African poetry written in the major European languages. I
hope it gives, too, a glimpse of the vast panorama of themes and styles, of the
influences and examples, the strengths and weaknesses, in much of the significant body of work in nearly three hundred years of literary effort. The
indisputable conclusion that a critic is bound to reach after much reading and
a great deal of reflection upon this poetry, is that in Africa as elsewhere the
development of poetry is closely bound up with the social, economic and political development of society; that even styles and themes of this poetry often
reflect upon forces that are thought to be non-literary; but that, in fact, a careful analysis of these forces will often unmask much that lies hidden behind the
tortured obscurities of style and the frequent recurrence of themes.

REFERENCES

1 See Introduction to Ulli Beier and Gerald Moore, *Modern Poetry from Africa*, Penguin, London, 1963.
2 *Translations From the Night* (Selected Poems) by Jean-Joseph Rabearivelo, ed. John Reed and Clive Wake, African Writers Series, Heinemann, London, 1975, p.xiv.
3 Robert Boudry, *Jean-Joseph Ravearivelo et la mort*, Présence Africaine, Paris, 1958, with a preface by Jean Amrouche, p.79.
4 *Ibid.*, p.80
5 Rabearivelo, *Translations*, p.xvii.
6 See Ulli Beier's 'Ravearivelo, in Ulli Beier (ed.), *Introduction to African Literature*, Longman, London, 1964, p.89.
7 Edouard Eliet, *Panorama de la Littérature Negro Africaine*, Présence Africaine, Paris, 1965, p.32.
8 Boudry, *Ravearivelo*, p.56.
9 *Ibid.*
10 Rabearivelo, *Translations*, p.9.
11 *Ibid.*, p.12.
12 *Ibid.*, p.11.
13 *Ibid.*, p.44
14 *Ibid.*, p.xvii.
15 *Ibid.*, p.xv.
16 *Ibid.*
17 L.G. Damas, *Poétes d'expression française, 1900-1945*, Editions du Seuil, Paris, 1947, pp.224-5.
18 See Mazisi Kunene's paper, 'Culture Under Conditions of Conflict with Special Reference to Southern Africa', delivered in his absence by this writer to the York University Conference on Southern Africa, 1975.
19 *Ibid.*
20 Jean Paulhan, 'Les Hain-Teny: Poésie Obscure' (a paper read to the conference of the Société des Conférences Monaco, 6 January 1930).
21 Rev. James Sibree, *Madagascar Before the Conquest*, T. Fisher Unwin, London, 1896, p.193.
22 *Ibid.*, p.195.
23 *Ibid.*
24 See Léopold Sédar Senghor's Preface to *Chansons sur mon pays* by Flavien Ranaivo contained in the 1970 Kraus Reprint of the author's work.
25 See O. Mannon's preface to *L'Ombre et le Vent* in the same volume.
26 Ranaivo, *Chansons sur mon pays*, p.20
27 See Senghor's Preface to *Chansons*.
28 Flavien Ranaivo, *Le retour au Bercail*, Kraus Reprint, Nendeln, 1970, p.37.
29 See the interesting comments contained in his chapter, 'The Rebellion of 1947: Three Malagasy Martyrs' in Arthur Stratton's book, *The Great Red Island, a Biography of Madagascar*, Macmillan, London, 1965, p.264.
30 *Ibid.*
31 *Ibid.*
32 Jacques Rabmananjara, *Les Ordarlies*, Présence Afrcicaine, 1972, p.15.
33 *Ibid.*
34 *Les Ordarlies* (Akanin'ny Nofy), p.25
35 Rabemananjara, *Antsa*, Présence Africaine, 1961, p.19.
36 *Ibid.*, p.64.
37 *Ibid.*, p.37.
38 David Diop, *Coups de Pilon*, Présence Africaine, 1973, p.26.
39 *Ibid.*, p.36.
40 *Ibid.*, p.21.
41 *Ibid.*, p.14.
42 *Ibid.*, pp.14−15.

43 *Ibid.*, p.13.
44 Bernard B. Dadié, *Legendes et Poémes*, Seghers, Paris, 1966 and 1973, p.27.
45 *Ibid.*, p.244.
46 Lamine Diakhate, *Primordiale du Sixième Jour*, Présence Africaine, 1963, p.11.
47 Norman R. Shapiro (ed), *Negritude: Black Poetry from Africa and the Caribbean*, October House, New York, 1970, p.137.
48 Léopold Sédar Senghor, *Selected Poems: A Bilingual Text and an Introduction* by Craig Williamson, Rex Collings, London, 1976.
49 *French African Verse*, with English Translations by John Reed and Clive Wake, African Writers Series, Heinemann, 1972, p.181.
50 Diop, *Coups de Pilon*, p.33.
51 W. E. Abraham in an interview with Lewis Nkosi and Wole Soyinka for National Educational Television.
52 See Introduction to Léopold Sédar Senghor, *Selected Poems*, translated and introduced by John Reed and Clive Wake, Oxford University Press, 1964, p.ix.
53 Senghor, *Selected Poems*, p.50.
54 *Ibid.*
55 See Jacques Chevrier's discussion of these issues in *Littérature Nègre*, Armand Colin, Paris, 1974, p.207.
56 *Ibid.*, p.29.
57 *Ibid.*, p.12.
58 Léopold Sédar Senghor, *La parole chez Paul Claudel et chez les Nègro-Africains*, Les Nouvelles Editions Africaines, NEA, Dakar, 1973, p.7.
59 Tchicaya U'Tamsi, *Brush Fire*, Mbari Publications, Ibadan, 1964, (unpaginated).
60 Tchicaya U'Tamsi, *Selected Poems*, translated by Gerald Moore, AWS, Heinemann, 1970, p.114.
61 From 'Against Destiny' in U'Tamsi, *Brush Fire* (unpaginated).
62 *Ibid.*, p.25
63 *Ibid.*, p.1.
64 See Claire Clea's introduction to *Arc Musical and Epitome*, Pierre Jean Oswald, 1970, p.23.
65 U'Tamsi, *Selected Poems*, p.7.
66 D. Dathorne, *The Black Mind*, University of Minnesota, Minneapolis, 1974, p.379.
67 See Arthur Rimbaud's 'Les Premières Communions' in *The Penguin Book of French Verse*, Penguin revised edn., 1975, p.464.
68 *Ibid.*, p.73
69 *Ibid.*, p.112.
70 See Gerald Moore, 'Surrealism on the River Congo' included in *African Literature and the Universities*, Ibadan University Press, 1965, p.49.
71 U'Tamsi, *Selected Poems*, p.19.
72 Kofi Awoonor, *Night of My Blood*, Doubleday, New York, 1971, pp.52-3.
73 Mazisi Kunene, *Zulu Poems*, André Deutsch, London, 1970, p.80
74 *Ibid.*, p.87.
75 *Ibid.*, pp.34−5
76 See Timothy Wangusa's 'East African Poetry' in *African Literature Today, 6*, Heinemann, London, 1973, p.46.
77 See Gerald Moore's 'The Language of Poetry' in *African Literature and the Universities*.
78 Okot p'Bitek, *Song of Lawino*, East African Publishing House, Nairobi, 1968, p.16.
79 'African Easter' is included in *West African Verse*, ed. Donatus Nwoga, Longman, 1967.
80 *Ibid.*
81 'Piano and Drums' in Nwaga (ed.), *West African Verse*, p.36
82 See G. Adali-Mortty's poem, 'The Brink of Another Day', in *Messages: Poems from Ghana*, ed. Kofi Awoonor and G. Adali-Mortty, Heinemann, 1971.
83 *Ibid.*, p.102.
84 V. N. Volosinov, *Marxism and the Philosophy of Language*, trans. by Ladislav Matejka and I. R. Titunik, Seminar Press, New York and London, 1973, p.19.
85 Christopher Okigbo, *Labyrinths*, (poems including 'Heavensgate', 'Limits', 'Silences', 'Distances' and 'Path of Thunder'), AWS, Heinemann, 1971, p.6.
86 *Ibid.*, p.5.

87 *Ibid.*, p.65.
88 A detailed exposition of the ideas contained in Okigbo's poetry is to be found in Sunday O. Anozie's pioneering study, *Christopher Okigbo: Creative Rhetoric*, Evans, London, 1972.
89 See Introduction to Okigbo, *Labyrinths*, p.xi.
90 Okigbo, *Labyrinths*, p.24.
91 See Wole Soyinka's 'The Writer in a Modern African State' delivered at the African – Scandinavian Writers' Conference, Stockholm, 1967. Papers published by The Scandinavian Institute of African Studies, Uppsala, 1968, under the title, *The Writer in Modern Africa*, ed. Per Wastberg.
92 Wole Soyinka, *A Shuttle in the Crypt*, Rex Collings/Eyre Methuen, London, 1972, pp.6–7.
93 Wole Soyinka, *The Interpreters*, André Deutsch, London, 1965, p.12.
94 Wole Soyinka, *The Road*, Oxford University Press, 1965, p.11.
95 Soyinka, *A Shuttle in the Crypt*, p.10.
96 Eldred D. Jones: *The Writing of Wole Soyinka*, Heinemann, 1973, p.32.
97 Wole Soyinka, *Idanre and other Poems*, Methuen, London, 1967, p.82.
98 *Ibid.*, p.53.
99 See for example Bernth Lindfors's paper to the Association for Commonwealth Literature and Language Studies, 1974, at Makerere University, Uganda.
100 See Stanley Macebuh's 'Poetics and the Mythic Imagination', in *Transition*, ix, 50, (October 1975/March 1976).
101 *Ibid.*
102 Gerald Moore, *Wole Soyinka*, Evans, London, 1978, p.96.
103 Soyinka, *A Shuttle in the Crypt*, p.84.
104 J. P. Clark, *A Reed in the Tide*, Longman, 1965, p.5.
105 *Ibid.*, p.1.
106 J. P. Clark, *Casualties: Poems*, Longman, 1970, p.37.
107 N. J. Udoeyo, *Three Nigerian Poets*, Ibadan University Press, 1973, p.89.
108 *Ibid.*, p.3.
109 Margaret Dickinson (ed.), *When Bullets Begin to Flower*, East African Publishing House, Nairobi, 1972, p.52.
110 *Ibid.*, pp.60–1.
111 Agostinho Neto, *Sacred Hope*, Tanzania Publishing House, Dar es Salaam, 1974, p.47.
112 *Ibid.*, p.35.
113 See Hugh MacDiarmid's Foreword in Barry Feinburg (ed.), *Poets to the People*, Allen and Unwin, 1974.
114 Dennis Brutus, *A Simple Lust: Collected Poems*, Heinemann, 1973, p.12.
115 *Ibid.*, p.24.
116 *Ibid.*, p.27.
117 See Leroi Jones's 'A Dark Bag' in *Poetry* vol 103, 6, March 1964.
118 Don Mattera's 'Six Poems' appeared in *Index on Censorship*, iii,4,1974.
119 Oswald Mbuyiseni Mtshali, *Sounds of a Cowhide Drum: Poems*, Oxford University Press, London, 1972, p.12.
120 Mongane Wally Serote, *Tetslo*, Ad Donker, Johannesburg, 1974, p.9.
121 *Ibid.*, p.16.
122 *Ibid.*, p.10.
123 Arthur Nortje, *Dead Roots: Poems*, Heinemann, 1971, p.139.

CHAPTER EIGHT

AFRICAN DRAMA: ITS THEMES AND STYLES

1

As in our study of African poetry, this chapter is designed to cast a quick glance at the growing output of African drama, to pinpoint its main themes and styles, and to determine some of the major influences at work. Whenever this seems necessary, we will also speculate about future directions. Above all, we should try, as far as this is possible, to look beneath the surface of the actual theatre at certain levels of aesthetic and ideological formations.

African drama presents us with an initial problem. This problem is one of definitions. What is African drama? Where and when does it begin and what are its perimeters? In essence, this problem is an academic one because the need to describe and define an activity which goes on independently of these definitions arises out of the peculiar academicism of our time, with its compulsions to discover the outlines of art forms and their rules of operation, and also implies a need to talk about them in firmer tones.

The first major distinction to be made in African drama is that which separates traditional forms from the Western-orientated drama of the scripted play: within these two main categories further divisions and subdivisions can be endlessly made but will prove finally less significant than this initial division.[1] In this regard we must make the further important observation that traditional theatrical forms as such are not entirely obsolete; they have not become mere objects of historical inquiry, but continue to coexist with the new drama of the scripted play. This *simultaneity* of modern and traditional forms is itself not accidental but reflects the conditions of contemporary society in its transitional stage. Indeed, it is this *contemporaneity* of forms, the coexistence of the traditional with the modern drama, which makes for an immensely rich environment. However, this very richness creates its own problems; it also accounts for the inevitable confusion and bias which plagues any discussion of African drama.

Parading under the guise of academic neutrality, a great deal of this bias is merely ideological, motivated by scarcely veiled antipathy for, if not a fear of, political drama, in favour of the 'kola nut school' of writing, with its inevitable apparatuses of African fetish priests and 'tribal' gods. For example, Graham-White's refusal to discuss South African drama in a recent book[2] is accompanied by the odd explanation: 'Within sub-Saharan Africa, Ethiopia and the Republic of South Africa have not shared the typical experience of the succession of colonialism and independence.' More astonishingly, in trying to account for what he considers the greater creativity of West Africa, the author has to fall back on the old and discredited theory of 'geographical factors':

'West Africa enjoys a moderate rainfall and the forest is less dense than in the Congo basin.'

How to talk coherently about African drama, which, as well as the modern play, may encompass anything between the *Engungun* ritual of the Yoruba to the *Ntsomi* performance of the Xhosa in South Africa, is the kind of dilemma that only patient scholarship can hope to resolve. The first piece of prejudice that we clearly shall have to abandon is the notion that only that drama which takes as its province the world of African spirits, fetish priests and divinities is worthy of the name; that modern industrial society, because it too often reminds many Western commentators of the unsolved problems of their own societies, is somehow not a legitimate domain of the African playwrights.

2

We have already argued that African drama, traditional drama in particular, raises problems of definition. Not so long ago Claude Pairault alluded to some of these difficulties[3] when he spoke of the need to discover a terminology which would adequately describe the sort of activities covered by the notion of 'drama' in an African setting. Such an inquiry would have to begin with an inventory in the proper African languages of those terms which we could rightly consider as forming part of 'a vocabulary of the theatre'.[4] But why such an inventory? Pairault rightly argues that terms borrowed from European languages such as 'theatre', 'tragedy', 'comedy', 'scene', 'director' and 'actor', are too rigid and severely restricted to describe all the activities and functions associated with traditional African drama. For example, the word 'theatre' implies a distinction between the 'object' considered as 'spectacle' on the one hand and the subject who considers this spectacle on the other.[5]

The confusion deepens, becomes more perplexing the moment we try to isolate the most essential features of traditional African drama. As we have already suggested, any attempt to characterise modern African drama too narrowly in accordance with some of the usual classificatory definitions comes up against the initial hurdle of the *multiplicity* as well as the *simultaneity* of forms. When we read, for example, that theatre in Africa is 'more functional'[6] than in Europe and Amercia, we have to ask ourselves not only the question *which* African theatre, but in what way it is possible to speak of, say, *The Road*, as more 'functional' than *A View from the Bridge*.

Of course, 'cult' and 'ritual dramas' are 'functional' in a precise and obvious way − in a manner in which drama in Europe and America has ceased to be functional. Traditional forms of drama can only be apprehended in their mode of functioning within the framework of ritual, of religious festivals and other ceremonial activities: seasonal changes, harvesting, birth, initiation, marriage and death, have all been occasions for dramatic performance of one from or another.

Ulli Beier has given us a vivid description of a 'ritual drama' in performance among the Yorubas. Not only has Beier given us a vivid description of such a performance, but he himself has made a succinct but creditable transposition of one such drama, *The Imprisonment of Obatala*. Even a sketchy outline of the plot will give some indication of the imaginative flair of African myth which, in turn, is the source of so much of indigenous African drama.

Obatala, the Yoruba god of Creation, it is said, against the advice of the Oracle decided to pay a visit to Shango, the God of Thunder, who ruled at Oyo. Recognised everywhere by the spotlessly white garments he wore, on this occasion Obatala, it is said, employed neither heralds nor drummers to announce his coming; so it was that tricked by a mischievous minor deity, Eshu, into spilling palm oil over his raiments, Obatala was mistaken for a horse thief at his arrival at Oyo, and promptly thrown into prison. Meanwhile Shango knew nothing of the visitor's fate. Months passed and at last the choleric god, normally a munificent deity of all growing things, caused the rain to dry up. For a time no child could be born, seeds could not germinate, and there was much sadness in the land. It was only after the Oracle had been consulted and Shango had learned of the harsh treatment meted out to a fellow-deity that Obatala was set free with much apology. The world was once again restored to its former regularity and life and vegetation once again began to bloom anew.

In the hands of Ijimere and Beier this Yoruba myth gains a new lease of life. The vigour and directness of the language, as well as the austere economy of the plot, bring to the story a verve and freshness which quicken our enjoyment. Beier's English rendition of the play, especially, has the boldness as well as the immense dignity of African speech in a traditional setting. Of the vividness of this language we have a good example in the harsh eloquence of Eshu, the mischief-maker, following the frustration of his diabolic plots:

> Obatala's children must suffer the iron
> On their cheeks and penises
> As soon as they can walk.
> The goat offered to the father of laughter
> Suffer Ogun's iron on its throat.
> The child that Obatala moulds in the womb
> Is begot and born with blood.
> Ogun's iron is merely sleeping,
> For a while it is satisfied
> With a mere trickle of blood.
> Ogun is like the baby lizard
> Whose head is camouflaged with the female green;
> But when the penis stiffens between his scaly legs
> His true red colour will blaze out on his head
> Proving battle; and his deadly tail will be ready
> To slash his opponent's belly.[7]

Here and there, scattered fruits of preliminary scholarship can provide us with other examples of African drama in the traditional setting which will form the raw material for the kind of theoretical work which is necessary in piecing together a picture of traditional drama in precolonial African society. The annual *Igogo* festival at Owo in Western Nigeria, the Dahomey 'cult dramas', and the masquerades of the Ekine societies, have already been the object of close anthropological scrutiny. In fact, throughout Africa, whether it is the seven-day *Ozidi* epic staged by the Ijaw people of the Niger Delta, the *mmo* mask dramas of the Ibos or the elaborate dance-operas of the Zulus, traditional theatre is still very much alive in Africa and would repay a more painstaking study. These traditional forms have not only survived but continue to fertilise the new written drama whose principal exponents are the new generation of playwrights most of whom are university-trained.

A word of caution is due here. Contrary to what Banham and Wake tell us[8] African plays written in English and French are not merely an extension of this tradition; in many respects they represent a decisive break with that tradition. Nor is it merely a question of language. Were *A Dance of the Forests* or *Ozidi* (as reworked by J.P.Clark from its traditional materials) to be written in Yoruba and Ijaw respectively, they would still represent a significant rupture with tradition. The evolution of artistic forms does not always resemble the unbroken line of parentage between father and son; it is not simply a question of previous forms predetermining new aesthetic forms in a kind of seamless continuity. A decisive break may occur which cannot entirely be accounted for by what has gone on before!

What we ought to examine in particular is a whole ensemble of social, economic and political conditions in which one type of drama (the Western-orientated play) comes into production, is consumed, interpreted, and assimilated into African systems of belief. *Ozidi* by J. P. Clark and *A Dance of the Forests* by Wole Soyinka may rely on ritual sources but this does not entitle someone[9] to argue from this fact that they are 'traditional' plays if by 'traditional' he means those plays which continue the theatrical practice associated with precolonial forms of drama. What writers of plays as different as *A Dance of the Forests* and *Renga Moi* may succeed in doing in one case, is simply to use raw materials of myth, and in the other to extract from traditional art forms certain formal properties which are then acted upon to produce something new and sometimes wholly unexpected.

We are forced to conclude, therefore, that in Africa we are now faced not with a single, continuous line of development, linking modern drama to traditional dramatic forms; but rather we are confronted by two phenomena which may touch but more often than not merely exist side by side. In societies undergoing class formation we cannot talk of African theatre, as Banham and Wake tend to do, as *functional*, without also posing the question *for whom* this theatre functions. We must then deal with traditional theatre as a separate entity, inspired by certain necessities, both economic and spiritual (ideological), which simultaneously made certain types of African sculpture and carving possible. It is true, for example, that the characteristic of traditional African drama is its communal aspect, a collective working out in symbolic language of the fears, hopes and wishes of an organic community, a placation of the gods (the natural elements) and a placebo for the dead who are called upon to intercede for the living. There is no proper 'script' and therefore no single author, sometimes not even a proper audience since the audience itself is fluid and indefinable, constantly merging with the performers.

When we move into the area of modern scripted drama, with its theatre buildings, its networks of relationships between author, producer, director and actors, we are also confronted with the reality of the script as the initial act of literary creation. That is to say: drama as literature. This division between the traditional unscripted drama, often fused with ritual, and the modern scripted play, originating from the fertile imagination of its author, is not simply arbitrary, accidental and unexpected. On the contrary, the division is both economically and politically determined: the development of contemporary drama, frequently located in the theatre, confronting the audience as the *other* which is initially conceived as hostile, at best as indifferent; which must then be wheedled, persuaded, and if necessary coerced into approbation; this schism between audience and players is itself linked to class formations and group conflict which are increasingly becoming evident in the modern African state.

Whereas traditional drama speaks for the community as a whole, and whereas its purpose is to express the community's shared beliefs actualised in certain religious practices, now drama becomes the ideological projections of the social frustrations of the new middle classes to which African writers in general are invariably attached as a group even as they continue to express dissatisfaction with the hostility toward this class. The plays of R. Sarif Easmon of Sierra Leone are a primary example of how a drama already determined by its role within the development of a certain class, attempts to stage a phoney revolt only to return more securely into the soft bosom of the class of its own origins.

3

A number of dramatic texts, though written by modern African playwrights, seem uncertain how to mediate the oppositions between traditional systems of African belief and the modern critical spirit fostered by Western analytical thought. This uncertainty may reveal itself at the level of plot; it may also disclose itself at the level of method; but both difficulties are only symptomatic of a wider problem in which writers who are at best sceptical toward African religion try to situate themselves within the cosmos of African gods and spirit. 'What is said in a literary text,' Macherey tells us, 'does not necessarily correspond to the life of the author . . . some writers attach themselves to the secondary tendencies of their epochs, or to survivals of epochs already completed.'[11]

Tsegaye Gabre-Medhin's tragic drama, *Oda-Oak Oracle*, is one case in point. The play is clearly of the same provenance as J.P. Clark's *Ozidi*, Ama Ata Aidoo's *Anowa* and other mythologically based plays. The story which is drawn from traditional Ethiopian sources concerns an unequal struggle between, on the one hand, the hero and heroine, and the other, all the forces of conservatism and superstition represented in the drama by the *Oda*-priest and the elders. This short play briefly evokes the qualities of epic. In particular what the drama shares with *Obatala* as reworked by Ijimere and Beier is a certain concision in its exposition, though the unvaried pace and length of Gabre-Medhin's verse makes for occasional monotony. Nevertheless, when it is most effective the language has the same restrained dignity, the same profane candour, with the same hint of oracular power, as in Beier's translation of the Yoruba play. A striking example of this use of language can be seen in Shanka's plaintive cry as he twists and writhes in the grip of a sexual desire he and Ukutee, his betrothed, dare not assuage for fear of giving birth to a son fated to be sacrificed to the ancestral spirits:

> To draw
> Our burning thighs together
> Is to rouse
> The ghost of plagues
> That will attack
> The foetus in her womb[11]

However, despite its affinity with the traditional forms of African drama Gabre-Medhin's play is recognisably modern, written with a modern audience in mind. Harshly critical of tradition, it is also 'sceptical' in a way that no traditional African play can be sceptical without being considered sacrilegious. For instance, Goaa, Shanka's closest friend, urges sexual union between the hero and his betrothed in terms which can only be described, at the very least, as slighting to the ancestral spirits:

> The anger of our forefathers
> Is only a nightmare
> From the world of our dead,
> While the bitterness
> Of an ignored woman
> Is the truer hell
> Raging inside your hut,
> Take your bride into your arms
> Strong man, now:
> The desire of a lonely woman
> Is in the nature of a wild cat.[12]

We feel this throughout the play: that the anger of the African gods is a 'nightmare' from which we can awake if we wish; but the real drama is that being worked out between human beings in the triangle of sexual frustration and appeasement which has brought together Shanka, Ukutee and Goaa. Nevertheless, in spite of its unused potentiality for drama of richer and deeper meaning, *Oda-Oak Oracle* nearly succeeds and only fails at certain crucial points.

Gabre-Medhin's conception of the character of his hero is imperfect to a degree which seriously diminishes the impact of the play. Though he is several times described as 'the strong son of the Valley tribe' Shanka remains a cipher, weak and passive, to whom things happen rather than a strong individual who is able to initiate action. Since the play centres around the conflict between the forces of modernism on the one hand and those of tradition and conservatism on the other, the lack of strong will and purpose in the principal protagonist for one side badly enfeebles the action. Indeed, Shanka's single instance of defiance is his refusal to have sexual relations with Ukutee, an act which constitutes rebellion precisely because it is an attempt to frustrate the workings of a divine Fate. In the event, it is Ukutee herself who, desiring a baby, initiates action by having sexual relations with Shanka's best friend, Goaa. Ukutee is thus able to conceive. In a delightful twist of irony, instead of the expected male child who might have served splendidly for sacrificial purposes, a baby daughter is born who is immediately denounced by one angry elder as a thing 'too profane even for sacrifice'.[13]

A closer reading of the play, however, shows that the weaknesses in its structure are merely symptomatic of deeper problems: at the centre of the play is a hidden ideology, Christian in nature, which because it remains hidden, creates an unresolved discord and dissonance. Goaa, for example, is not a consistent character. In his essential character as *agent provocateur* he is a rebel against both tradition and the imported religion of the White strangers. There is a suggestion elsewhere that he once deserted the Valley to go with white people in 'their big floating huts'; and from these strangers he received 'The Word' which he in turn imparted to his friend, Shanka, but in the end it is Goaa himself who becomes disillusioned with the 'white strangers' while Shanka clings sentimentally to a quasi-Christian system of beliefs already thoroughly betrayed by its own confessors:

> They blow
> The name of their strange Word
> Whichever way the wind carries It,
> For they bear It.
> On the tip of their tongues,
> And not in their hearts
> Which are filled with fears . . .
>
> They market Its name
> To our kind, for gold; and
> For shame,
> While their frightened hearts
> Regard us
> As their open-day nightmares.[14]

And yet the play offers us no clear-cut choice between the cruel inflexibility of indigenous religion and the all too flexible uses to which Christianity is put by European colonisers: the criticism is well directed but the nature of the play's resolution is to leave us uncertain with which of the two characters we are supposed to identify, Shanka who reluctantly kills Goaa in a combat he did not seek, or Goaa, the spurner of tradition who simultaneously denounces any co-operation with the White strangers. After all, Goaa shows no perception of a third way out which might form the basis of a rationally ordered society.

It is this same failure to resolve what is, in its fullest implications, an ideological conflict between a modern critical spirit and a belief in traditional systems of religious faith and magic, which accounts for the lack of coherence in two dramas by two Ghanaian playwrights, Ama Ata Aidoo and Efua Sutherland. Both plays, *Anowa* by Ama Aidoo and *Edufa* by Efua Sutherland, require us to submit ourself to a system of belief which is partly undermined by the realistic mode in which the two plays are cast. More pertinent still to our argument is the failure of the two playwrights, who happen to be both women, to make explicit what remains in the text an implicit criticism of a male-dominated society, a dimly perceived wrong done to women. To make this criticism more explicit, one supposes, would require in the two heroines a fully developed consciousness of what their disadvantaged position might mean, what causes it and what might alleviate it, a consciousness which neither Anowa nor Ampoma is permitted to develop.

All in all, it is the enforced marriage between the supernatural and the realistic mode which undoes Efua Sutherland's play. The play's debt to Greek tragedy is obvious enough, but its attempts to incorporate the supernatural fail to meet our scepticism. Having been told by a diviner that he is to die unless someone else dies a 'substitute death' for him, Edufa, a wealthy businessman, tries to escape his fate by tricking his own father into taking his place as a scape-goat. He does so by casually asking his gathered family who among them loves him well enough to die for him. As the old man tells it:

How could we have known it was not a joke when you suddenly leaned back and asked which of us loved you well enough to die for you, throwing the question into the air with studied carelessness? Emancipated one, how could we have known of your treachery?

You have willed that some old wheezer like me should be the victim. And I was the first to speak. 'Not me, my son,' said I, joking. 'Die your own death. I have mine to die.' And we all laughed. Do you remember? My age was protecting me. Then Ampoma spoke. Yes, I see you wince in the same manner as you did when she spoke the fatal words that day and condemned her life. 'I will die for you, Edufa,' she said, and meant it too, poor doting woman.[15]

In panic, Edufa tries to get Ampoma, his wife, to forswear the oath, but it is too late; the charm is already working. When the play opens she is already slowly dying in the place of her husband. Given the nature of this plot, which mixes reality with fantasy, the play does not rise above the 'fairy tale' quality of myth; it thus sacrifices a wonderful opportunity for examining the nature of moral responsibility in terms which are fully acceptable to a modern audience.

Aidoo's play, Anowa, is more ambitious in scope, but it too hints at a world psychologically in conflict with its realistic mode. The play seems to be about the corrosive effects of acquisitiveness and slavery; it also seems to be a protest about the situation of women in African society. Nevertheless, Anowa's attack on her husband, Kofi Ako's materialism, on his exploitation of slaves as well as his 'conspicuous consumption' of wealth, is deprived of much of its force by the simple fact that Anowa's source of disaffection is not clearly brought out. In the end we are left with the vague impression that Kofi Ako's sexual impotence, the cause of which is mystically attributed to his cupidity in the pursuit of material wealth, matters more to Anowa than their ideological conflict which stems from Ako's views on slavery and the subjection of women.

As in Gabre-Medhin's drama Anowa rejects her prescribed role within traditional society without coming to any deeper understanding of what it is her rebellion implies. In the end, it is her mother, Badua, who refusing to sanction her daughter's apprenticeship to a priestess, hints at a profounder criticism of African religious tradition. 'My daughter shall not be a priestess,' she tells

Osam, '. . . in the end, they [priestesses] are not people. they become too much like the gods they interpret'.[16] There are other inconsistencies which indicate a play based on an imperfectly realised vision of the society; contradictions that float to the surface but remain unresolved.

One such contradiction immediately springs to mind: though Anowa attacks her husband's purchase of slaves, his rapacious accumulation of wealth; her disapproval does not, apparently, compel her to do without the slave service she so obviously abominates. All along she has co-operated, however reluctantly, with the amassing of that wealth which has become a millstone around her neck.

An ambitious playwright, who has made a magnificent contribution to the language of African drama, to the way ordinary village people speak when this language is cast into a foreign tongue, it is nevertheless a sad observation that Ama Aidoo has not yet succeeded in devising plots and characters whose interaction add up to a coherent view of society, which can reveal to us in dramatic form what she wishes African society to become in the light of its traditional past. In her first published play, *Dilemma of a Ghost*, this incoherence is more crippling to her art, for nothing in that thin gruel, supported by a wholly indigestible human pasty in the form of the black American woman, Eulalie, quite holds together. Again it is only the dialogue as spoken by the traditionalists, its combination of a bare rural simplicity with an occasional levening of proverbs and oracular wisdom, which carries the authority of African creation.

4

In English-speaking Africa the most exciting drama which, though conscious of Western techniques, tries to explore the indigenous tradition, has been undertaken in West Africa, especially Nigeria, and its two well-known exponents are the two Nigerian playwrights, Wole Soyinka and John Pepper Clark; but it is no exaggeration to say that while independence has liberated enormous energies in terms of artistic production, it has also revealed the unexpected hesitations and social ambivalence in writers who, by the nature of their education and professional interest, live too close to the social power of the new ruling class not to disclose certain social compulsions within their works that such a proximity engenders. In this connection we can cite certain plays which make a pretence of striking out against the claims of the new ruling class, but which confirm in their most intimate preoccupations an identity of interests between these writers and the new rulers. These plays are unable to tell us anything of value about the lives of ordinary people because in the main their imaginative capital is mortgaged to the remnants of bourgeois colonial culture which in turn is merely the extension of European metropolitan culture.

It is no exaggeration, I suppose, to say that the most astonishing manifestation of the emergence of European middle-class values on African soil is to be found in the plays of R. Sarif Easmon of Sierra Leone and J. C. De Graft of Ghana: surprising because in Europe where the middle class has been most triumphant, the writers who celebrate the virtues of this class can be counted on the fingers of one hand. The rest, in spite of their association with this class, feel obliged to mount an attack on what they regard as its essential philistinism, its single-minded dedication to the accumulation of wealth and material comfort, and its subordination of all spiritual needs to the requirements of production 'in the service of unlimited acquisition and accumulation'. Indeed, since the writings of Baudelaire and Flaubert, to say nothing of Engels and the young Marx, we have become accustomed to the most strident attacks on the so-called bourgeois life.

The really surprising thing about a playwright like Easmon is not that he writes with such apparent approval of the dominant values of his class, but that he seems unaware of some of the most stringent criticism that has been made of it. Fanon's attack on the new middle class which takes over from the departing colonial masters, for example, is that it is merely a pale reflection of an actual bourgeois class in the Western countries: it cannot create a national culture because its position as an agency of foreign domination renders it unable to; by this analysis the African middle class is simply a puppet class, sometimes aping its European masters, sometimes acting as agents of foreign capital but lacking real autonomy and originality.

It is, therefore, startling to find a play like *Dear Parent and Ogre* which seems to be written as a perfect illustration of the social physiognomy of this class. The very description of the interior decor of the play, the clothes and the buckets of champagne, are indices of unashamed bourgeois privilege. In the play itself these material objects, the furniture and the decor, are matched only by an ensemble of gestures which link the physical movements of the characters to the thoughts and feelings of every middle class character in the bourgeois novels or plays we have ever read or seen before: '*Deep in thought, he moves round end of settee to back. Bends over, rests his arms on back of settee, his head near Siata's.*'[17] Like the character of a West African novel who runs his hand through his short curly hair in imitation of his English lecturers at Oxford or Cambridge, these gestures are not as innocent as they may at first appear. They register certain emotions and appetites which may be new in an African context. In Scene 2, Act 3, of *Dear Parent and Ogre*, as a result of a victory at the elections which is achieved with the support of the trade unions, Dauda Touray, a lawyer-politician of impeccable aristocratic background, is about to assume the post of prime minister of Luawaland. We first see him sitting in his 'favourite arm-chair'; 'there is a glass of wine — one of those with elegant long stems — on the small table beside him'. Dauda is in 'white tuxedo, dress trousers and shoes', and he is reading through the congratulatory telegrams from many quarters; however, none brings him as much satisfaction as the one from an English friend of his student days. At his approval David Touray's pleasure bursts all bounds. He soliloquises: 'Dear English John, true philosopher, guide and friend of my student days! Yours is the most precious of all the messages I have received . . . The rest are but the chaff of this country's history.'[18] True, Dauda wants to do something for his country and for Africa, 'much more than fill your children's bellies with three square meals a day'.[19] He also wants to enshrine the principle of law and justice in the process of government: 'Dear Luawaland. The English brought you, and have left us, a standard. In whatever else I may fail may NEVER one of my countrymen stand up in a court of law and say: I NEVER KNEW THE ENGLISH TO DO THIS.'[20]

Dauda not only comes from the traditionally ruling aristocratic families of Luawaland, he is also engaged in a wearing struggle with his headstrong daughter, Siata, who seems determined to marry a successful pop-singer, Sekou Kuyateh, the descendant of Yalie slaves. Dauda himself is married to Françoise, a French woman, to whom he gave his heart when, after being widowed, he first 'saw her among the chestnuts in the Champs Elysees'. A *haute bourgeoise* to her finger tips, given to lacing her dialogue with such Gallic expressions as 'Bête — comme toujours!' — Françoise's marriage to Dauda Touray is symbolically speaking, the most perfect embodiment of the alliance between the European bourgeoisie and the emergent ruling class in Africa. It is to this union that her stepson, Saidu, armed with an inevitable bottle of champagne, pays tribute on the occasion of his and Sekou's return from a triumphant tour of France:

Your health, dear Mamman.
And may you always have the inspiration to combine your France and our Africa in the same genial way you have brought together our native costume and your country's best beverage to welcome us today . . .[21]

This toast, I may add, is not offered in any sardonic spirit. Saidu's notion of culture is quintessentially *bourgeois* in the worst sense of the term, revelling as it does in the mere possession of commodities or conspicuous consumption of them: 'Parents', he says at one time, 'owe their children the obligation of bringing them up in an atmosphere of culture. Champagne is a physical essential to that background.[22] This view of 'culture' as the mere surface glitter and polish is never once challenged; indeed, it is constantly reinforced; by among others, Sekou Kuyateh, Siaka's suitor, who remembers visiting the Touray household in the old days which 'gave me a peep beyond the horizon of my life into a realm of light, colour and magic'; by the trade union leader, Mahmoud Saweneh who, gazing at the room in which he has just been admitted, declares with all the force of his being:

This IS a beautiful room. I see it. I feel it. It speaks a kind of civilisation that I hunger for, hate and desire with a bitterness and longing I cannot describe. Deep down, I suppose all human beings aspire to this kind of culture . . .[23]

Given these attitudes which are fundamental to the life depicted in the play, the conflict between Dauda Touray, the 'father and ogre' of the title, and his two children, Saidu and Siata, is no more than a reworking of a rather trite theme of what is now called the 'generation gap'. Enmeshed as it is in its 'inauthentic values', even on the level of method the play is unable to offer anything more dynamic than the usual format of English drawing room comedy; or anything, for that matter, which faintly suggests the actual rhythms of African life. The revolt of the young is as 'phoney' as the lives led by their elders. What Sekou Kuyateh, whose artistic creativity consists of setting to music Byron's 'So, we'll go no more a-roving/So late at night', will be able to contribute to national culture, is not very clear. On the other hand, Easmon's writing is not incompetent or unconfident, and what this play is finally able to show us is a glimpse of life among the ruling classes of the new Africa, their newly acquired toy-gadgets and tastes, their appetite for power and the liberal sentimentality which cloaks this appetite.

The theme of 'generation conflict' is taken up by J.C. de Graft of Ghana with the same disastrous results, disastrous because, like Easmon, where De Graft is standing he cannot possibly see where the battle begins and where it ends. This time the 'father and ogre' is a self-made businessman, James Ofusu, who wants his son, Aaron, to become a mechanical engineer, and his daughter, Maanan, to become 'Ghana's first lady lawyer'. The elder Ofusu states the case clearly and uncompromisingly:

> If I know anything, it is that this world is moved by men in bigger positions; men who have been to college and university; men who know, and who because they know are entrusted with bigger responsibilities: trained men like your lawyers and accountants and engineers and doctors. [24]

Both Aaron and Maanan have different ideas; the former wishes to be a painter, the latter wants to be a dancer; but their revolt carries them no further than the mere repetition of the tired clichés about the sanctity of art; because Aaron, for one, while he rejects the connection between artistic success and financial reward, he cannot see that artistic activity and the kinds of rewards which a society offers its artists are inseparable from the mode of economic activity which dominates the life of the country. Though De Graft clearly sees − and that he is able to do this is surely to his credit − that the life of the new middle class is constricting and stifling to the best that is imaginative in the society he writes about, he is nevertheless unable to see any form of alternative life; as a result his protest, never very emphatic, dwindles into a muted cry of rage by two thwarted individuals who cannot even understand that it is in the very nature of this new 'money-making class' not to want to promote any art which works at a deeper level of inspiration, which would then truly reflect the aspirations of the people.

Through A Film Darkly is even less of a play than its self-conscious narrative method at first promises. De Graft has a way of picking up important issues and then not making much of them. Ostensibly the play is about *racism*, the psychological damage done to the personality of Ghanaian students in England; in the character of John we see that the wounds opened in England continue to fester long after his return home. The play is therefore about the memory of racism; but racism itself is only superficially examined. After the bit of melodrama between John and Rebecca, the most incredible relationship in the entire play, Fenyinka's long harangue about the corrosive effects of racism has echoes of real feeling, but its didactic quality has at best a tenuous relationship with the rest of the play. Perhaps because he is such an uninteresting character, which is but another way of saying that as a character he is not properly motivated, nothing that has happened to John, the alleged victim of English prejudice, has any power to move us. For example, it is difficult to see why John should be so inconsolable at the discovery that Molly, the English girl he had begun to love in England, was keeping anthropological notes about him and his culture, at best a clumsy indiscretion, at worst a bizarre form of academic curiosity. Certainly there is no suggestion that for all that the girl did not love him. Therefore, to say, as John does 'what of the wreck Molly made of my life?' seems a preposterous exaggeration.

In this play as in the other plays we have been looking at, the problem, as usual, seems always to lie elsewhere other than in the actual dramatic form. This kind of play is always worrying continuously on the edges of what may become, if properly realised, a core of significant social consciousness but without ever really plunging in. Though De Graft constantly hints at something more fundamentally wrong with society than the memory of racial insult, something infinitely more corrupt and corrupting than the failure of love — 'It's money that matters in Ghana now, you know. Money and big cars' — the play-wright is unable to relate such a perception to the central concern of the play. The petit-bourgeois lives which the playwright unfolds before us; the claustro-phobic, self-consuming paranoia and frustration, the quest for status which fails to satisfy the feelings of personal impoverishment and limitation; the end-less discussions of the villainy of house-servants and the malevolence of unfriendly neighbours; all this and more, alert us to certain social formations in the society which are related to class and other material conditions, but whose connections and interpenetration remain unexamined in the drama. It is for this reason that the play's constant striving toward 'modernity' remains an empty yearning like the desire for a new car model which, when it is finally delivered, proves to be the same old one, only painted over and slightly tarted up. Properly speaking, these plays cannot break away from the stifling frame of the drawing room drama because there is nothing in the lives of the individuals they portray which demands either the enlargement of the form or the explosion of the dramatic frame.

5

Such an enlargement, if it can be detected anywhere, is to be found in the work of two Nigerian playwrights, Wole Soyinka and John Pepper Clark. Both of them products of the University College of Ibadan, and having largely pioneered modern literature of the post-independence phase, they have become something of elder statesmen to a younger generation of poets and dramatists who were at school when the Clark and Soyinka generation began to publish. Both Soyinka and Clark write drama as well as poetry, but Soyinka is indisputably the dramatist whose poetry is only occasionally successful, while Clark is the poet whose drama works better between the pages of a book than on the stage. But even when we take into account their limitations in certain individual fields of literary activity, their contribution to the change in the direction the literature of their country has taken since the hesitant beginnings of the 'pioneers' of the 1940s, has been immense.

An Ijaw from the Delta region of the Niger, John Pepper Clark first gained attention as a dramatist with the production of his *Song of a Goat* (1962), a verse tragedy about a man's sexual impotence and the passions aroused by his wife's adultery with his brother. During the purification ceremony guilt is established when Zifa, the husband, cuts off the head of the goat and compels his brother, Tonye, to thrust the head into the pot until the pot breaks. Realising at once the symbolic import of this, Ebiere, already pregnant by Tonye, her brother-in-law, faints and miscarries, bleeding to death. In remorse, Tonye runs into the hut and, locking himself inside, hangs himself. Zifa, Ebiere's husband, is last seen walking into the sea where, in the play's final catastrophe, he drowns himself. While Clark is able to recreate the 'feel' of traditional African society in tight verse forms, no mean achievement in itself, he has often been criticised for his inability to create dramatic action; certainly this criticism applies with greater force to his two subsequent dramas, *The Masquerade* and *The Raft*, both of which are rather static as theatre; they are vehicles for a poetic sensibility which might have been found a more suitable outlet in radio drama than on the stage. But for all its occasional echoes of Elizabethan blank verse and Greek classical tragedy, *Song of a Goat* is a real achievement, evocative of much of the poetry of village life in a traditional African setting, with its moral certainties, its strict adherence to a time-tested code of honour and social regularity; its rigorous pursuit of justice and, inevitably, the severe punishment meted out for crimes which appear to us now only forms of moral offence. There is nothing particularly African in all this except in the specific detail of social organisation and the fidelity to local colour.

There is a sense in which Clark's previous dramatic works can be said to have been a preparation for his *Ozidi* (1966) an epic work which has not only strengthened his reputation as a poet of the theatre but has also clearly demonstrated his power to break new ground. *Ozidi* is a revenge tragedy. The plot turns around the story of a child brought up by his grandmother, Oreame, the witch, in order to avenge his father, an aspirant to the throne who was treacherously killed by his clansmen. Having been invested with magical powers Ozidi II embarks on his murderous career, slaying the guilty and the innocent alike, until no longer able to arrest the process, he kills his grandmother. The recasting of this annual festival drama, first taped and filmed by Clark in his own Ijaw region, has had a revitalizing effect on his earlier, rather precious Elizabethan blank verse; the language is looser, freer, the handling of the larger scenes has the fascination of the pomp and pageantry of all masquerade drama. There are lapses, of course; the use of English slang words like 'thug' and 'sucker' in a traditional drama have a jarring effect; on the other hand, they are more than compensated for by the rich imagery contained in some of the excellent passages when the playwright's considerable powers as a poet are given their full stretch; note how he uses and extends the 'yam' metaphor in Scene 7 of Act III:

Ofe:	I was such a fool, believing the catfish cannot come Out of a bamboo trap. Now I am pricked on All sides by its thorns.
First Citizen:	(*stepping forward from behind Ewiri*) You led the tilling of the land.
Second Citizen:	Alone you carried the head of the yam That you all planted.
Third Citizen:	Now it is harvest time, and the yam Has thrown such a tuber it taps The bowels of the earth.

Fourth Citizen:	Above the ground, its leaves and
	Tendrils spread so wide, if you do not shore up
	The plant, it certainly will choke all the land,
First Citizen:	So please trim down this blossom.
Second Citizen:	Dig up the treasure to its last root.[25]

The play provides many other examples of Clark's superb gift for imagery. Nevertheless, in spite of some very positive elements, doubts about the play remain. Though in this play Clark has given himself a greater freedom than in any of his previous work, the freedom has been at the expense of a tighter unity and economy, the absence of which risks a considerable diffusion of energy. For example, Act I by itself has nine scenes, Act III has eight; such criticism raises, of course, the question of how close Clark's version of the drama is to the original and whether the plea of fidelity to the original epic is a sufficient ground for exonerating a modern playwright from criticism for what seems in the end a very loose and rambling play. Then there is a more serious problem which applies with equal force to everything Clark has written. Clark's *oeuvre* is, I would say, less satisfying because of a lack of controlling idea or philosophy of society behind it; his work always seems to lack an organising principle: nothing gives it personal stamp; no obsession, no physic wounds, no vision of society beyond a tepid humanism, gives us a perspective from which to judge his writing. Whatever dissatisfactions it may arouse, this is not a charge that can be made against the work of his compatriot, Wole Soyinka.

Of the modern school of African dramatists, Wole Soyinka is by far the most internationally well-known. He was only 23 when his first plays were staged in London and Nigeria but it was not until 1959 that Soyinka emerged as a playwright of note with the production at the Ibadan Arts Theatre in Nigeria of his first two plays *The Swamp Dwellers*, a drama in which village life is seen under the stresses of social change; and his flawless comedy, *The Lion and the Jewel*, which tells the story of an ageing chief, a reactionary old lecher who, against all the expectations of modern audiences grown accustomed to witnessing the triumph of the new against the old Africa, wins a local belle from his rival, a progressive but ineffectual school teacher. Baroka's courtship of Sidi, the village 'jewel', is one of the most effective pieces of comic writing in all of African drama:

> Yesterday's wine alone is strong and blooded, child,
> And though the Christians' holy book denies
> The truth of this, old wine thrives best
> Within a new bottle. The coarseness
> Is mellowed down, and the rugged wine
> Acquires a full and rounded body . . .
> Is this not so — my child?[26]

The Trials of Brother Jero, a light-hearted farce, concerning the activities of a false beach prophet, shows Soyinka to be continuing his development in the direction of comic satire that world culminate in *Kongi's Harvest*, a bitter attack on power corruption in what seems a composite of two African states.

187

This play won him the Drama Prize at the 1966 Dakar Festival of Negro Arts.

A Dance of the Forests is Soyinka's first major work in which the author's highly developed satirical talent is given full play. Writing for the Nigerian independence celebration in 1960, the author turns a jaundiced eye on the 'gathering of the tribes' and mocks the august ceremony as an occasion for unsavoury bickering among the potentates, royal prostitutes and power-hungry artists recalled from the other world to share in the state proceedings. *A Dance of the Forests* is a many-layered play, with different levels of meaning, but already in this drama Soyinka brings into focus some of the main themes which have become central to his work ever since.

In one form or another, his most serious plays deal with the African past, with the need to clarify and understand this past, if it is to be used as a basis for the future, an understanding which, for Soyinka, especially in this play, means accepting the glorious as well as the inglorious aspects of national history. He is also concerned with the corrupting influence of power upon artists and states-men alike; and, finally, with the indissoluble link between death and destruc-tion on the one hand and the principle of creation or renewal on the other. As in his nearly unfathomable tragedy *The Road,* first presented in London's Stratford East, the writing in *A Dance of the Forests* is dense, enigmatic, gnomic, with symbols and motifs drawn mainly from Yoruba lore, especially the ancestor-worship ceremonies of the Yoruba *Egungun.*

Soyinka has sometimes been justly criticised for being too cryptic in his use of symbols for his plays to yield their full meaning; but happily what stands him in good stead is his ability to create strong characters and strong dramatic situation; usually, his plays absorb our interest, even though the ultimate meaning may be lost on us; it is, indeed, very rare that a Soyinka play, however dense its language, loses completely its hold upon an audience. This says a great deal for Soyinka's instinctive sense of the dramatic. He himself has stated as his primary purpose giving theatrical pleasure to his audiences: 'My prime duty as a playwright', he has said, 'is to provide excellent theatre . . . to make sure they the audience do not leave the theatre bored.'[27]

It is not easy to sum up Soyinka's achievements. A versatile and prolific writer; a teacher, an actor, and producer; an editor and controversial speaker, he has done so many things, some so well that it is not easy to see just how anyone could have done them better; others so badly that it is fair to say no one could have done them worse. His ventures into critical comment, for example, are usually tense, exhibitionistic affairs written in impenetrably dense and pre-tentious language; his fiction alternates between passages of immense power and acute psychological insights and stretches of extremely tortuous and verbose writing. However, it is as a dramatist that Soyinka's reputation will come to rest; and here his immense contribution to modern African theatre, if there is still any doubt about it, will come to be truly recognised for what it is.

There is, first of all, the question of his contribution to language. It is true that the critical response to Soyinka's handling of language has been mixed, some finding in his work a great 'feeling for words',[28] while some deprecate what they consider wilful obscurity clothed in 'esoteric idiom';[29] some praise the 'Johnsonian richness'[30] and the 'verve of his language' which 'continually suggests another world of sounds, lying beyond it,'[31] while others speak of 'lapses into an ensnaring verbal facility and mannered obscurities of expression'.[32] Although there is some truth on both sides of the argument – even Soyinka's most unrestrained admirer, E.D. Jones, has spoken of a self-conscious violence of imagery which ranges from the beautiful to the absurd – neither point of view can be wholly justified without taking into account the general context in which the Soyinka language functions: for example, in a poem his difficult, 'archaic' and contorted syntax can seem a gratuitous obfuscation of meaning whereas in a play, with the aid of subtle characterisation and appropriate situation, the same passage can exercise a near hypnotic power. Above all, we must be wary of the kind of criticism which rests purely on the fact that Soyinka is 'difficult'. A great number of important literary texts are 'difficult' and obscure and we can only derive full enjoyment in our reading of them through painful and earnest labour, repeated over a number of times.

As a satirist, Soyinka's gift for epigram is rightly celebrated; he has trenchant wit and a great power for invective language. In his plays, moreover, Soyinka's chronic struggle with language, finds partial solution not by offering meaning on the literal plane, but simply by providing a dramatic context through which meaning can usually be worked out. It may be, of course, that even after situating the utterances of certain characters within the context of an arcane traditional theology we can find no satisfactory meaning; certainly attempts to decipher the meaning of some of the obscurer speeches of the Professor in *The Road* may be as mistaken as they are doomed to failure; but in my opinion, such difficulties are not as exasperating in the plays as they are in the novels. This is simply because, whereas in the expository passages of the novel these difficulties can be attributed to the author's failure to communicate properly, in a play they may be legitimately blamed on a character's idiosyncratic use of a language. With Professor we are never sure, for example, whether some of the flights into metaphysical fancy are backed by the author or whether we are meant to regard them as the ravings of a madman. Whatever reservations there may be on this point, there is no doubt that in many passages of his plays – especially *The Road*, and *A Dance of the Forests*, Soyinka's language, in its very lunatic twists and turns, can sometimes attain the heights of poetry. This is particularly true where dailogue is used to reveal some important psychic depth of personality or a moment of intense moral light and illumination. Such a moment comes at the end of *A Dance of the Forests* when 'Forest Head' contemplates the unceasing folly of men and the gods:

> My secret is my eternal burden – to pierce the encrustations of soul-deadening habit, and bare the mirror of original nakedness – knowing full well, it is all futility. Yet I must do this alone, and no more, since to intervene is to be guilty of contradiction, and yet to remain altogether unfelt is to make my long-rumoured ineffectuality complete; hoping that when I have tortured awareness from their souls, that perhaps, only perhaps, in new beginnings . . . Aroni, does Demoke know the meaning of his act?[33]

In the past ten years the glossing of Soyinka's dramatic texts has gone on apace and his work has, no doubt, provided much useful employment for many grateful scholars and commentators; yet for all the scholarly theses, for all the unsolicited explanations and indifferent commentaries, the question of what Soyinka's plays are truly about; of what, given the totality of his work and output, his general philosophical position amounts to is never made clear; what attitudes he means us to take to the perennial issues he raises surrounding the meaning of death, self-sacrifice, and redemption, remain only superficially indicated or largely unanswered.

He is, we are told often enough, preoccupied with the theme of 'conflict between the values of the old society and the new'.[34] There are other pre-occupations which are usually mentioned in relation to Soyinka's work. One that immediately comes to mind is the all too obvious concern with the cyclical nature of human suffering: 'the sense of the repetitive futility, folly and waste of human history'[35] and, given this condition, the need for redemption. According to his most loyal and devoted annotator, Soyinka is also interested in 'individuals who doggedly pursue their vision in spite of the opposition of the very society they seek to save'.[36] Self-sacrifice, individual quest, the isolation of the gifted or maimed individual from society, and the greater likelihood that such an isolation will produce an individual with vision, capable of discovering the abiding truths of human existence, are all common themes in Soyinka's plays. The most illuminating commentator on the playwright's Yoruba heritage speaks of the author's exploration of 'the role of the spiritually elect in a human community'.[37]

There is no doubt from his many pronouncements, that Soyinka endorses this view of the artist as somehow belonging to some kind of special priesthood, periodically susceptible to temptation, like Demoke and Court poet in *A Dance of the Forests*, but at his best capable of dragging society screaming toward the summit of human consciousness from where, if not actually saved, special individuals might glimpse the possibilities of their own salvation. What this salvation consists of besides leading society to something very nearly like a theatrical purgation it has never been clear. Whatever it is, it is not political. For a writer who mentions the word 'revolution' as often as Soyinka does in his public pronouncements, his distrust of politics and politicians has been as remarkable as it is perplexing. Soyinka is undoubtedly a committed writer, but we have yet to learn to what exactly he is committed. Comparing the Nigerian with John Arden, the British playwright, Graham-White comments that 'both are sceptics in the face of ideology and write plays about governing from *extra-political viewpoints* of the individual's human needs and aspirations'.[38] (Italics mine) Indeed, it is this religious tendency in his work, the quest for the salvation of society, not in political struggle to which ordinary people can be drawn, but in some metaphysical scheme of things, which is a disturbing and dangerous element in Soyinka's work; its link to elitism, to the worship of death and nihilistic gesture, have not been pointed out often enough.

What, then, to use Lucien Goldmann's term, is the 'world-view' contained in Soyinka's work? Soyinka, it seems to me, is often showing us a group of individuals, usually educated, usually artists; individuals, at any rate, who are gifted in some extraordinary way; who are frustrated and at war with the social order. Isolated, 'alienated' and burdened with extreme self-consciousness, these individuals frequently seek salvation not in politics but in quasi-religious solutions. Very often the plays are built on an opposition between a messianic individual on the one side and an indifferent humanity on the other, between a group of enlightened intellectuals and a group of bungling bureaucrats, whether academic, government or business men.

We can, if we wish, say that Soyinka's plays are a continuous attempt to resolve certain contradictions in African society during its transitional stage between colonial tutelage and political independence. Indeed, it is possible to see the attempts to find a solution to the conflict between traditionalism and modernism in plays like *The Swamp Dwellers, The Lion and the Jewel,* and *Kongi's Harvest* as related to this larger struggle; and Soyinka's tendency to come down on the side of traditionalism, sometimes no more than a mischievous prank to tease the committed modernist, only increases the fun but should never be taken as more serious than that. How to reconcile the scientism of the modern age with traditional African beliefs is what Soyinka, like most African writers, appears to be truly engaged in; but it is also worth noting that Soyinka's preoccupation with religion, his mania for the deification of our gross lusts and social ambitions as somehow a revelation of a clash of wills among various divine powers leads him away from what is potentially his greatest strength: the portraiture of a sub-class whose presence is swelling numbers at the outskirts of our cities is the source of an unending nightmare for the ruling elites.

It is the collective portrait of spivs and small-time criminals in *The Road* which endows the play with its harrowing air of menace as well as its peculiar energy. Professor dominates the play, it is true, but he is only palpable as a character through his manipulation of this dangerous underworld that teeters always on the edge of revolt. An absurd windbag, a pettifogging bureaucrat and religious poseur, Professor has no reality outside theirs; but his frustrations as a one-time lay preacher, his successes as a forger, and his eternal quest for meaning in a meaningless universe makes him the most poetic emblem for a group of African intellectuals whose relation to the state and civil society is extremely problematical and ambiguous. Soyinka's great achievement has been to find theatrical forms and an idiom varied enough to dramatise the frustrations of a certain group in African society; his weakness has been his constant striving after metaphysical formulas which merely mask these frustrations.

6

Although the quality is patchy, and the level of general achievement is not as high as in Ghana and Nigeria, French-speaking West Africa has a well-established modern theatrical tradition, which received impetus with the setting up in Senegal in the 1930s, of the Daniel Sorano National Theatre at the William Ponty School. During the vacations the pupils of William Ponty were charged with the task of gathering African traditional folklore and local legends; these were later used as the basis of plays which, although written in French, were suffused with the feelings of traditional African culture. Due to the fact that all the French-speaking African states were then under the French colonial umbrella, pupils of the William Ponty came from many states outside Senegal. In Mali elements of the William Ponty were amalgamated with those of the Bambara traditional theatre.

Since the days of the William Ponty there have been three Senegalese plays worthy of our attention: *Les derniers jours de Lat Dior* by Amadou Asse Dia (1965), *L'exil d'Albouri* by Cheik N'Dao (1967) and *El Hadj Omar* by Gérard Chenet. All three plays deal with some aspects of African history. For example, *L'exil d'Albouri*, which won the author the Gold Medal at the Algiers Festival of African Arts, deals with the conflict between the French colonisers and the last of the Joloff sovereigns, who chooses exile rather than submission to the European victors.

Drama woven around historical personages, usually ancient heroes of African empires, is a favourite with African playwrights. President Senghor has written a drama about *Shaka*, the Zulu king, which was presented in Nigeria at the Ife Festival in 1966. Plays like *La recontre secrète de l'Almany Samory et de Tieba* by the Malian writer, Mamadou Outtara, *Tanimoune* by Andre Salifou of the Niger Republic, and in South Africa the historical plays about Zulu kings by the late poet and playwright, H.I.E. Dhlomo, are all part of the same genre. In popularity the historical play is rivalled only by the play of 'culture conflict' of which *L'Oracle* by Paul Mayenga of Congo-Brazzaville or *L'appel du fétiche* by Moctar Fofana of Mali are good examples. Both plays deal with the pull exerted by witchcraft and the supernatural upon a hero and heroine who wish to live modern lives.

To end this critical survey of African drama, it is necessary to mention a few important developments in connection with the future of African theatre. The first of these lies in the emergence of political theatre of great vitality and resourcefulness exemplified by the work of Ngugi wa Thiong'o and Micere Githae, *The Trial of Dedan Kimathi* (1976).

It is not clear how much Ngugi was responsible for the writing of the play and what portion is the work of Micere Mugo; perhaps it does not matter that much except the desire to appease our curiosity. What is certain is that *The Trial of Dedan Kimathi*, more than *Petals of Blood*, is one of the most perfect exhibitions of a revolutionary impulse seeking and finding its true and proper form. *The Black Hermit* was a feeble and unconvincing work, with a hollow, improperly articulated figure at its centre. The choice of Dedan Kimathi as the hero of this play allows us to focus our attention around a figure of great political interest.

Dedan Kimathi was one of the greatest heroes of the freedom struggle for nationhood in Kenya. Ngugi and Micere Mugo's choice of the subject is itself an indication of their concern to recover for theatre and for literature what will remain an important event in the history of Kenya, the country's transformation from a colonial possession to an independent status. By refusing to confine the play within the frame of a trial, hence within a fixed and static theatrical frame, Micere Mugo and Ngugi have created a free-wheeling work, restlessly eloquent, allowing workers and peasants to speak in words and in songs with a power rarely heard before in the African theatre. In *The Trial of Dedan Kimathi* the African revolution has found its true voice.

The second development concerns the exploration of indigenous forms to be seen in the work of Robert Serumaga and the Abafumi Theatre Company of Uganda, with its attempts to integrate various disciplines – speech, music, dance, mime − into a unified vehicle of communication. I was perhaps one of the first writers on the theatre to point out both the relevance and the fructifying potential of other artistic forms, such as African carving, to the development of indigenous African theatre.[39] Since then Serumaga has gone so far as to attempt a complete elimination of human speech from his plays.

> European theatre gives us only part of a human being − intellect and speech as a creator of logical sense. We view the human being as the capsule from which can be released a tremendous energy. His body is the clay from which we create sculptured forms. We exploit sounds other than those of actual speech and that is why you'll find that in our plays we hardly ever rely on dialogue to convey the story.[40]

Critics of Serumaga have been quick to point out that in view of the political climate in Uganda at the time that he was writing, 'speech', being so explicit, was to a particularly inconvenient means of expression. Be that as it may, there is no denying the visual power of a play like *Renga Moi*. The initial response to this play is one of incredulous astonishment at the plasticity and power of bodies moving with the lithe precision of prowling panthers and just as suddenly the mute frozen stillness of bodies grouped like carved figures on the stage. It is a theatre of constant, restless movement which is paradoxically capable of immense stillness and aching immobility. Leaning heavily on traditional African modes of drama, the sound, shape, colour and movement are so closely textured to the purposes of the drama as to make it nearly impossible to isolate any one element from the total expression of its meaning.

Although quite compelling in themselves, the achievements of the Abafumi Company cannot be viewed in isolation from the development of African theatre elsewhere on the continent. Indeed, Serumaga's theatre company came to the 1975 World Theatre Season at the Aldwych, London, in the track of an even bigger critical success by the National Theatre Workshop of South Africa for their presentation of a Zulu version of *Macbeth*, which was memorable for its marriage of Western styles with traditional 'dance opera' techniques, a performance which led one English critic to speculate that 'apart from the splendid dancing and singing' the company had shown 'the possibility of a valid African acting coupled with a sophisticated literary script'. This return to traditional forms of theatre for ideas and inspiration is a process which is going on simultaneously in different parts of Africa. Folk opera in Nigeria has become a veritable movement, with the plays of Kola Ogunmola, Herbert Ogunde, Daro Lapido and Obatunde Ijimere, leading the field; these 'folk operas', together with the *hira-gasy* players of Malagasy and the *Agerfikir* theatre of Ethiopia, provide a useful bridge between the 'elitist' drama which caters for educated audiences and popular forms of entertainment aimed at ordinary people. The strength of this kind of theatre is that it usually employs the vernacular, and the dialogue is interspersed with songs and dances all of which help to reinforce the central theme. For the bulk of the African population only just emerging from illiteracy, this form of popular theatre offers the best means of communication between the artist and his audience; and not surprisingly in almost every instance of its manifestation, in the *hain-*

teny song of Malagasy as much as in the popular song of the Nigerian folk opera, this entertainment has become a source of vigorous 'social criticism' which falls somewhere between the Western 'morality play' and the 'satirical review' of the modern theatre. Here is part of a popular song from Kola Ogunmola's *The Love of Money*:

> Yo! Yo! Yo!
> Yorubas think!
> Yorubas have turned themselves into a football
> They kick you up
> They kick you down.
>
> Don't trust your luck:
> The girls of nowadays are bad you know;
> The girls of nowadays are hard.
> They merely come to eat you clean,
> They shave your head and paint it black.
> Beware of them!
> If the world rewards you, live wisely!
> Money does not stay in the same place for generations to come:
> Fear the son of man.

REFERENCES

1   See Oyin Ogumba's paper 'Modern Drama in West Africa' in C. Heywood (ed.), *Perspectives on African Literature*, Heinemann, London, 1968 p.81. See also the introduction to Anthony Graham-White's book, *The Drama of Black Africa*, Samuel French, New York, 1974, p.2.
2   Graham-White. *The Drama of Black Africa*.
3   See Claude Pairault's, 'Où trouver le theâtre?' in *Le Theâtre Nègro-Africain: Actes du colloque d'Abidjan – 1970*, Présence Africaine, Paris, 1971, p.16.
4   *Ibid.*
5   *Ibid.*
6   Martin Banham with Clive Wake, *African Theatre Today*, Pitman, London, 1976, p.1
7   Obotunde Ijimere and Ulli Beier, *The Imprisonment of Obatala and other plays*, Heinemann, 1969, p.43.
8   Banham and Wake, pp.1 – 3
9   See Ola Rotimi's 'Traditional Nigerian Drama' in Bruce King (ed.), *Introduction to Nigerian Literature*, University of Lagos/Evans, 1971 p.36
10 Pierre Macheray, *Pour une Théorie de la Production Littéraire*, Francois Maspero, Paris 1978, p.128.
11 Tsegaye Gabre-Medhin, *Oda-Oak Oracle*, Oxford University Press, 1976, p.11.
12 *Ibid.*, p.3
13 *Ibid.*, p.49
14 Ibid., p.39
15 'Edufa' by Efua T. Sutherland is included in Fredric M. Litto (ed.), *Plays from Black Africa*, Hill and Wang, New York, 1968, p.225.
16 Ama Ata Aidoo, *Andwa*, Longman, London, 1970, pp.11 – 12.
17 R. Sharif Easmon, *Dear Parents and Ogre*, Oxford University Press, 1964, p.75.
18 *Ibid.*, p.75.
19 *Ibid.*
20 *Ibid.*, p.30.

21   *Ibid.*, p.29.
22   *Ibid.*, p.21.
23   *Ibid.*, p.26.
24   J.C. De Graft, *Sons and Daughters*, Oxford University Press, 1964, p.45.
25   J.P. Clark, *Ozidi*, Oxford University Press, 1966, p.81.
26   Wole Soyinka, *Collected Plays 2*, Oxford University Press, 1974, p.49.
27   See an interview with Wole Soyinka by Lewis Nkosi included in Dennis Duerden and Cosmo Pieterse (eds.) *African Writers Talking*, Heinemann 1972, pp.172 − 3.
28   See Eldred Jones's review of *The Interpreters* in *African Literature Today*, 2, January 1969.
29   See 'Towards The Decolonisation of African Literature', by Chinweizu Onwuchekwa Jemie and Ihechukwu Madubuike, in *Okike*, 6.
30   Graham-White, *The Drama of Black Africa*, p.97.
31   Gerald Moore, *Wole Soyinka*, Evans, London, 1978, p.19.
32   Ogumba, 'Modern Drama in West Africa', pp.47 − 8.
33   See Wole Soyinka, 'A Dance of the Forests' in *Five Players*, Oxford University Press, 1964, p.88.
34   Margaret Laurence, *Long Drums and Cannons*, Macmillan, London, 1968, p.74.
35   Eldred D. Jones, *The Writing of Wole Soyinka*, Heinemann, 1973, p.11.
36   *Ibid.*
37   See Oyin Ogumba's article 'Traditional Content of the Plays of Wole Soyinka', in *African Literature Today*, 4, Heinemann, 1972, p.16.
38   Graham-White, *The Drama of Black Africa*, p.145.
39   See Lewis Nkosi's chapter, 'Toward a New African Theatre', in *Home and Exile*, Longman, London, 1965.
40   Robert Serumaga, in an unpublished interview with Lewis Nkosi.

INDEX

Abrahams, Peter, 31
  A Wreath for Udomo, 47–51
  Tell Freedom, 81
  Wild Conquest, 47–51
Abafami Theatre Company, 192–3
Achebe, Chinua, 4, 6–7, 30, 46, 53, 67
  Arrow of God, 31, 32–9
  Things Fall Apart, 31, 32–9
Adali-Mortty, G., 154
Afolayan, A., 56
African culture/civilization, writers'
  attitudes to, 11–12, 47–51, 131–2,
  138, 147–62
Afrikaner writing, 77–8
Aidoo, Ama Ata
  Anowa, 177, 179–81
  Dilemma of a Ghost, 181
Aiken, Henry D., *The Age of Ideology*,
  19
alienation, of African writers, 6, 21,
  55–6, 62–3, 74, 108–11, 129, 131
Allen, Samuel W., 10, 14
Aluko, T.M., 82
American influence, on South African
  writing, 81–2, 169
Amo, Anton Wilhelm, 110
Andrade, Costa, 165
Andrade, Mario de, 26
anguish, as theme, 60–1, 65, 82
anti–colonial writing, 1, 2, 23–6,
  163–5
Arden, John, 190
Armah, Ayi Kwei, *The Beautyful Ones
  Are Not Yet Born*, 54, 62–3, 64–7
Armattoe, R.E.G., 116, 121–4
  Between the Forest and the Sea, 122
  Deep Down the Blackman's Mind, 121
  'A Letter to an African Poet in 5000
    AD' 123–4
  'Negro Heaven', 122
  'Our God is Black', 122
  'The Human Race', 123
  'The White Man's Grave', 121

authenticity, as judgmental concept, 7
autobiographical novels, 94–5, 102
Awoonor, Kofi, 126, 127, 148
  This Earth, My Brother, 3, 54, 55
    62–4, 94

Banham, Martin and Wake, Clive, 176
Bastide, Roger, 26–7
Beier, Ulli, 94. 128, 161
  The Imprisonment of Obatala (with
    Ijimere), 174–5, 177
Bereng, 112
black consciousness movement, 27, 139,
  168
Blake, William, 24
Blixen, Karen, 3
  Out of Africa, 7
Blok, Alexander, 168
Bognini, Joseph Miezan, 138
Bolamba, Antoine–Roger, 138
  'Bonguemba', 141
Boudry, Robert, 128–9
bourgeois society
  frustration with, philosophical, 19–23
  in drama, 181–5
  seen as an evil, 5, 23
Brazilian writing, 25–26
Breton, André, 24
Brew, Kwesi, 154
  'Ancestral Faces', 154
Breytenbach, 77
Brutus, Dennis, 101, 114, 166–7
  China Poems, 166
  Letters to Martha, 166
  Poems from Algiers, 166
  Siren, Knuckles, Boots, 166
  Thoughts Abroad, 166
  'Off the Campus: Wits', 166

Capitein, James Eliza John, 110
Carim, Enver, 78, 79–80, 81–2

A Dream Deferred, 83−5, 86−91
Golden City, 82−3, 95
Casely-Hayford, Gladys, 116, 118, 124
censorship, 78
Césaire, Aimé, 10−11, 17, 22, 23−4,
   26−7, 146−7
   Cahier d'un retour au pays natal, 11,
   24
Chenet, Gérard, *El Hadj Omar*, 192
Christianity
   effects on traditional society, 34−8
   influence on early poets, 111−18, 145
Cissoko, Siriman, 142
Clark, John Pepper, 148, 154−7, 161−2,
   181
   A Reed in the Tide, 161
   Casualties, 162−3
   Ozidi, 176, 177, 185−7
   Song of a Goat, 185−6
   The Masquerade, 3, 186
   The Raft, 186
   'Agbor Dancer', 161−2
   'Casualties', 162
   'Child Asleep', 161
   'Cry of Birth', 161
   'For Granny', 161−2
   'Fulani Cattle', 161
   'Girl Bathing', 161
   'Imprisonment of Obatala', 161−2
   'Night Rain', 161−2
   'Olokun', 161
   'Song', 162
class struggle, 41−2, 73, 114
   drama as instrument in, 176−7,
   181−5
Claudel, Paul, 144
Clea, Claire, 146
colonialism, effects on traditional
   society, 33−9
Conrad, Joseph, 80
Craveirinha, José, 26, 163
   'I want to be a Drum', 164
Cuguano, Ottalah, 108
Cullen, Countee
   From the Dark Tower, 123
   Heritage, 21−2
   cynicism, in modernism, 64

Dadié, Bernard, 126, 137, 140−1
   'Afrique debout', 140
   'Confession', 141
   'Je vous remercie mon Dieu', 140
   'La ronde des jours', 140
   'La vie n'est pas un rêve', 140

'Sèche tes pleurs', 140
Damas, Léon, 23
   Limbe, 25
Darthorne, O.R., 67, 109, 146
De Graft, J.C., 181
   Through A Film Darkly, 184−5
Dei-Anang, Michael, 118
   Ghana Glory, 119−20
   'Awake, Ye Gold Coast Sons!', 119
   'Come to Ghana', 120−1
   'Inside and Outside', 120
Depestre, René, 10
Dhlomo, Herbert I.E., 192
   Valley of a Thousand Hills, 114−16
Dhlomo, R.R.R., 51
Dia, Amadou Asse, *Les derniers jours de
   Lat Dior*, 192
Diakhathe, Lamine, 138, 141
Diallo, A.Y., 142
Dickens, Charles, 65
Dickinson, Margaret, *When Bullets
   Begin to Flower*, 163
didacticism, 41−6, 71−4, 118−24
Dikobe, Modikwe, *The Marabi Dance*,
   80−1
Diop, Alioune, 92
Diop, Birago, 126, 137−8
   'Diptyque', 140
   'Leurres et lueurs', 140
   'Souffles', 140
Diop, David, 126, 137−8, 165
   Coups de Pilon, 139−40
   'Africa', 142
   'Black Dancer', 142
   'Certitude', 139
   'La route véritable', 139
   'Vagues', 139
Dos Santos, Marcelino, 165
drama
   as instrument in class struggle, 176−7,
   181−5
   functional, 176
   historical themes, 192
   linguistic experimentation, 188−9
   Ntsomi, 174
   political, development of, 192
   popular, 193−4
   satire, 187−8
   traditional/Western coexistence,
   173−7
   treatment of traditional religion,
   177−81
   vocabulary of, 174
Drum, 91, 99

INDEX

Easmon, R. Sarif, 177, 181
  Dear Parent and Ogre, 182–4
Egungun, ritual, 174, 188
Eliet, Edouard, 128
Eliot, T.S., 155
elite, intellectual
  alienation of, 4, 6, 21, 55–6, 62–3,
    74, 131, 190–1
  and Western values, 124, 181–5
  literary satirizing of, 42
elite, political, 66, 68
  literary satirizing of, 70–1
  poetry praising, 120
  writers' identification with, 181–5
Encisco, Diego Jimene de, 109
Equiano, Olaudah, 108
L'Etudiant Noir, 10
European languages
  Anglophone *cf* Francophone poetry,
    126–7
  difficulty of representing African
    concepts in, 3
  dominance in African literature, 1–2
  novel and, 53
  poetry in, 107–8, 111
experimental writing, 6–7
  poetic technique, 127, 154

Fall Malick, 138, 141
Fanon, Frantz, 18, 182
Flather, Newell, 16
Fofana, Moctar, *L'appel du fétiche*, 192
Freudianism, and negritude, 22
functionalism, drama, 176

Gabre-Medhin, Tsegaye, *Oda-Oak
  Oracle*, 177–9
Gakwandi, Shatto Arthur, 62, 67
Galton, Sir Francis, 121
Goldblatt, John, 103
Goldmann, Lucien, 190
Gordimer, Nadine, 45–6, 77, 78
Graham-White, Anthony, 173–4, 190
Guardian, 93
Gwala, Pascal, 167

hain-teny, 132–4
harmonisation, as ideal in traditional
  art, 5
Head, Bessie, 78, 99
  A Question of Power, 101–2
  Maru, 100–1
  When Rain Clouds Gather, 100
Head, Norman, 114

historical novels, 30–51
  creation of myth, 31–2
  English *cf* French traditions, 40
Hoffman, Frederick J. 22

Ibo, 53
Ijaw, 55, 57
Ijimere, Obotunde, 175, 193
  The Imprisonment of Obatala (*with*
    Beier), 174–5, 177
imprisonment, writing arising from,
  103–4, 135–6, 164
independence, political
  and growth of literature, 1, 55, 79,
    148
  corruption following, 62, 64, 68–69
    187–8
intellectual tradition, negritude as,
  19–23
Irele, Abiola, 7, 12–13

Jacinto, Antonio, 'Letter from a
  Contract Worker', 163–4
Jacobson, 77
Jeanpierre, W., 92
Joachim, Paulin, 138
Jolobe, J.J.R., 112, 113, 116–18
  Thuthula, 117
  'To Light', 118
  'To the Fallen', 118
Jones, E.D., 189
Jones, LeRoi, 167
Joyce, James, 32

Kafka, Franz, *The Castle*, 59–60
Kant, Immanuel, *Critique of Pure
  Reason*, 19
Kayira, Legson, 82
Kayper-Mensah, A., 154
Kgositsile, Keorapetse, 81
Kgotsisile, Willie, 167
Kunene, Mazisi, 114, 116, 124, 126, 131,
  148, 167
  Zulu poems, 149
  'The Day of Treachery', 149
  'The Night', 149

La Guma, Alex, 87
  A Walk in the Night, 85–6
  And A Threefold Cord, 85
  In the Fog of the Seasons' End, 85–6
  The Stone Country, 85
Laleau, Léon, *Trahison*, 20–1
languages, African

difficulties of translating, 3–4
overlaid on to classical novel, 53–5, 56–7
reluctance to write in, 3
vernacular poetry, 112–15
Lapido, Daro, 193
Latino, Juan, 108–10
Austriad, 109
Epigrammatum Liber, 109
Laurence, Margaret, 39
Laurenson, Diana, 58
Lawrence, D.H., 24, 45, 95
Laye, Camara
L'enfant noir, 53
Le regard du roi (*The Radiance of the King*), 7, 53, 58–60
Légitime défense, 23
Lero, Etienne, 23
Lero, Thelus, 23
Lessing, Doris, *The Grass is Singing*, 76–7, 88–9
linguistic experimentation, 53–5, 56–7, 62, 71
development in poetry, 151–62
in drama, 188–9
literacy, 1, 8
Lo Liyong, 127
Lodge, David, 59
Lukacs, George, 41
Luna, Jorge de, 26

Macaulay, Thomas B., 30, 103
Macebuh, Stanley, 160
Macheray, Pierre, 177
Maimane, Arthur, 91
Malraux, André, 40
Mandela, Nelson, 103
Maquet, Jacques, 13
Marxism
and negritude, 14–15, 16
in the novel, 40–1
influence on poetry, 139
Mattera, Don, 167
Matthews, James, 166–7
Mayenga, Paul, *L'Oracle*, 192
Memmi, Albert, 2
Menil, René, 23
Mercer, Colin, 55
Micere Mugo, *The Trial of Dedan Kimathi* (*with* Ngugi), 192
modernism, in the novel, 53–74
anguish, 60–1, 65
cynicism, 64
linguistic experimentation, 53–5,

56–7, 62, 71
place of religion, 70
self-consciousness, 58
style, deliberate application of, 54
Modisane, Bloke, 91, 95, 96
Mofolo, Thomas, *Chaka*, 51
Monnerot, Jules, 23
Moore, Gerald, 3, 32, 56, 79, 147, 161
Mootry, Maria K., 115
Motsisi, Casey, 91, 95
Mphahlele, Ezekiel, 16–19, 78, 91–9, 115
Down Second Avenue, 91, 94
In Corner B, 93
Man Must Live, 93
The Living and the Dead, 93
The Wanderers, 82, 91, 93–8
Mqhayi, 112, 116
Mtshali, Oswald, 167
music, influence on South African writing, 79, 81–2

Naipaul, V.S., 99
N'Dao, Cheik, *L'exil d'Albouri*, 192
Ndebele, Njabulo, 167
negritude, 10–27, 92, 122, 135
and intellectual tradition, 19–23
as political reaction, 11
attacks on, 15–19
effect on literature, 17–19
Marxism and, 14–15, 16
philosophy of, 10–15
poles of, post-independence, 138–41
seen as encouraging racism, 16–17
surrealist movement, 23–7
Negro Caravan, 21
Neto, Angostinho, 163
'Bamako', 165–6
New African, The, 99
New Statesman, The, 99
Ngugi wa Thiong'o, 2, 31, 53, 71
A Grain of Wheat, 31, 39–46, 72
Petals of Blood, 54, 72–3, 192
Secret Lives, 73
The Black Hermit, 192
The River Between, 73
The Trial of Dedan Kimathi (*with* Micere Mugo), 192
Weep Not, Child, 72
Nicol, Abioseh, 127
'African Easter', 151–2
Nietzsche, Friedrich, 51
Nkosi, Lewis, 78
Nkrumah, Kwame, 120, 121

INDEX

Nortje, Arthur, 114, 167
  'Questions and Answers', 169
novel
  appropriateness to African society,
    5–6
  autobiographical, 94–5, 102
  comic, 82
  commitment in, 49
  historical, 30–51
  modernism, 53–74
  socialist/didactic, 41–6, 71–4
Ntsomi, 174
Nwoga, Donatus I., 121

O'Flinn, J.P., 61, 71
Ogunde, Herbert, 193
Ogunmola, Kola, 193
  The Love of Money, 194
Okara, Gabriel, 127
  The Voice, 54, 57–8, 60–2
  'The Snow Flakes Sail Gently Down',
    153
Okigbo, Christopher, 7, 127, 148, 149
  Labyrinths, 155
  'Heavensgate', 157
  'Limits', 157
  'The passage', 155
Olson, Charles, 131
Osadebay, Dennis Chukude, 116, 118
  'Young Africa's Explanation', 118–19
Ouologuem, Yambo, 31–2
  Le devoir de violence (Bound to
    Violence), 47–51, 54
Ousmane, Sembene, 8, 15–16, 31, 86
  Les bouts de bois de Dieu (God's Bits
    of Wood), 31, 39–46
Outtara, Mamadou, La rencontre
  secrète de l'Almany Samory et de
  Tieba, 192

Pairault, Claude, 174
Pan-Negro cultural universe, concept of,
  12–13
Paton, Alan, 77
Paulhan, Jean, 131
p'Bitek, Okot, 126, 148
  Song of Lawino, 149, 150
Peters Lenrie, 127, 153
Pilotin, Michel, 23
Poètes d'expression française, 131
poetry
and development of society, 169

Anglophone cf Francophone, 126–7
  as expressive medium for negritude,
    14
  development of modern style, 126–7,
    139, 147
  didacticism, 118–24
  'difficult', 155
  experiment with technique, 127, 154
  form/content dichotomy, 22
  from slavery to colonialism, 107–24
  glorification of blackness in, 24–6,
    122, 141–2
  hain-teny, 131–3
  in oral tradition, 81, 107–8, 148–50
  influence of Christianity, 111–18, 144
  linguistic development, 151–62
  'literary' style, 114–15, 118
  modern, 126–69
  modernist/traditional conflicts,
    147–51
  of slavery, 108–11
  patriotic, 120
  post-independence, problems, 138
  protest as theme, 112, 114, 163–9
  satire, 121–5
  South African, 165–9
  vernacular, 112–15
Pompidou, Georges, 143
Pope, Alexander, 110
Post, 99
Pound, Ezra, 131, 155
Povey, John, 34
praise–poetry, 81, 114, 115, 149
Price–Mars, Jean, 20
protest
  as writer's function, 76
  in poetry, 112, 114, 163–9

Quitman, Maurice-Sabat, 23

Rabearivelo, Jean–Joseph, 127–32
  Chants pour Abeone, 129
  La Coupe de Cendres, 129
  Prèsque Songes, 129
  Sylves, 129
  Traduit de la Nuit, 131
  Vieilles chansons des pays d'Imerina,
    132
  Volumes, 129
  'Daybreak', 130
  'Filao', 130
  'Postlude', 130
  'Zahana', 130
  'Zebu', 129

Rabemananjara, Jacques, 128, 134–7
  Antsa, 134–7
racism
  as theme, 76–8, 80–1, 98, 100–1,
    166, 184
  negritude seen as encouraging, 16–17
  white women in context of, 88–90
Ranaivo, Flavian, 128, 132
  Mes chansons de toujours, 132
  'Chant pour deux Valiha', 132–4
reason
  African *cf* European, 12
  English *cf* French, 17–19
  irrationalist movements, 20
rebelliousness, of African writers, 20–2,
  23–6
Rebelo, Jorge, 165
Reed, John and Wake, Clive, 16, 128,
  131, 143
relevance, of writings in European
  languages, 1–2, 6
religion, traditional
  effects of Christianity on, 34–8
  optimism of, 4
  treatment of, in drama, 177–81
Rimbaud, Arthur, 146
Roumain, Jacques, 25
  Guinée, 21

Salifou, André *Tanimoune*, 192
Sancho, Ignatius, 108
Sartre, Jean–Paul, 13–14, 18
  Orphée Noir, 17
satire, 42, 70–1, 121–5, 187–8
Senghor, Léopold, 10–12, 23, 26, 92,
  126, 132–3, 137–8, 141–4
  Anthologie de la Nouvelle Poésie
    Nègre et Malgache de Langue
    *Fran*çaise, 14, 138
  Chants d'ombre, 143
  Chants pour Naett, 143
  Ethiopiques, 143
  Hosties noires, 142–3
  Manhattan, 25
  Nocturnes, 143
  Shaka, 192
  'Femme noire', 142
Serote, Mongane Wally, 167
  No Baby Must Weep, 168
  Tsetlo, 168
  Yakhal'inkomo, 168
  'Night-time', 168
Serumaga, Robert, 192–3
  Renga Moi, 176, 193

Sibree, James, 131–2
slavery
  memoirs of, 1
  poetry written during, 108–11
society, African
  as living organism, 30
  function of intellectuals within, 55
  instability, 55–6
  literature as reflection of development,
    169, 191
  post-independence, as corrupt, 62, 64,
    68
  pre-colonial, as decaying/degenerate,
    34, 47–51
  South African, 76, 163
  urban/rural dichotomy, depth of,
    80–1
Sousa, Noemia de, 163
South African writing, 51, 76–105,
  165–9
  Afrikaner, 77–8
  American influence, 81–2, 169
  as mirror of society, 76, 163
  influence of music, 79, 81–2
  lack of range, 78–9
  state and, 76, 77
  urban bias, 79–81
Soyinka, Wole, 3, 8, 19, 127, 148,
  157–61, 181, 187–91
  A Dance of the Forests, 157–8, 176,
    188–90
  A Shuttle in the Crypt, 157
  Idanre, 157, 159–60
  Kongi's Harvest, 187, 191
  The Interpreters, 54, 62, 67–72, 157,
    159
  The Lion and the Jewel, 157, 187, 191
  The Road, 157, 159, 174, 188, 189,
    191
  The Swamp Dwellers, 72, 187, 191
  The Trials of Brother Jero, 187
  'Après la guerre', 161
  'Civilian and Soldier', 160
  'Conversation at night with a
    Cockroach', 158
  'Death at Dawn', 161
  'Massacre October '66', 161
  'Season', 161
  'Telephone Conversation', 160, 161
  'The Other Immigrant', 160
Spratlin, V.B., 110
story-telling, traditional, 6, 55, 58
  oral poetry, 81, 107–8, 148–50
style

INDEX

deliberate application of, 54
development in modern poetry,
126–7, 139, 147
'literary', in poetry, 114–15, 118
surrealism, 23–7, 56, 139
Sutherland, Efua, *Edufa*, 179–80
Swingewood, Alan, 65

Tati-Loutard, J.–B., 138
Themba, Can, 91, 95, 96
Thomas, Dylan, 56
Thompson, John, 4
Transition, 5
Trek, 93
Tutuola, Amos, 6–7
  The Palm-Wine Drinkard, 53, 56–8

Udoeyo, N.J., 162
urban bias, in South African writing,
79–81
U'Tamsi, Tchicaya, 15, 138, 144–7
  Brush Fire, 145
  Cahier, 147
  'The Promenade', 145

Vaughan, Henry, 120
victim theme, 32
Vilakazi, B.W., 115
  'Because', 112
  'On the Gold Mines', 112–14
vocabulary of drama, 174
Volosinov, V.N., 154

Wade, Michael, 47–8
Wake, Clive, *see* Banham and Wake;
  Reed and Wake
Wali, Obi, 5–6
Walsh, William, 99
Wanodi, 127
Wheatley, Phillis, 110–11
women, status of, 88–90, 179–80

Yoruba, 6, 56, 160
Yoyotte, Simone, 23

Zulu, 112-14, 148–9
Zwelonke, D.M., 78, 103
  Robben Island, 103–4